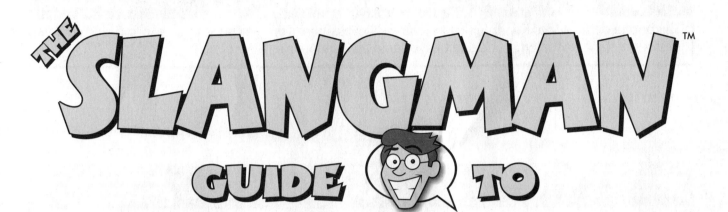

THE SLANGMAN GUIDE TO

BIZ SPEAK 2

SLANG, IDIOMS, & JARGON USED IN BUSINESS ENGLISH

Front cover:

ca... someone (to) ... to fire someone from a job.

SLANGMAN D...D BUR...

DEDICATION

This book is dedicated to Kenny Smith and Nancy Nieves – two of the best people you can find, and endless sources of slang and idioms. I couldn't have done this without them.

A SPECIAL THANKS

I'd like to give a very special thanks to Hemera Technologies, Inc. for their invaluable contribution to this book. The tailor-made clipart they created for us was no less than astounding. Their illustrations went far beyond my expectations of simply conveying the meaning of each slang term and idiom – each was wonderfully clever, creative, and most important, downright hilarious. I feel fortunate to have the opportunity to work with a group of people that is so professional, accommodating, and so very talented.

490 St-Joseph Boulevard, Suite 301 • Hall, Quebec • Canada J8Y 3Y7 • Contact: info@hemera.com • Tel: (819) 772-8200 • Fax: (819) 778-6252

For more information about Hemera™ and their products, including Hemera Photo-Objects 50,000 Volumes I & II and The Big Box of Art, please go to www.hemera.com

ACKNOWLEDGEMENTS

I'd like to give a special thanks to thank our talented "slang gang" of actors who are always at the ready when called in to record the audio portions of our SLANGMAN books. Their skill, support, and friendship mean the world to me: Grant Beehler, Nancy Burke, Noah Manne, and Debbie Wright.

Kathy Jones of United Audio/Video is *da bomb!* I just can't thank her enough for her attention to the duplication phase of our audio CDs and cassettes. Her professionalism, service, wit, and kindness is always a treat.

There's no way I could give my publishing guru, Kim Hendrickson, the thanks she deserves. Throughout the years, she's given me invaluable guidance, insight, and never-ending support. I thank her so much for her help and cherished friendship.

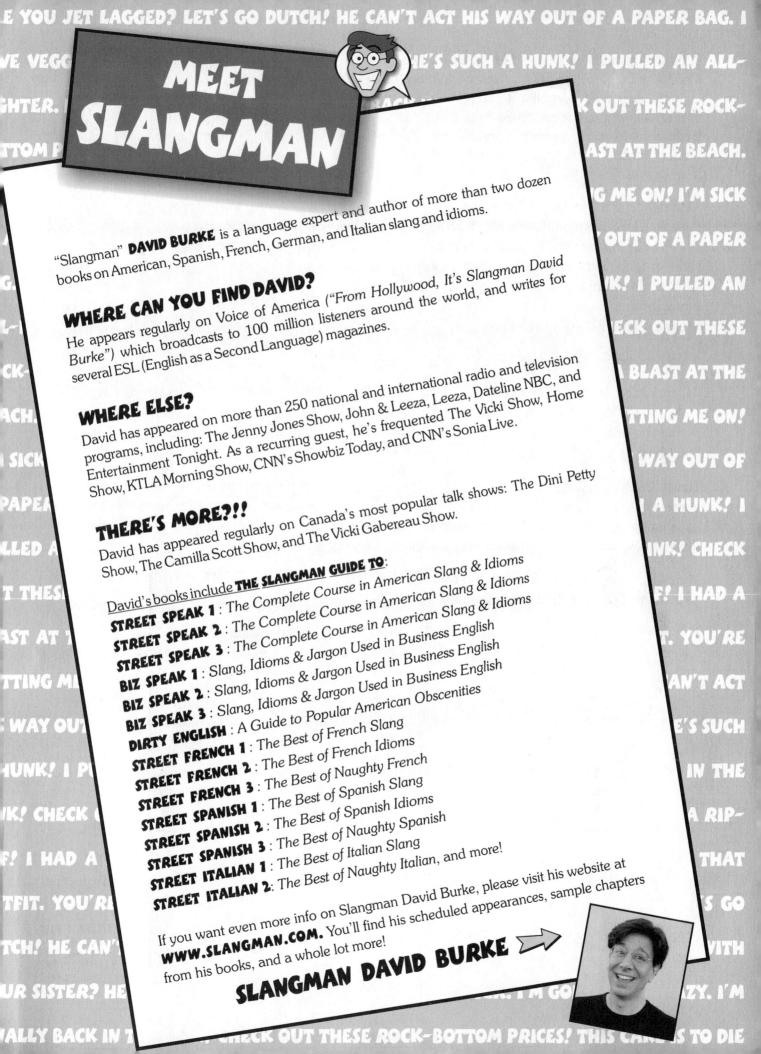

MEET SLANGMAN

"Slangman" **DAVID BURKE** is a language expert and author of more than two dozen books on American, Spanish, French, German, and Italian slang and idioms.

WHERE CAN YOU FIND DAVID?

He appears regularly on Voice of America ("From Hollywood, It's Slangman David Burke") which broadcasts to 100 million listeners around the world, and writes for several ESL (English as a Second Language) magazines.

WHERE ELSE?

David has appeared on more than 250 national and international radio and television programs, including: The Jenny Jones Show, John & Leeza, Leeza, Dateline NBC, and Entertainment Tonight. As a recurring guest, he's frequented The Vicki Show, Home Show, KTLA Morning Show, CNN's Showbiz Today, and CNN's Sonia Live.

THERE'S MORE?!!

David has appeared regularly on Canada's most popular talk shows: The Dini Petty Show, The Camilla Scott Show, and The Vicki Gabereau Show.

David's books include **THE SLANGMAN GUIDE TO**:

STREET SPEAK 1 : The Complete Course in American Slang & Idioms
STREET SPEAK 2 : The Complete Course in American Slang & Idioms
STREET SPEAK 3 : The Complete Course in American Slang & Idioms
BIZ SPEAK 1 : Slang, Idioms & Jargon Used in Business English
BIZ SPEAK 2 : Slang, Idioms & Jargon Used in Business English
BIZ SPEAK 3 : Slang, Idioms & Jargon Used in Business English
DIRTY ENGLISH : A Guide to Popular American Obscenities
STREET FRENCH 1 : The Best of French Slang
STREET FRENCH 2 : The Best of French Idioms
STREET FRENCH 3 : The Best of Naughty French
STREET SPANISH 1 : The Best of Spanish Slang
STREET SPANISH 2 : The Best of Spanish Idioms
STREET SPANISH 3 : The Best of Naughty Spanish
STREET ITALIAN 1 : The Best of Italian Slang
STREET ITALIAN 2 : The Best of Naughty Italian, and more!

If you want even more info on Slangman David Burke, please visit his website at **WWW.SLANGMAN.COM.** You'll find his scheduled appearances, sample chapters from his books, and a whole lot more!

SLANGMAN DAVID BURKE ⟹

Book Design and Production: Slangman Publishing
Managing Partner/Brand & Marketing Director: Jason Reese
Design (Logo/Web): Jennifer Reese
Illustrator – Outside cover: Ty Semaka
Illustrator – Main inside illustrations: Hemera Technologies
Photographer – Outside back cover: Rick Olson
Icon Design: Sharon Kim

Copyright © 2002 by David Burke
Published by Slangman Publishing • 12206 Hillslope Street • Studio City, CA 91604-3603 • USA
Toll Free Telephone from the USA & Canada: 1-877-SLANGMAN (1-877-752-6462)
From outside North America: 1-818-769-1914
Worldwide Fax number: 1-413-647-1589
Email: editor@slangman.com
Website: http://www.slangman.com

This publication is designed to provide accurate and authoritative information in regard to the subject matter covered. It is sold with the understanding that the publisher is not engaged in rendering legal, accounting, or other professional services. If legal advice or other expert assistance is required, the services of a competent professional person should be sought.

The persons, entities and events in this book are fictitious. Any similarities with actual persons or entities, past and present, are purely coincidental.

This publication includes images from CorelDRAW® 10 and ArtToday.com which are protected by the copyright laws of the U.S., Canada and elsewhere. Used under license.

ISBN 1-891888-15-3
Printed in the United States of America
10 9 8 7 6 5 4 3 2 1

LEGEND

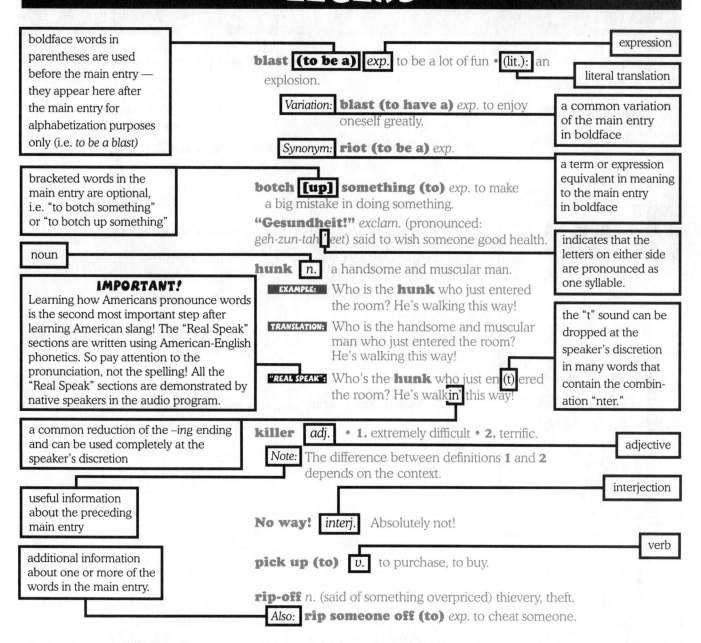

boldface words in parentheses are used before the main entry — they appear here after the main entry for alphabetization purposes only (i.e. *to be a blast*)

blast [(to be a)] *exp.* to be a lot of fun • **(lit.):** an explosion.

Variation: **blast (to have a)** *exp.* to enjoy oneself greatly.

Synonym: **riot (to be a)** *exp.*

expression

literal translation

a common variation of the main entry in boldface

bracketed words in the main entry are optional, i.e. "to botch something" or "to botch up something"

botch [up] something (to) *exp.* to make a big mistake in doing something.

"Gesundheit!" *exclam.* (pronounced: geh-zun-tah['eet) said to wish someone good health.

a term or expression equivalent in meaning to the main entry in boldface

noun

hunk [n.] a handsome and muscular man.

indicates that the letters on either side are pronounced as one syllable.

IMPORTANT!
Learning how Americans pronounce words is the second most important step after learning American slang! The "Real Speak" sections are written using American-English phonetics. So pay attention to the pronunciation, not the spelling! All the "Real Speak" sections are demonstrated by native speakers in the audio program.

EXAMPLE: Who is the **hunk** who just entered the room? He's walking this way!

TRANSLATION: Who is the handsome and muscular man who just entered the room? He's walking this way!

"REAL SPEAK": Who's the **hunk** who just en[t]ered the room? He's walkin' this way!

the "t" sound can be dropped at the speaker's discretion in many words that contain the combination "nter."

a common reduction of the –*ing* ending and can be used completely at the speaker's discretion

killer [adj.] • **1.** extremely difficult • **2.** terrific.

Note: The difference between definitions **1** and **2** depends on the context.

adjective

useful information about the preceding main entry

interjection

No way! [interj.] Absolutely not!

additional information about one or more of the words in the main entry.

verb

pick up (to) [v.] to purchase, to buy.

rip-off *n.* (said of something overpriced) thievery, theft.

Also: **rip someone off (to)** *exp.* to cheat someone.

EXPLANATION OF ICONS

These exercises reinforce visual recognition of the slang terms and idioms presented throughout this book.

These exercises include fill-ins, crossword puzzles, word matches and many other fun word games to help you use the new terms in context.

These exercises help you to understand not only *what* Americans speak, but *how* they speak! These exercises can all be found on the audio program. (*See back pages for details*)

These oral exercises are designed to help you to begin speaking and thinking like a native.

TABLE OF CONTENTS

ACTIVITIES		FROM THE SLANGMAN FILES

TABLE OF CONTENTS

LESSON TITLE	WORDS PRESENTED

LESSON 1

KYLE'S MAKING BIG BUCKS!

General Workplace Slang & Idioms *(Part 1)*

THIS LESSON FEATURES 10 NEW SLANG WORDS & IDIOMS

LET'S WARM UP!

MATCH THE PICTURES

As a fun way to get started, see if you can guess the meaning of the new slang words and expressions on the opposite page by using the pictures below and following the context of the sentences.

1. Donald has been doing the same job for thirty years. He's tired of the **daily grind**!
   "daily grind" means: . . . . ❑ coffee at the office . . . . ❑ work routine

2. Phil has been **working around the clock** to finish the project.
   "working around the clock" means: . . . ❑ working day and night. . . . . . ❑ work all day

3. Jeff got promoted. Now he's **top dog**!
   "top dog" means: . . . . ❑ boss . . . . ❑ veternarian

4. I'm earning **big bucks** at my new job. I'll finally be able to afford that new car!
   "big bucks" means: . . . . ❑ large deer. . . . . ❑ a lot of money

5. Jerry wants a promotion. That's why he's always **brown nosing** the boss.
   "brown nosing" means: . . . . ❑ throwing mud at . . . . ❑ trying to earn the favor of

6. Carl **stepped on Shelley's toes** by selling merchandise to one of her clients!
   "stepped on Shelley's toes" means:. . . . ❑ trespassed into Shelley's. . . . . ❑ broke Shelley's toes
   area of authority

7. If we finish the project, we can go to **happy hour** and get a few drinks!
   "happy hour" means:. . . . . ❑ a bar with after-work specials. . ❑ a one-hour comedy show

8. I've been **climbing the corporate ladder** for years. Now I'm a vice president!
   "climbing the corporate ladder" means: . ❑ getting fired. . . . . ❑ getting promoted

9. Before I got promoted, I was working for **chicken feed**!
   "chicken feed" means: . . . . ❑ a small amount of money . . . . ❑ a small amount of food

10. You'd better **knuckle down**! The boss needs that report in an hour!
    "knuckle down" means: . . . . ❑ use your knuckles . . . . ❑ work very hard

General Workplace Slang & Idioms (Part 1)

LET'S TALK!

A. DIALOGUE USING SLANG & IDIOMS

The words introduced on the first two pages are used in the dialogue below. See if you can understand the conversation. *Note:* The translation of the words in boldface is on the right-hand page.

CD-A: TRACK 2

Melissa: Kyle got promoted to **top dog**. I heard that he **stepped on people's toes** and **brown-nosed** the Board of Directors to get there. Now he's getting **big bucks** while we're still earning **chicken feed**.

Tony: Well, if we **knuckled down** and **worked around the clock**, maybe we could **climb the corporate ladder**, too.

Melissa: But who wants to spend one's life working all the time? I'm sick of the **daily grind**.

Tony: Me, too. In fact, let's leave early and go to **happy hour**.

Melissa: I'm right behind you!

B. DIALOGUE TRANSLATED INTO STANDARD ENGLISH

LET'S SEE HOW MUCH YOU REMEMBER!
Just for fun, move around in random order to the words and
expressions in boldface below. See if you can remember their
slang equivalents without looking at the left-hand page!

Melissa: Kyle got promoted to **a powerful executive**. I heard that he **trespassed into a lot of other people's area of authority** and **tried shamelessly to earn the favor of** the Board of Directors to get there. Now he's getting **a lot of money** while we're still earning **a small amount of money**.

Tony: Well, if we **worked very hard** and **worked all day and night**, maybe we could **get promoted**, too.

Melissa: But who wants to spend one's life working all the time? I'm sick of the **daily work routine**.

Tony: Me, too. In fact, let's leave early and go to a **bar with after-work specials**.

Melissa: I'm right behind you!

C. DIALOGUE USING "REAL SPEAK"

The dialogue below demonstrates how the slang conversation on the previous page would *really* be spoken by native speakers!

CD-A: TRACK 2

Melissa: Kyle got pr'moded da **top dog**. I heard th'd 'e **stepped on people's toes** 'n **brown-nosed** the Board 'a Direcders da get there. Now 'e's gedding **big bucks** while w'r still earning **chicken feed**.

Tony: Well, 'ef we **knuckled down** 'n **worked aroun' the clock**, maybe we could **climb the corp'rit ladder**, too.

Melissa: B't who wansta spen' one's life working all the time? I'm sick 'a the **daily grind**.

Tony: Me, too. In fact, let's leave early 'n go da **happy hour**.

Melissa: I'm right behin' ja!

LET'S LEARN!

VOCABULARY

The following words and expressions were used in the previous dialogues. Let's take a closer look at what they mean.

CD-A: TRACK 3

big bucks *n.* a lot of money.

EXAMPLE:	Trisha is smart and works harder than everyone else. That's why she makes **big bucks**.
TRANSLATION:	Trisha is smart and works harder than everyone else. That's why she makes **a lot of money**.
"REAL SPEAK":	Trisha's smart 'n works harder th'n ev'ryone else. That's why she makes **big bucks**.

NOW YOU DO IT. COMPLETE THE PHRASE ALOUD:

You don't really start making **big bucks** until you get promoted to...

brown nose (to) *exp.* to try shamelessly to earn the favor of someone.

EXAMPLE:	Kyle laughs at all of the boss's jokes because he wants a promotion. I could never **brown nose** like that!
TRANSLATION:	Kyle laughs at all of the boss's jokes because he wants a promotion. I could never **try shamelessly to earn someone's favor** like that!
"REAL SPEAK":	Kyle laughs 'id all 'a the boss's jokes b'cuz 'e wants a pr'motion. I could never **brown nose** like that!
Synonym:	**suck up to someone (to)** *exp.*
Also:	**brown noser** *n.* one who tries shamelessly to earn the favor of someone else.

NOW YOU DO IT. COMPLETE THE PHRASE ALOUD:

Jessica **brown nosed** the boss when she...

chicken feed *n.* a small amount of money.

EXAMPLE: I work six days a week, but I only earn **chicken feed**. I need to find another job.

TRANSLATION: I work six days a week, but I only earn **a small amount of money**. I need to find another job.

"REAL SPEAK": I work six days a week, b'd I only earn **chicken feed**. I need da find another job.

Synonym 1: **chicken scratch** *n.*

Synonym 2: **peanuts** *n.*

Synonym 3: **squat** *n.*

NOW YOU DO IT. COMPLETE THE PHRASE ALOUD:
Toby makes **chicken feed** working as a...

climb the corporate ladder (to) *exp.* to get promoted.

EXAMPLE: I'm going to be the new manager in the office! I'm finally starting to **climb the corporate ladder**!

TRANSLATION: I'm going to be the new manager in the office! I'm finally starting to **get promoted**!

"REAL SPEAK": I'm gonna be the new manager 'n the office! I'm fin'lly starding da **climb the corp'rit ladder**!

Synonym: **move up the ranks (to)** *exp.*

NOW YOU DO IT. COMPLETE THE PHRASE ALOUD:
...is really **climbing the corporate ladder**. She'll be vice president in less than a year!

daily grind *exp.* one's daily work routine.

EXAMPLE: I'm tired of the **daily grind**. I need a new challenge, or maybe a vacation!

TRANSLATION: I'm tired of the **daily work routine**. I need a new challenge, or maybe a vacation!

"REAL SPEAK": I'm tired 'a the **daily grind**. I need a new challenge, 'er maybe a vacation!

NOW YOU DO IT. COMPLETE THE PHRASE ALOUD:
Joseph hates the **daily grind**, so he's going to...

happy hour *n.* a bar with after-work specials, usually inexpensive alcohol and food.

EXAMPLE: Let's go to **happy hour**. I had a terrible day at the office and could really use a drink.

TRANSLATION: Let's go to **a bar with after-work specials**. I had a terrible day at the office and could really use a drink.

"REAL SPEAK": Let's go da **happy hour**. I had a terr'ble day 'it the office 'n could really use a drink.

NOW YOU DO IT. COMPLETE THE PHRASE ALOUD:
I had a long day doing... Let's go to **happy hour**.

knuckle down (to) *exp.* to work very hard.

EXAMPLE: We're not going to make our goal unless we skip some lunches and really **knuckle down**.

TRANSLATION: We're not going to make our goal unless we skip some lunches and really **work hard**.

"REAL SPEAK:" W'r not gonna make 'ar goal unless we skip s'm lunches 'n really **knuckle down**.

NOW YOU DO IT. COMPLETE THE PHRASE ALOUD:
… should **knuckle down** if he wants to keep his job!

step on someone's toes (to) *exp.* to trespass into someone else's area of authority.

EXAMPLE: Dave really **stepped on Heather's toes** when he made the decision to hire a manager without consulting her first.

TRANSLATION: Dave really **trespassed into Heather's area of authority** when he made the decision to hire a manager without consulting her first.

"REAL SPEAK:" Dave really **stepped on Heather's toes** when 'e made the decision da hire a manager without consulting 'er first.

NOW YOU DO IT. COMPLETE THE PHRASE ALOUD:
Carla **stepped on my toes** when she...

top dog *n.* the ower or boss of a company.

EXAMPLE: It took Leslie six years of hard work, but now he's **top dog** and determines all of the company's policies.

TRANSLATION: It took Leslie six years of hard work, but now he's **the boss** and determines all of the company's policies.

"REAL SPEAK:" It took Leslie six years 'a hard work, b't now 'e's **top dog** 'n determines all 'a the comp'ny's policies.

Synonym 1: **big cheese** *n.*

Synonym 2: **head honcho** *n.*

Synonym 3: **top brass** *n.*

NOW YOU DO IT. COMPLETE THE PHRASE ALOUD:
I'll be **top dog** if I...

work around the clock (to) *exp.* to work all day and night.

EXAMPLE: I've been **working around the clock** for five days in order to finish this report for our meeting! I can't wait to go home and see my family again.

TRANSLATION: I've been **working all day and night** for five days in order to finish this report for our meeting! I can't wait to go home and see my family again.

"REAL SPEAK:" I' been **working aroun' the clock** fer five days 'n order da finish th's report fer 'ar meeding! I can't wait ta go home 'n see my fam'ly again.

NOW YOU DO IT. COMPLETE THE PHRASE ALOUD:
I've been **working around the clock** to finish...

LET'S PRACTICE!

A. CHOOSE THE RIGHT WORD
Underline the word that best completes the phrase.

CD-A: TRACK 4

1. If you work hard, you'll get promoted and start earning big (**dogs**, **bugs**, **bucks**).

2. Elliot didn't deserve a promotion, but he brown (**mouthed**, **nosed**, **eared**) the boss until he got one.

3. Now I make a lot of money, but I used to earn (**chicken**, **horse**, **cow**) feed.

4. If you want to (**paint**, **climb**, **make**) the corporate ladder, you have to work very hard.

5. If the (**monthly**, **weekly**, **daily**) grind gets too boring, you can always take a vacation.

6. If we finish our assignment early, we can go to (**happy**, **sad**, **funny**) hour and get a beer.

7. If Janine knuckles (**up**, **down**, **over**), she might get promoted by the end of the year.

8. Trevor stepped on my (**face**, **feet**, **toes**) and hired an assistant without getting my permission.

9. When I got hired, I started out at the lowest position, but now I'm top (**cat**, **dog**, **elephant**).

10. If we work around the (**clock**, **toaster**, **phone**), we'll be able to finish the project by next week.

B. CONTEXT EXERCISE

Read the short conversations. Decide whether the slang used makes sense or doesn't make sense. Circle your answer.

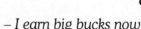

CD-A: TRACK 5

– I'm going on a vacation.
– Have fun at the daily grind!

MAKES SENSE   DOESN'T MAKE SENSE

– I need a beer to relax.
– Let's go to happy hour!

MAKES SENSE   DOESN'T MAKE SENSE

– I earn big bucks now.
– How can you afford to pay rent?

MAKES SENSE   DOESN'T MAKE SENSE

– I'm working around the clock.
– The boss will be angry!

MAKES SENSE   DOESN'T MAKE SENSE

– I want a promotion.
– Try brown nosing the boss!

MAKES SENSE   DOESN'T MAKE SENSE

– The boss needs the report soon.
– Then we should knuckle down.

MAKES SENSE   DOESN'T MAKE SENSE

– I got promoted to top dog!
– I thought you didn't like animals.

MAKES SENSE   DOESN'T MAKE SENSE

– Tony stepped on my toes.
– You must be so happy!

MAKES SENSE   DOESN'T MAKE SENSE

– I'm tired of earning chicken feed.
– You need to ask for a raise.

MAKES SENSE   DOESN'T MAKE SENSE

C. CREATE YOUR OWN SENTENCE

Read Person A's questions or statements aloud and use
the suggested words to create your response for Person B.

SPEAKING
CD-A: TRACK 6

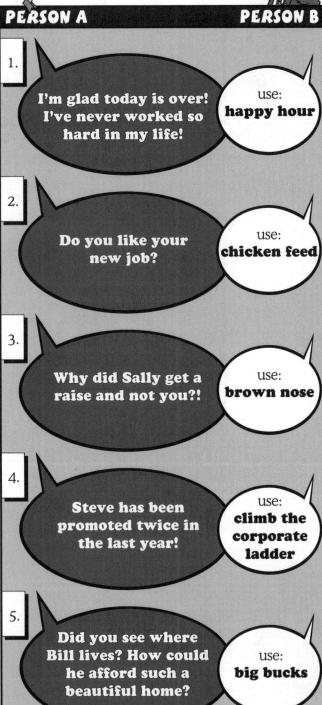

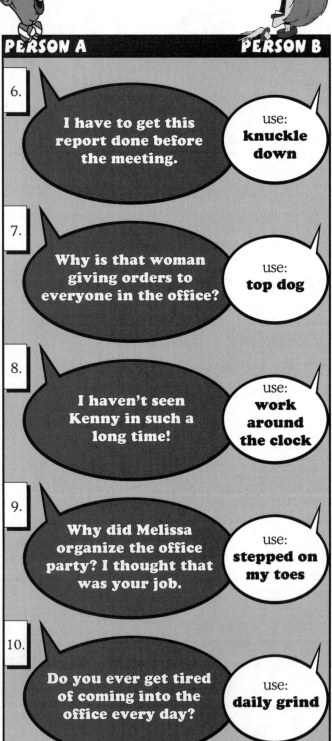

PERSON A	PERSON B
1. I'm glad today is over! I've never worked so hard in my life!	use: **happy hour**
2. Do you like your new job?	use: **chicken feed**
3. Why did Sally get a raise and not you?!	use: **brown nose**
4. Steve has been promoted twice in the last year!	use: **climb the corporate ladder**
5. Did you see where Bill lives? How could he afford such a beautiful home?	use: **big bucks**
6. I have to get this report done before the meeting.	use: **knuckle down**
7. Why is that woman giving orders to everyone in the office?	use: **top dog**
8. I haven't seen Kenny in such a long time!	use: **work around the clock**
9. Why did Melissa organize the office party? I thought that was your job.	use: **stepped on my toes**
10. Do you ever get tired of coming into the office every day?	use: **daily grind**

General Workplace Slang & Idioms (Part 1)

D. COMPLETE THE PHRASE

Complete the phrase by choosing the appropriate word from the list below.

BROWN	GRIND	LADDER
CLOCK	HOUR	TOES
FEED	KNUCKLE	TOP

1. Every day at the office is the same. I'm so tired of the daily _____.

2. If you want to be _____ dog, you'd better start working harder so you can get promoted.

3. I can't even pay my bills because I'm earning chicken _____. I need to find a new job!

4. We need to finish this project by Friday, so let's _____ down.

5. The boss assigned me to organize the convention, but Isaac did it instead. He really stepped on my _____!

6. Wendy bought the president lunch for the third time this week. She's trying to _____ nose him in order to get a promotion!

7. Chris started working in the sales department then got promoted three times within a year. Now he's vice president! It's nice to see a good person climb the corporate _____ like that.

8. We need to finish the project quickly. Everyone is going to happy _____ after work, and I don't want to be late!

9. I feel sorry for Natalie. She's been working around the _____ lately and hasn't spent any time with her husband.

FROM THE SLANGMAN FILES

More General Workplace Slang & Idioms (A-G)

You probably know by now that even after studying English for ten years, if you don't know the popular slang used by virtually *everyone*, you're going to miss what people are saying. Once you have learned everyday slang and idioms, you'll find that understanding American television shows and movies is a **breeze** (*very easy*)!

But there is still one more piece of the puzzle to this "secret language" that must be mastered, especially if you work in the U.S. — business slang, jargon and idioms. You'll discover that most of the business slang throughout this book is so commonly used in the workplace that much of it has crept its way into our everyday conversations!

back to square one (to go) *exp.* to restart from the beginning.

> **EXAMPLE:** I explained to John all the changes the client wanted him to make, but he didn't understand. I had to **go back to square one** and explain it all again!

> **TRANSLATION:** I explained to John all the changes the client wanted him to make, but he didn't understand. I had to **restart from the beginning** and explain it all again!

> **"REAL SPEAK":** I explain' da John all the changes the client wan'ed 'im da make, b'd 'e didn' understand. I had da **go back ta square one** 'n explain id all again!

backstab someone (to) *v.* to sabotage someone else's career intentionally, usually for personal gain.

> **EXAMPLE:** Julie deserved that promotion, but Carlos **backstabbed her** so he'd be promoted instead. He told the boss she has a drinking problem.

> **TRANSLATION:** Julie deserved that promotion, but Carlos **intentionally sabotaged her career** so he'd be promoted instead. He told the boss she has a drinking problem.

> **"REAL SPEAK":** Julie deserved that pr'motion, b't Carlos **backstabbed 'er** so 'e'd be pr'moded 'nstead. He told the boss she has a drinking problem.

bad-mouth someone (to) *exp.* to say negative things about someone.

> **EXAMPLE:** I don't like Ann in accounting, but I would never **bad-mouth her**.

> **TRANSLATION:** I don't like Ann in accounting, but I would never **say negative things about her**.

> **"REAL SPEAK":** I don't like Ann 'n accoun(t)ing, b'd I'd never **bad-mouth 'er**.

beef up (to) *v.* to expand, to make stronger.

> **EXAMPLE:** Our competition is getting tough. We'd better **beef up** our products quickly!

> **TRANSLATION:** Our competition is getting tough. We'd better **expand and improve** our products quickly!

> **"REAL SPEAK":** 'Ar competition's gedding tough. We'd bedder **beef up** 'ar produc's quickly!

big gun *n.* a very skilled person.

> **EXAMPLE:** The project isn't going well, so management is hiring some **big guns** to help us.

TRANSLATION: The project isn't going well, so management is hiring some **very skilled people** to help us.

"REAL SPEAK": The project isn't going well, so management's hiring s'm **big guns** da help us.

big shot *n.* an important person.

EXAMPLE: Even though Dennis just started with the company, he acts like a **big shot** and tries to tell me what to do.

TRANSLATION: Even though Dennis just started with the company, he acts like an **important person** and tries to tell me what to do.

"REAL SPEAK": Even though Dennis jus' starded w'th the comp'ny, he ac's like a **big shot** 'n tries da tell me what ta do.

bite the bullet (to) *exp.* to confront a difficult situation.

EXAMPLE: Pat has been annoying me a lot lately. I need to **bite the bullet** and talk to him about it.

TRANSLATION: Pat has been annoying me a lot lately. I need to **confront the situation** and talk to him about it.

"REAL SPEAK": Pat 's been annoying me a lot lately. I need da **bite the bullet** 'n talk ta him aboud it.

biz dev *abbrev.* an abbreviation for "the business development department."

EXAMPLE: If you have any questions about the project, talk to Phil in **biz dev**. He's in charge.

TRANSLATION: If you have any questions about the project, talk to Phil in **the business development department**. He's in charge.

"REAL SPEAK": If ya 'ave any questions about the project, talk ta Phil 'n **biz dev**. He's 'n charge.

boot camp *n.* an intense training program • (lit.): the military training camp from which all new recruits must graduate.

EXAMPLE: We send all of our new employees through **boot camp** to learn about our company.

TRANSLATION: We send all of our new employees through **an intense training program** to learn about our company.

"REAL SPEAK": We send all 'ev 'ar new employees through **boot camp** ta learn aboud 'ar comp'ny.

brick and mortar store *exp.* an actual store (traditionally made of brick and mortar) with a physical location as compared to an on-line store that exists only on the Internet.

EXAMPLE: Let's focus our marketing efforts on **brick and mortar stores**. They need our services to develop an Internet presence.

TRANSLATION: Let's focus our marketing efforts on **stores with physical locations**. They need our services to develop an Internet presence.

"REAL SPEAK": Let's focus 'ar markeding efferts on **brick 'n morder stores**. They need 'ar services ta develop 'n In(t)ernet presence.

burn one's bridges (to) *exp.* to cause permanent, irreparable damage to a relationship.

EXAMPLE: Don't **burn your bridges** with Jeff. He'll be the president of this company soon.

TRANSLATION: Don't **cause any permanent damage to your relationship** with Jeff. He'll be the president of this company soon.

"REAL SPEAK": Don't **burn yer bridges** w'th Jeff. He'll be the president 'a this comp'ny soon.

burn the candle at both ends (to) *exp.* to work on too many tasks at once.

EXAMPLE: Carol's been **burning the candle at both ends** in order to get promoted. She looks exhausted!

TRANSLATION: Carol's been **working on too many tasks at once** in order to get promoted. She looks exhausted!

"REAL SPEAK": Carol's b'n **burning the candle 'it both enz** 'n order da get pr'moded. She looks exhausted!

burn the midnight oil (to) *exp.* to work late into the night.

EXAMPLE: There's a big meeting tomorrow, so we need to **burn the midnight oil** in order to finish the reports in time.

TRANSLATION: There's a big meeting tomorrow, so we need to **work late into the night** in order to finish the reports in time.

"REAL SPEAK": There's a big meeding damarrow, so we need da **burn the midnide oil** 'n order da finish the r'ports 'n time.

burned out (to be) *exp.* to be exhausted, especially as a result of long-term stress.

EXAMPLE: I've been working on this project every day for two months. I'm completely **burned out**!

TRANSLATION: I've been working on this project every day for two months. I'm completely **exhausted**!

"REAL SPEAK": I've been working on th's project ev'ry day fer two munts. I'm completely **burned out**!

"Business is booming!" *exp.* "The company is doing extremely well."

EXAMPLE: **Business is booming**! We've had the most profitable year of all.

TRANSLATION: **The company is doing extremely well**! We've had the most profitable year of all.

"REAL SPEAK": **Bizness 'ez booming**! We've had the most profidable year 'ev all.

carte blanche *n.* (from French, meaning "blank check") complete freedom or authority to do something.

EXAMPLE: The boss must really trust me. He gave me **carte blanche** to hire anyone I want!

TRANSLATION: The boss must really trust me. He gave me **complete authority** to hire anyone I want!

"REAL SPEAK": The boss mus' really trust me. He gay me **cart blonch** ta hire anyone I want!

casual Friday *n.* a Friday when employees are allowed to dress more casually than normal.

EXAMPLE: I'm so glad the company has **casual Fridays**. I hate wearing suits every day!

TRANSLATION: I'm so glad the company **allows us to dress more casually on Fridays**. I hate wearing suits every day!

"REAL SPEAK": I'm so glad the comp'ny has **casual Fridays**. I hate wearing suits ev'ry day!

catch 22 *exp.* an unresolvable situation where you lose no matter what choices you make.

> **EXAMPLE:** If I hire Joe for the job instead of Chris, Chris will be mad at me. If I hire Chris, Joe will be mad at me. And if I hire someone else, they will both be mad at me! It's a **catch 22**!

> **TRANSLATION:** If I hire Joe for the job instead of Chris, Chris will be mad at me. If I hire Chris, Joe will be mad at me. And if I hire someone else, they'll both be mad at me! It's an **unresolvable situation**!

> **"REAL SPEAK":** If I hire Joe fer the job 'nstead 'a Chris, Chris'll be mad 'it me. If I hire Chris, Joe'll be mad 'it me. And if I hire someone else, they'll both be mad 'it me! It's a **catch twen'y-two**!

chew out (to) *exp.* to reprimand.

> **EXAMPLE:** The boss **chewed me out** for an hour because I forgot about this morning's meeting.

> **TRANSLATION:** The boss **reprimanded me** for an hour because I forgot about this morning's meeting.

> **"REAL SPEAK":** The boss **chewed me out** fer 'n hour b'cuz I fergod about th's morning's meeding.

come full circle (to) *exp.* to return to the beginning of an argument or process.

> **EXAMPLE:** After talking about the problem for two hours, the argument **came full circle** and we chose the first solution we had discussed.

> **TRANSLATION:** After talking about the problem for two hours, the argument **returned to where it had started** and we chose the first solution we had discussed.

> **"REAL SPEAK":** After talking about the problem fer two hours, the argument **came full circle** 'n we chose the firs' solution we'd discussed.

con call *abbrev.* (an abbreviation for "conference call") a telephone call involving multiple people in multiple locations.

> **EXAMPLE:** The only way we can organize this project across our six offices is with a **con call**.

> **TRANSLATION:** The only way we can organize this project across our six offices is with a **conference telephone call**.

> **"REAL SPEAK":** The only way we c'n organize this project across 'ar six offices 'ez w'th a **con call**.

cream of the crop (the) *exp.* the best, most desired people.

> **EXAMPLE:** We always get **the cream of the crop** to work for us because our company offers the highest salaries.

> **TRANSLATION:** We always get **the best people** to work for us because our company offers the highest salaries.

> **"REAL SPEAK":** We ahweez get **the cream 'a the crop** ta work fer us b'cuz 'ar comp'ny offers the highes' saleries.

> *Synonym:* **crème de la crème** *exp.* from French literally meaning "the cream of the cream."

cup of joe *n.* cup of coffee.

> **EXAMPLE:** Carl can't get motivated to work in the morning until he's had his **cup of joe**.

TRANSLATION:	Carl can't get motivated to work in the morning until he's had his **cup of coffee**.
"REAL SPEAK":	Carl can't get modivaded da work 'n the morning 'til 'e's had 'is **cup 'a joe**.
Synonym:	**cup of java** *exp.*

cut corners (to) *exp.* to do something in the easiest or most inexpensive way; to reduce expenses.

EXAMPLE:	The office manager really **cut corners** when he bought our furniture. This chair hurts my back!
TRANSLATION:	The office manager really **took the easiest, least expensive option** when he bought our office furniture. This chair hurts my back!
"REAL SPEAK":	The office manager really **cut corners** when 'e bod 'ar furniture. This chair hurts my back!

do something quick and dirty (to) *exp.* to complete a task quickly but not necessarily correctly.

EXAMPLE:	Jessica **does everything quick and dirty**. She always finishes on time, but I have to go back and fix all the problems.
TRANSLATION:	Jessica **completes her tasks quickly but not necessarily correctly**. She always finishes on time, but I have to go back and fix all the problems.
"REAL SPEAK":	Jessica **does ev'rything quick 'n dirty**. She ahweez finishes on time, b'd I hafta go back 'n fix all the problems.

dog-and-pony show *exp.* a simple presentation which often insults the intelligence of its audience.

EXAMPLE:	I can't believe the boss liked Jack's **dog-and-pony show**! He didn't give any details and completely ignored all the important issues.

TRANSLATION:	I can't believe the boss liked Jack's **simplistic presentation**! He didn't give any details and completely ignored all the important issues.
"REAL SPEAK":	I can't believe the boss liked Jack's **dog-n-pony show**! He didn' give any details 'n completely ignored all the important issues.

down (to be) *adj.* broken; not functional.

EXAMPLE:	My computer is **down** again. I don't know how I'm going to get this report finished in time for our meeting!

TRANSLATION:	My computer is **broken** again. I don't know how I'm going to get this report finished in time for our meeting!
"REAL SPEAK":	My compuder's **down** again. I dunno how I'm gonna get th's report finished 'n time fer 'ar meeding!
Note:	When applied to a person, **to be down** means "to be depressed."

easy street *exp.* a state of financial security or independence.

EXAMPLE:	Now that Susan inherited all that money from her grandmother, she's on **easy street**.
TRANSLATION:	Now that Susan inherited all that money from her grandmother, she's in **a state of financial security**.

"REAL SPEAK": Now th't Susan inherited all that money fr'm 'er gran'mother, she's on **easy street**.

ego trip (to be on an) *exp.* to love drawing attention to one's own importance.

EXAMPLE: All Diane does is talk about her accomplishments. She's **on a ego trip**.

TRANSLATION: All Diane does is talk about her accomplishments. She **loves drawing attention to her own importance**.

"REAL SPEAK": All Diane does 'ez talk aboud 'er accomplishments. She's **on 'n ego trip**.

eyeball something (to) *v.* to look at something.

EXAMPLE: Make sure that Steve **eyeballs** the report. He always has valuable suggestions.

TRANSLATION: Make sure that Steve **looks at** the report. He always has valuable suggestions.

"REAL SPEAK": Make sher th't Steve **eyeballs** the r'port. He always has val'yable suggestions.

fall between the cracks (to) *exp.* to be forgotten.

EXAMPLE: We were supposed to have a big office party next month but it **fell through the cracks**. We all got busy with so many new projects.

TRANSLATION: We were supposed to have a big office party next month but **everyone forgot about it**. We all got busy with so many new projects.

"REAL SPEAK": We were saposta have a big office pardy nex' month b'd it **fell through the cracks**. We all got busy w'th so many new projects.

fallout *n.* the accidental result of an action.

EXAMPLE: Catherine should not have argued with the executives. The **fallout** is that she'll probably never get another promotion.

TRANSLATION: Catherine should not have argued with the executives. The **accidental result of her action** is that she'll probably never get another promotion.

"REAL SPEAK": Catherine shouldn't 'ev argued w'th the execudives. The **falloud** 'ez that she'll prob'ly never ged another pr'motion.

fast track (the) *exp.* a career path which leads to rapid advancement.

EXAMPLE: Pete works hard and people like him. He's definitely on **the fast track** at this company.

TRANSLATION: Pete works hard and people like him. He's definitely on **a career path which leads to rapid advancement** at this company.

"REAL SPEAK": Pete works hard 'n people like 'im. He's definitely on **the fas' track** 'it this comp'ny.

flesh out (to) *v.* to elaborate on, to give more detail.

EXAMPLE: This report is terrible! Tell Joseph **to flesh out** the section involving our yearly profits.

TRANSLATION: This report is terrible! Tell Joseph **to elaborate on** the section involving our yearly profits.

"REAL SPEAK": This r'port 'ez terr'ble! Tell Joseph **ta flesh out** the section involving 'ar yearly profits.

flip side (on the) *exp.* the other side of an argument.

EXAMPLE: I really like Janet, but **on the flip side**, she's always late for work.

TRANSLATION: I really like Janet, but **on the other side of the argument**, she's always late for work.

"REAL SPEAK": I really like Janet, b'd **on the flip side**, she's ahweez late fer work.

Synonym: **on the other hand** *exp.*

get down to business (to) *exp.* to talk about an important topic or situation.

EXAMPLE: We need to **get down to business**. How are we going to make more money next year?

TRANSLATION: We need to **talk about an important topic**. How are we going to make more money next year?

"REAL SPEAK": We need da **get down da bizness**. How 'er we gonna make more money next year?

Synonym: **get cracking (to)** *exp.* to start work.

get more bang for the buck (to) *exp.* to get more benefit for the same amount of money.

EXAMPLE: It's going to cost us one thousand dollars to advertise our new book in this magazine. But if we advertise our entire series of books, we can **get more bang for the buck**!

TRANSLATION: It's going to cost us one thousand dollars to advertise our new book in this magazine. But if we advertise our entire series of books, we can **get more benefit for the same amount of money**!

"REAL SPEAK": It's gonna cost us one thousan' dollers ta advertise 'ar new book 'n th's magazine. B'd if we advertise 'ar entire series 'a books, we c'n **get more bang fer the buck**!

get off someone's back (to) *exp.* to stop harassing someone.

EXAMPLE: I want Hannah **to get off my back**. I told her I would have the report finished by noon!

TRANSLATION: I want Hannah **to stop harassing me**. I told her I would have the report finished by noon!

"REAL SPEAK": I want Hannah **da get off my back**. I told 'er I'd have the r'port finished by noon!

get-rich-quick scheme *exp.* a plan to make a lot of money very quickly.

EXAMPLE: Jerry is always inventing new **get-rich-quick schemes** because he hates to work.

TRANSLATION: Jerry is always inventing new **plans to make a lot of money very quickly** because he hates to work.

"REAL SPEAK": Jerry's ahweez inven'ing new **get-rich-quick schemes** b'cuz 'e hates ta work.

get right on something (to) *exp.* to begin work immediately.

EXAMPLE: I need that report as soon as possible, so **get right on it**!

TRANSLATION: I need that report as soon as possible, so **begin work on it immediately**!

"REAL SPEAK": I need that r'pord 'ez soon 'ez possible, so **get ride on it**!

get to the bottom of something (to) *exp.* to discover the origin of a problem.

EXAMPLE: My computer isn't working! Tell Laurie **to get to the bottom of this**.

TRANSLATION: My computer isn't working! Tell Laurie **to discover the origin of this problem**.

"REAL SPEAK": My c'mputer isn't working! Tell Laurie **da get ta the boddom 'a this**.

give someone a heads up (to) *exp.* to tell someone a piece of information before it becomes official.

EXAMPLE: I heard that Sandy is going to get fired. I'm going **to give her a heads up**, so she can start looking for another job.

TRANSLATION: I heard that Sandy is going to get fired. I'm going **to tell her about it before it becomes official**, so she can start looking for another job.

"REAL SPEAK": I heard th't Sandy's gonna get fired. I'm gonna **give 'er a heads up**, so she c'n start looking fer another job.

give something a once-over (to) *exp.* to look at something briefly.

EXAMPLE: I didn't see any misspellings in your report, but I only **gave it a once-over**.

TRANSLATION: I didn't see any misspellings in your report, but I only **looked at it briefly**.

"REAL SPEAK": I didn' see any misspellings 'n yer r'port, b'd I only **gave id a once-over**.

go belly up (to) *exp.* to go out of business; to go bankrupt.

EXAMPLE: It's been hard to find a job this year. So many companies are **going belly up**.

TRANSLATION: It's been hard to find a job this year. So many companies are **going out of business**.

"REAL SPEAK": It's been hard da find a job th's year. So many comp'nies 'er **going belly up**.

go over someone's head (to) *exp.* to go to the person above one's direct superior with a problem or concern.

EXAMPLE: If Thomas won't give me a raise, I'll simply **go over his head**.

TRANSLATION: If Thomas won't give me a raise, I'll simply **go to the person above him with my concern**.

"REAL SPEAK": If Thomas won't gimme a raise, a'll simply **go over 'is head**.

go public (to) *exp.* to make secret information widely known.

EXAMPLE: I heard that one of the executives is stealing from the company, but I'm too afraid **to go public**. I might get fired!

TRANSLATION: I heard that one of the executives is stealing from the company, but I'm too afraid **to make the secret information widely known**. I might get fired!

"REAL SPEAK": I heard th't one 'a the execudives 'ez stealing fr'm the comp'ny, b'd I'm too afraid **da go public**. I might get fired!

grapevine (the) *n.* the gossip, rumors, and informal information circulating throughout an office.

EXAMPLE: I heard through **the grapevine** that the boss wears women's underwear!

TRANSLATION: I heard through **the rumors circulating throughout the office** that that the boss wears women's underwear!

"REAL SPEAK": I heard through **the grapevine** th't the boss wears women's underwear!

Synonym: **rumormill** *n.*

LESSON 2

DEBBIE TALKS SHOP!

More General Workplace Slang & Idioms *(Part 2)*

THIS LESSON FEATURES 10 NEW SLANG WORDS & IDIOMS

LET'S WARM UP!

MATCH THE PICTURES

As a fun way to get started, see if you can guess the meaning of the new slang words and expressions on the opposite page by using the pictures below and following the context of the sentences.

1. Carl and Steve are always **talking shop**, even after work!
   - ❏ talking about shopping
   - ❏ talking about work

2. Brian made a **snap judgment** that lost us money. He should have read the report more carefully first!
   - ❏ hasty decision
   - ❏ loud noise

3. As a **rule of thumb**, you should never yell at your boss.
   - ❏ general guideline
   - ❏ rule about fingers

4. Gary has never done an assignment like this before. He's just **flying by the seat of his pants**!
   - ❏ moving around like he's flying
   - ❏ improvising

5. Lionel finally **got the hang of** the computer program! He's been trying to understand it for weeks.
   - ❏ became proficient at
   - ❏ broke

6. Nathan **gave me some pointers**. Now I'm working more efficiently.
   - ❏ gave me some sharp sticks
   - ❏ gave me some advice

7. I slept through the meeting. What did I miss, **in a nutshell**?
   - ❏ in detail
   - ❏ in summary

8. Rob is **going over the problem in his head**, but he hasn't thought of a solution yet.
   - ❏ thinking about the problem carefully
   - ❏ ignoring the problem

9. Tim **showed Paul up** by correcting him in front of the boss.
   - ❏ made himself appear more competent than Paul
   - ❏ made himself appear taller than Paul

10. I'm hungry! I'm taking my **lunch break**.
   - ❏ time allotted for breaking things during lunch
   - ❏ time allotted for eating lunch

More General Workplace Slang & Idioms (Part 2)

LET'S TALK!

A. DIALOGUE USING SLANG & IDIOMS

The words introduced on the first two pages are used in the dialogue below. See if you can understand the conversation. *Note:* The translation of the words in boldface is on the right-hand page.

CD-A: TRACK 8

Karen: I can't **get the hang of** this new job. Jeff told me what to do and I keep **going over it in my head**, but I feel like I'm just **flying by the seat of my pants** most of the time. Will you **give me some pointers**?

Debbie: As a **rule of thumb**, I don't like to **talk shop** on my **lunch break**, but I'll make an exception for you. Here's my advice **in a nutshell**. Don't make any **snap judgments** and try not to **show anyone up**. The rest is easy!

More General Workplace Slang & Idioms (Part 2)

B. DIALOGUE TRANSLATED INTO STANDARD ENGLISH

LET'S SEE HOW MUCH YOU REMEMBER!
Just for fun, move around in random order to the words and
expressions in boldface below. See if you can remember their
slang equivalents without looking at the left-hand page!

Karen: I can't **become proficient at** this new job. Jeff told me what to do and I keep
thinking about it carefully, but I feel like I'm just **improvising** most of
the time. Will you **give me some advice**?

Debbie: As a **general guideline**, I don't like to **discuss work** on my **time allotted
for lunch**, but I'll make an exception for you. Here's my advice **in summary**.
Don't make any **hasty decisions** and try not to **appear more competent
than anyone else**. The rest is easy!

C. DIALOGUE USING "REAL SPEAK"

The dialogue below demonstrates how the slang conversation on the previous page would *really* be spoken by native speakers!

Karen: I can't **get the hang 'a** this new job. Jeff told me what ta do 'n I keep **going over id in my head**, b'd I feel like I'm jus' **flying by the seat 'a my pants** most 'a the time. Will ya **gimme s'm poin(t)ers**?

Debbie: As a **rule 'a thumb**, I don't like ta **talk shop** on my **lunch break**, b'd a'll make 'n exception fer you. Here's my advice **in a nutshell**. Don't make any **snap judgments** an' try not ta **show anyone up**. The rest 'ez easy!

LET'S LEARN!

VOCABULARY

The following words and expressions were used in the previous dialogues. Let's take a closer look at what they mean.

fly by the seat of one's pants (to) *exp.* to improvise.

EXAMPLE: Matthew never spends enough time checking facts or researching. He always **flies by the seat of his pants** when he makes decisions.

TRANSLATION: Matthew never spends enough time checking facts or researching. He always **improvises** when he makes decisions.

"REAL SPEAK": Matthew never spenz anuf time checking facts 'er researching. He ahweez **flies by the sead 'ev 'is pants** when 'e makes decisions.

Synonym: **make something up as one goes (to)** *exp.*

NOW YOU DO IT. COMPLETE THE PHRASE ALOUD:
If you don't have time to research..., just try to **fly by the seat of your pants**.

get the hang of something (to) *exp.* to become proficient.

EXAMPLE: After reading the manual a dozen times, I finally **got the hang of** using my new computer!

TRANSLATION: After reading the manual a dozen times, I finally **became proficient at** using my new computer!

"REAL SPEAK": After reading the manual a dozen times, I fin'lly **got the hang 'ev** using my new c'mpuder!

NOW YOU DO IT. COMPLETE THE PHRASE ALOUD:
This job is too hard! I can't **get the hang of** doing....

give someone some pointers (to) *exp.* to give someone someone advice.

EXAMPLE: If you need help writing this report, ask Albert to **give you some pointers**. He's the best manager in this company.

TRANSLATION: If you need help writing this report, ask Albert to **give you some advice**. He's the best manager in this company.

"REAL SPEAK": If ya need help wriding this r'port, ask Albert ta **give ya s'm poin(t)ers**. He's the best manager 'n th's comp'ny.

NOW YOU DO IT. COMPLETE THE PHRASE ALOUD:
If you want to learn how to ..., I can **give you some pointers**.

go over something in one's head (to) *exp.* to think about something carefully.

EXAMPLE: If I have to fire someone, I'll fire Ted. I've **gone over it in my head** several times, and Sandra is definitely a better worker.

TRANSLATION: If I have to fire someone, I'll fire Ted. I've **thought about it carefully** several times, and Sandra is definitely a better worker.

"REAL SPEAK": If I hafta fire someone, a'll fire Ted. I've **gone over id in my head** sev'ral times, 'n Sandra's definitely a bedder worker.

Synonym 1: **mull something over (to)** *exp.*

Synonym 2: **think on it (to)** *exp.*

NOW YOU DO IT. COMPLETE THE PHRASE ALOUD:
I keep **going over ... in my head**.

in a nutshell *exp.* in summary.

EXAMPLE: If you miss the meeting today, don't worry about it. **In a nutshell**, we're opening a new store in Los Angeles and we're going to start hiring some more employees.

TRANSLATION: If you miss the meeting today, don't worry about it. **In summary**, we're opening a new store in Los Angeles and we're going to start hiring some more employees.

"REAL SPEAK": If ya miss the meeding taday, don't worry aboud it. **In a nutshell**, w'r opening a new store 'n LA 'n w'r gonna start hiring s'm more employees.

Synonym 1: **gist (the)** *n.* the basic idea.

Synonym 2: **in short** *exp.*

Synonym 3: **make a long story short (to)** *exp.*

NOW YOU DO IT. COMPLETE THE PHRASE ALOUD:
In a nutshell, the report was about...

More General Workplace Slang & Idioms (Part 2)

lunch break *n.* the time allotted to employees for eating lunch which is typically an hour.

EXAMPLE: The bank is always closed by the time I leave work at the end of the day. I'm going to go during **lunch break**.

TRANSLATION: The bank is always closed by the time I leave work at the end of the day. I'm going to go during **the time allotted to employees for eating lunch**.

"REAL SPEAK": The bank's ahweez closed by the time I leave work 'it the end 'a the day. I'm gonna go during **lunch break**.

Synonym: **lunch hour** *n.*

NOW YOU DO IT. COMPLETE THE PHRASE ALOUD:
Let's go eat at... on our **lunch break**.

rule of thumb *exp.* a general guideline.

EXAMPLE: As a **rule of thumb**, you should never question a decision made by a superior unless you want to get fired.

TRANSLATION: As a **general guideline**, you should never question a decision made by a superior unless you want to get fired.

"REAL SPEAK": As a **rule 'a thumb**, you should never question a decision made by a saperier unless ya wanna get fired.

Origin: One time in American history, husbands were allowed to hit their wives with sticks no thicker than their thumbs, thus the "rule of thumb."

NOW YOU DO IT. COMPLETE THE PHRASE ALOUD:
As a **rule of thumb**, you should never...

show someone up (to) *exp.* to make oneself appear more competent than someone else.

EXAMPLE: Oliver **showed me up** in front of the whole team. He answered all the questions before I had a chance to.

TRANSLATION: Oliver **made himself look more competent than me** in front of the whole team. He answered all the questions before I had a chance to.

"REAL SPEAK": Oliver **showed me up** 'n fronna the whole team. He answered all the questions b'fore I had a chance to.

NOW YOU DO IT. COMPLETE THE PHRASE ALOUD:
I **showed up my boss** when I …

snap judgment *exp.* a hasty decision made without having all the necessary facts.

EXAMPLE: I wish Ralph would stop making **snap judgments**. He should listen to both sides of an argument before reaching a conclusion.

TRANSLATION: I wish Ralph would stop making **hasty decisions**. He should listen to both sides of an argument before reaching a conclusion.

"REAL SPEAK": I wish Ralph 'ed stop making **snap judgments**. He should listen da both sides 'ev 'n argument b'fore reaching a c'nclusion.

NOW YOU DO IT. COMPLETE THE PHRASE ALOUD:
I made a **snap judgment** about...

talk shop (to) *exp.* to discuss work.

EXAMPLE: Charles is no fun to eat lunch with. I like to get away from the office, but he always wants to **talk shop**.

TRANSLATION: Charles is no fun to eat lunch with. I like to get away from the office, but he always wants to **discuss work**.

"REAL SPEAK": Charles 'ez no fun da eat lunch with. I like ta ged away fr'm the office, b't he ahweez wansta **talk shop**.

NOW YOU DO IT. COMPLETE THE PHRASE ALOUD:
Let's **talk shop**. What do think about... ?

More General Workplace Slang & Idioms (Part 2)

LET'S PRACTICE!

CD-A: TRACK 10

A. FIND THE MISSING WORDS

Complete the dialogue by filling in the blanks with the correct words using the list below.

BREAK	**RULE**
HANG	**SEAT**
HEAD	**SHOP**
NUTSHELL	**SHOW UP**
POINTERS	**SNAP**

Ken: Do you have time to talk _____? I've been going over the information in my

_____, but I just can't get the _____ of this new procedure. Do

you have time to give me some _____?

Shelley: Sure, no problem! Okay. As a _____ of thumb, you should always think

before you speak, don't make any _____ judgments when talking to clients,

don't _____ the other employees by making them look foolish in front of the

client, and don't take your lunch _____ when you're scheduled to have a

meeting. That's the new procedure in a _____.

Ken: I guess I can't just fly by the _____ of my pants anymore. Thanks!

B. CREATE YOUR OWN NEWSPAPER COLUMN

Without looking at the newspaper column at the bottom of the page, fill in the blank lines of 1-10 directly below. Next, transfer your answers to the empty boxes in the newspaper column. Make sure to match the number of your answer with the numbered box. Next, read your column aloud. Remember: The funnier your answers, the funnier your column will be!

1. Write down an "adjective" *(strange, tall, fat, etc.)*: _____

2. Write down a "thing" in plural form *(pencils, potatoes, toothbrushes, etc.)*: _____

3. Write down an "animal" *(dog, bear, giraffe, etc.)*: _____

4. Write down an "adjective" *(strange, tall, fat, etc.)*: _____

5. Write down a "place" *(market, movie theater, hospital, etc.)*: _____

6. Write down a "thing" *(pencil, potato, toothbrush, etc.)*: _____

7. Write down a "verb" *(play, sing, dance)*: _____

8. Write down a "verb" *(play, sing, dance)*: _____

9. Write down a "thing" *(pencil, potato, toothbrush, etc.)*: _____

10. Write down a "thing" *(pencil, potato, toothbrush, etc.)*: _____

THE WEEKLY

GOSSIP-MONGER GAZETTE

NEWS FOR PEOPLE WHO LIKE TO TALK ABOUT OTHER PEOPLE

"Dear Blabby..."

**by B. Blabby Barnet
Gossip Expert**

Dear Blabby...

In a nutshell, my boss is [____1.____]! He's always making **snap judgments**

about [____2.____] and taking really long **lunch hours** with his [____3.____] so he can **talk shop**. As a **rule of thumb**, he's [____4.____]! When we're at the [____5.____], he tries to **show me up** in front of my [____6.____]. I thought I would know how to [____7.____] with him by now, but I'm still **flying by the seat of my pants**.

I need you to **give me some pointers**! If I don't **get the hang of this** soon, I'll have to [____8.____] my [____9.____], which would be terrible. I keep **going over this in my head**, and I need your help! Please, Blabby, tell me what to do. It's a matter of life and [____10.____]!

Sincerely,
Frustrated in Fresno

C. **MATCH THE SENTENCES**

Match the numbered sentences below with the lettered
sentences on the opposite page. Write your answers in the
boxes at the bottom of the pages.

READING

CD-A: TRACK 11

1 Alice didn't study. She just guessed the answers.

2 Is it okay to date a coworker?

3 Peter is doing very well in his new job.

4 Did I miss anything important at the meeting?

5 I want to discuss the project but I'm late for a meeting!

6 Where's Isabelle? I can't find her.

7 Eric fired his assistant because she was late. Now he regrets it.

8 Can you help me with this project?

9 Kyle made Wendy look stupid in the meeting.

10 I'm worried that I'll forget my speech!

NUMBERS	1	2	3	4	5
LETTERS					

C. MATCH THE SENTENCES - *(continued)*

NUMBERS	6	7	8	9	10
LETTERS					

More General Workplace Slang & Idioms (Part 2)

FROM THE SLANGMAN FILES

More General Workplace Slang & Idioms (H-O)

half-baked *adj.* impractical and not well contemplated.

> **EXAMPLE:** All of Melissa's suggestions are **half-baked**. She needs to spend more time considering the problem before speaking.
>
> **TRANSLATION:** All of Melissa's suggestions are **impractice and not well contemplated**. She needs to spend more time considering the problem before speaking.
>
> **"REAL SPEAK":** All 'a Melissa's suggestions 'er **half-baked**. She needs da spen' more time c'nsidering the problem b'fore speaking.

have all one's ducks in a row (to) *exp.* to be very organized.

> **EXAMPLE:** This project is really complicated! I need **to have all my ducks in a row** or I'll lose control.

> **TRANSLATION:** This project is really complicated! I need **to be very organized** or I'll lose control.
>
> **"REAL SPEAK":** This projec's really complicaded! I need **da have all my ducks 'n a row** 'er a'll lose c'ntrol.

have the upper hand (to) *exp.* to have the advantage.

> **EXAMPLE:** I've been working here for ten years and Edward just started last fall. The boss will definitely listen to my suggestions before his. I clearly **have the upper hand**.
>
> **TRANSLATION:** I've been working here for ten years and Edward just started last fall. The boss will definitely listen to my suggestions before his. I clearly **have the advantage**.
>
> **"REAL SPEAK":** I' been working here fer ten years 'n Edward jus' starded las' fall. The boss'll def'nitely listen da my suggestions b'fore his. I clearly **have the upper hand**.

heads will roll *exp.* people will be punished.

> **EXAMPLE:** If we don't make our sales goals for this month, **heads will roll**!
>
> **TRANSLATION:** If we don't make our sales goals for this month, **people will be punished**!
>
> **"REAL SPEAK":** If we don't make 'ar sales goals fer this month, **heads'll roll**!
>
> *Note:* This expression refers to the era when the decapitation of criminals was common.

hustle (to) *v.* to work quickly.

> **EXAMPLE:** This report is due in an hour. We really need **to hustle** to get it done!
>
> **TRANSLATION:** This report is due in an hour. We really need **to work quickly** to get it done!
>
> **"REAL SPEAK":** This r'port's due 'n 'n hour. We really need **da hustle** ta ged it done!

in the hot seat (to be) *exp.* to be in an uncomfortable situation where you are being closely examined for mistakes you have made.

> **EXAMPLE:** Martin's **in the hot seat** because he forgot to schedule the meeting, and the boss wants to know why.

> **TRANSLATION:** Martin's **in an uncomfortable situation** because he forgot to schedule the meeting, and the boss wants to know why.

> **"REAL SPEAK":** Martin's **in the hot seat** b'cuz 'e fergot ta schedule the meeding b't didn't, an' the boss wansta know why.

in the know (to be) *exp.* to be fully informed.

> **EXAMPLE:** Lorraine **is in the know** because she and the president were friends in college and they talk all the time.

> **TRANSLATION:** Lorraine **is fully informed** because she and the president were friends in college and they talk all the time.

> **"REAL SPEAK":** Lorraine's **'n the know** b'cuz she 'n the president were frienz 'n college an' they talk all the time.

John Hancock *n.* signature.

> **EXAMPLE:** The deal will be completed as soon as you put your **John Hancock** on the dotted line.

> **TRANSLATION:** The deal will be completed as soon as you put your **signature** on the dotted line.

> **"REAL SPEAK":** The deal'll be compleded 'ez soon 'ez ya put cher **John Hancock** on the dodded line.

> *Note:* John Hancock was the first to sign the Declaration of Independence.

jump to conclusions (to) *exp.* to make assumptions based on too little information.

> **EXAMPLE:** Don't **jump to conclusions** about Adam. He seems naive sometimes, but he's actually very smart.

> **TRANSLATION:** Don't **make assumptions** about Adam. He seems naive sometimes, but he's actually very smart.

> **"REAL SPEAK":** Don't **jump ta conclusions** aboud Adam. He seems naive sometimes, b'd 'e's akshelly very smart.

jump start something (to) *exp.* to activate something stagnant and get it moving forward.

> **EXAMPLE:** I'm glad Brett is helping us. He **jump-started the project** with his fresh ideas.

> **TRANSLATION:** I'm glad Brett is helping us. He **got the project moving forward** with his fresh ideas.

> **"REAL SPEAK":** I'm glad Brett's helping us. He **jump-starded the project** with 'is fresh ideas.

> *Variation:* **jump-start** *n.*

jury-rig (to) *v.* to improvise a solution for something.

> **EXAMPLE:** Since the repair person can't come for a week, we need to **jury-rig** the computers right away.

> **TRANSLATION:** Since the repair person can't come for a week, we need to **improvise a solution for** the computers right away.

> **"REAL SPEAK":** Since the repair person can't come fer a week, we need da **jury-rig** the c'mpuders ride away.

keep a low profile (to) *exp.* to remain in the background; to be inconspicuous.

> **EXAMPLE:** Ever since Sue got reprimanded, she tries to **keep a low profile**, so she won't get fired.

> **TRANSLATION:** Ever since Sue got reprimanded, she tries to **remain in the background and be inconspicuous**, so she won't get fired.

> **"REAL SPEAK":** Ever since Sue got reprimanded, she tries da **keep a low profile**, so she won't get fired.

> *Synonym:* **lay low (to)** *exp.*

keep an eye on someone/something (to) *exp.* to watch someone/something very carefully.

> **EXAMPLE:** **Keep an eye on Ralph.** I have a feeling he's the one who has been stealing office supplies.

> **TRANSLATION:** **Watch Ralph very carefully.** I have a feeling he's the one who has been stealing office supplies.

> **"REAL SPEAK":** **Keep 'n eye on Ralph.** I have a feeling he's the one oo's been stealing office supplies.

> *Synonym:* **keep tabs on someone (to)** *exp.* to watch someone closely.

kiss a lot of frogs (to) *exp.* to try a lot of different ideas.

> **EXAMPLE:** If this plan doesn't work, we just need to try another one. You have to **kiss a lot of frogs** in this business.

> **TRANSLATION:** If this plan doesn't work, we just need to try another one. You have to **try a lot of different ideas** in this business.

> **"REAL SPEAK":** If this plan doesn' work, we jus' need da try another one. Ya hafta **kiss a lodda frogs** 'n th's bizness.

> *Note:* This is a reference to the fairy tale *The Frog Prince* where the princess kisses a frog and it turns into a prince.

knee-jerk reaction *n.* an instinctive response, usually made without thought.

> **EXAMPLE:** When Darryl found out that he didn't get the promotion, he started screaming. It was a **knee-jerk reaction** and now he regrets it.

> **TRANSLATION:** When Darryl found out that he didn't get the promotion, he started screaming. It was an **instinctive response** and now he regrets it.

> **"REAL SPEAK":** When Darryl found out th'd 'e didn' get the pr'motion, he starded screaming. It w'z a **knee-jerk reaction** 'n now 'e regrets it.

kudos *n.* praise.

> **EXAMPLE:** Nancy deserves a lot of **kudos** for her graphic design. Her work is always excellent.

> **TRANSLATION:** Nancy deserves a lot of **praise** for her graphic design. Her work is always excellent.

> **"REAL SPEAK":** Nancy deserves a lodda **kudos** fer her graphic design. Her work's ahweez excellent.

> *Synonym:* **props** *n.* (popular teen slang).

leading-edge technology *n.* the most recently discovered technology.

> **EXAMPLE:** If we only want to use **leading-edge technology**, we'll have to spend millions of dollars and train our personnel regularly. It's not worth it.

More General Workplace Slang & Idioms (Part 2)

TRANSLATION: If we only want to use **the most recently discovered technology**, we'll have to spend millions of dollars and train our personnel regularly. It's not worth it.

"REAL SPEAK": If we only wanna use **leading-edge technolagy**, we'll hafta spen' millions 'a dollers 'n train 'ar personnel regularly. It's not worth it.

leave someone holding the bag (to) *exp.* to force someone to be responsible for something.

EXAMPLE: Kimberly was supposed to be in charge of our last project, but she went on vacation and **left me holding the bag**!

TRANSLATION: Kimberly was supposed to be in charge of our last project, but she went on vacation and **forced me to be responsible for it**!

"REAL SPEAK": Kimberly w'z saposta be 'n charge 'ev 'ar las' project, b't she wen' on vacation 'n **left me holding the bag**!

lock horns with someone (to) *exp.* to argue over something.

EXAMPLE: I think we should spend more money on marketing, but Barry disagrees. I **lock horns with him** about everything.

TRANSLATION: I think we should spend more money on marketing, but Barry disagrees. I **argue with him** about everything.

"REAL SPEAK": I think we should spen' more money on markeding, b't Barry disagrees. I **lock horns w'th 'im** aboud ev'rything.

look out for number one (to) *exp.* to put one's own interests above everything else's.

EXAMPLE: Erica didn't tell her friends about the new job positions opened in the mall. She wanted to be the only one to apply. Erica always **looks out for number one**.

TRANSLATION: Erica didn't tell her friends about the new job positions opened in the mall. She wanted to be the only one to apply. Erica always **puts her own interests above everything else's**.

"REAL SPEAK": Erica didn' tell 'er friends about the new job pasitions opened in the mall. She wan'ed da be the only one to apply. Erica ahweez **looks out fer number one**.

make a living (to) *exp.* to earn enough money to sustain day-to-day life.

EXAMPLE: I don't have a big salary, but I **make a living**.

TRANSLATION: I don't have a big salary, but I **earn enough money to sustain day-to-day life**.

"REAL SPEAK": I don't have a big salery, b'd I **make a living**.

Variation: **it's a living** *exp.* It's enough to sustain day-to-day life.

make a name for oneself (to) *exp.* to earn public recognition.

EXAMPLE: I just started at the company, but I'm hoping **to make a name for myself** in a few months.

TRANSLATION: I just started at the company, but I'm hoping **to earn public recognition** in a few months.

"REAL SPEAK": I jus' starded 'it the company, b'd I'm hoping **da make a name fer myself** 'n a few munts.

More General Workplace Slang & Idioms (Part 2)

meet someone halfway (to) *exp.* to compromise with someone.

> **EXAMPLE:** Nathan and I just can't agree on what to do. I'm going to **meet him halfway**, so we can start making progress again.

> **TRANSLATION:** Nathan and I just can't agree on what to do. I'm going to **compromise with him**, so we can start making progress again.

> **"REAL SPEAK":** Nathan 'n I jus' can' agree on what ta do. I'm gonna **meed 'im halfway**, so we c'n start making progress again.

migrate (to) *v.* to move.

> **EXAMPLE:** The new computer system will be delivered in an hour. Just make sure to **migrate** all the data onto it before using it.

> **TRANSLATION:** The new computer system will be delivered in an hour. Just make sure to **move** all the data onto it before using it.

> **"REAL SPEAK":** The new c'mpuder system'll be delivered in 'n hour. Jus' make sher da **migrade** all the dada onto it b'fore using it.

> *Note:* Usually refers to people, birds, or animals, but now often refers to moving data from one database to another.

milk something for all it's worth (to) *exp.* to get the maximum benefit from something.

> **EXAMPLE:** The boss praised my last report, so I'm going to **milk it for all it's worth**. I'm going to ask him for a raise tomorrow.

> **TRANSLATION:** The boss praised my last report, so I'm going to **get the maximum benefit from it**. I'm going to ask him for a raise tomorrow.

> **"REAL SPEAK":** The boss praised my last report, so I'm gonna **milk it fer all it's worth**. I'm gonna ask 'im fer a raise tamorrow.

nepotism *n.* favoritism shown to relatives or friends in business.

> **EXAMPLE:** Our manager gives his nephew all the good assignments. I wish the president would stop the **nepotism** in this company.

> **TRANSLATION:** Our manager gives his nephew all the good assignments. I wish the president would stop the **favoritism shown to relatives** in this company.

> **"REAL SPEAK":** 'Ar manager gives 'is nephew all the good assignments. I wish the president 'ed stop the **nepatism** 'n this comp'ny.

netizen *n.* a person who uses the Internet (*net* is short for "Internet" and *-izen* is short for "citizen").

> **EXAMPLE:** With the growing popularity of computers and the Internet, there are more **netizens** every year.

> **TRANSLATION:** With the growing popularity of computers and the Internet, there are more **people who use the Internet** every year.

> **"REAL SPEAK":** W'th the growing popularidy of c'mpuders 'n the In(t)ernet, there 'er more **nedizens** ev'ry year.

network (to) *v.* • **1.** to form relationships with people who can help to advance one's career • **2.** in technology, a system of interconnected computers.

> **EXAMPLE 1:** I got this job because of Natalie's help. I'm glad I spent so much time **networking**!

More General Workplace Slang & Idioms (Part 2)

TRANSLATION: I got this job because of Natalie's help. I'm glad I spent so much time **forming relationships with people who can help to advance my career**.

"REAL SPEAK": I got this job b'cuz 'a Nadalie's help. I'm glad I spent so much time **networking**!

EXAMPLE 2: Can you connect my computer to the **network**? I need to access some information stored on Bob's machine.

TRANSLATION: Can you connect my computer to the **system of interconnected computers**? I need to access some information stored on Bob's machine.

"REAL SPEAK": C'n you connect my c'mpuder ta the **network**? I need da access s'm infermation stored on Bob's machine.

nip something in the bud (to) *exp.* to stop something at an early stage.

EXAMPLE: Some of the employees are expecting big raises this year, and I want to **nip that rumor in the bud**. No one will be getting a raise until next year.

TRANSLATION: Some of the employees are expecting big raises this year, and I want to **stop that rumor at an early stage**. No one will be getting a raise until next year.

"REAL SPEAK": Some 'a the employees 'er expecting big raises this year, 'n I wanna **nip that rumer in the bud**. No one'll be gedding a raise 'til next year.

off the cuff *exp.* without really thinking about it.

EXAMPLE: I don't know the answer, but **off the cuff**, I'd say we should hire someone new.

TRANSLATION: I don't know the answer, but **without really thinking about it**, I'd say we should hire someone new.

"REAL SPEAK": I dunno the answer, b'd **off the cuff**, I'd say we should hire someone new.

Synonym: **off the top of my head** *exp.*

on the downlow *adj.* supposed to be kept a secret.

EXAMPLE: That information I told you is **on the downlow**. If you tell anyone, I could get reprimanded.

TRANSLATION: That information I told you is **supposed to be kept secret**. If you tell anyone, I could get reprimanded.

"REAL SPEAK": Thad infermation I told ju's **on the downlow**. If ya tell anyone, I could get reprimanded.

Synonym 1: **keep something hush-hush (to)** *exp.* to keep something a secret.

Synonym 2: **keep something under one's hat (to)** *exp.*

on the same page (to be) *exp.* to have the same understanding about something.

EXAMPLE: Delia and I are **on the same page** about the project. We both think we need to hire some more people to help us finish it.

TRANSLATION: Delia and I **have the same understanding** about the project. We both think we need to hire some more people to help us finish it.

"REAL SPEAK": Delia 'n I 'er **on the same page** about the project. We both think we need da hire s'm more people da help us finish it.

org chart *abbrev.* organization chart; the graph depicting a company's hierarchy.

EXAMPLE: Have you seen the **org chart** lately? Now Pauline is in charge of the whole accounting team.

TRANSLATION: Have you seen the **graph depicting our company's hierarchy** lately? Now Pauline is in charge of the whole accounting team.

"REAL SPEAK": Have ya seen the **org chart** lately? Now Pauline's 'n charge 'a the whole accoun(t)ing team.

More General Workplace Slang & Idioms (Part 2)

LESSON 3

LISA GETS A FAIR SHAKE

Even More General Workplace Slang & Idioms *(Part 3)*

THIS LESSON FEATURES ⑩ NEW SLANG WORDS & IDIOMS

LET'S WARM UP!

MATCH THE PICTURES

As a fun way to get started, see if you can guess the meaning of the new slang words and expressions on the opposite page by using the pictures below and following the context of the sentences. Each answer can only be used once!

1. Hank's been working very hard for the last three months. If he doesn't get an assistant, he's going to **go postal**!

2. The same people have been working here for the last twenty years. We need some **new blood** to bring energy to the company.

3. Keith **gives everyone a fair shake**. He judges workers on their skills rather than their race or gender.

4. Everyone loves Raymond because he **does the lion's share of the work** and never complains.

5. Jenna works for a **dot com**. Her company sells toys over the Internet.

6. Our company has a great **corporate culture**. We dress casually, our managers respect us, and we enjoy our work.

7. On **dress-down days**, I can wear a t-shirt instead of a suit.

8. The **old boys' club** at our company only promotes Caucasian men, so Juan is going to quit.

9. Sandy wants to find a job that pays more money. That's why she's **polishing her résumé**.

10. Geoffrey's a **dinosaur**! He's been working here for fifty years and can't even use a computer!

A. Internet company

B. traditionally-minded executives

C. new employees

D. updating her résumé

E. become violently angry

F. gives everyone an equal chance to succeed

G. does most of the work

H. days where employees are allowed to dress casually

I. old-fashioned person

J. office mood

Even More General Workplace Slang & Idioms (Part 3)

LET'S TALK!

A. DIALOGUE USING SLANG & IDIOMS

The words introduced on the first two pages are used in the dialogue below. See if you can understand the conversation. *Note:* The translation of the words in boldface is on the right-hand page.

CD-A: TRACK 12

Lisa: I hate working for this **old boys' club** because I don't **get a fair shake**. I **do the lion's share of the work** and they expect me to work on this **dinosaur** of a computer! I swear I'm going to **go postal**!

Paul: You should work for a **dot com**. They have a fun **corporate culture** and a lot of **dress-down days**. They always need **new blood**.

Lisa: Great idea! I'll start **polishing my résumé** tonight.

B. DIALOGUE TRANSLATED INTO STANDARD ENGLISH

LET'S SEE HOW MUCH YOU REMEMBER!
Just for fun, move around in random order to the words and
expressions in boldface below. See if you can remember their
slang equivalents without looking at the left-hand page!

Lisa: I hate working for this **group of traditionally-minded, older executives** because I don't **get an equal opportunity to succeed**. I **perform most of the work** and they expect me to work on this **outdated** computer! I swear I'm going to **become violently angry**!

Paul: You should work for an **Internet company**. They have a fun **company mood** and a lot of **days when employees can wear casual clothes**. They always need **new employees with fresh ideas**.

Lisa: Great idea! I'll start **updating my résumé** tonight.

C. DIALOGUE USING "REAL SPEAK"

CD-A: TRACK 12

The dialogue below demonstrates how the slang conversation on the opposite page would *really* be spoken by native speakers!

Lisa: I hate working fer this **old boys' club** b'cuz I don't **ged a fair shake**. I **do the lion's share 'a the work** 'n they expect me da work on this **dinisor** 'ev a c'mpuder! I swear I'm gonna **go postal**!

Paul: You should work fer a **dot com**. They have a fun **corp'rit culture** an' a lodda **dress-down days**. They ahweez need **new blood**.

Lisa: Grade idea! A'll start **polishing my résumé** danight.

LET'S LEARN!

VOCABULARY

The following words and expressions were used in the previous dialogues. Let's take a closer look at what they mean.

CD-A: TRACK 13

corporate culture *exp.* a company's mood determined by its employees and policies.

> **EXAMPLE:** Our **corporate culture** is very fun and exciting. Most of the employees are young and the company allows us to wear whatever clothes we want.

> **TRANSLATION:** Our **company's mood** is very fun and exciting. Most of the employees are young and the company allows us to wear whatever clothes we want.

> **"REAL SPEAK":** 'Ar **corp'rit culture**'s very fun 'n exciding. Most 'a the employees 'er young 'n the company allows us ta wear whadever coze we want.

> **NOW YOU DO IT. COMPLETE THE PHRASE ALOUD:**
> My company's **corporate culture** is...

dinosaur *n.* an old-fashioned or outdated person or thing.

> **EXAMPLE:** Dino is a great author, but he still writes all of his books with pen and paper instead of with a computer. He's such a **dinosaur**!
>
> **TRANSLATION:** Dino is a great author, but he still writes all of his books with pen and paper instead of with a computer. He's such an **old-fashioned person**!
>
> **"REAL SPEAK":** Dino's a grade auther, b'd 'e still writes all 'ev 'is books w'th pen 'n paper 'nstead 'ev w'th a c'mpuder. He's such a **dinasaur**!
>
> *Synonym:* **relic** *n.*
>
> **NOW YOU DO IT. COMPLETE THE PHRASE ALOUD:**
> I'm a **dinosaur** because I....

do the lion's share of the work (to) *exp.* to perform most of the work.

> **EXAMPLE:** Jim deserves a raise. He **does the lion's share of the work**, but makes less money than everyone else.
>
> **TRANSLATION:** Jim deserves a raise. He **performs most of the work**, but makes less money than everyone else.
>
> **"REAL SPEAK":** Jim deserves a raise. He **does the lion's share 'a the work**, b't makes less money th'n ev'ryone else.
>
> **NOW YOU DO IT. COMPLETE THE PHRASE ALOUD:**
> .... is **doing the lion's share of the work** because...

dot com *n.* an Internet company (typically whose name ends in "dot com").

> **EXAMPLE:** I own a **dot com** that specializes in discounted textbooks. Students can go on-line and order any title without leaving their homes!
>
> **TRANSLATION:** I own an **Internet company** that specializes in discounted textbooks. Students can go on-line and order any title without leaving their homes!
>
> **"REAL SPEAK":** I own a **dot com** th't specializes in discoun(t)ed tex'-books. Students c'n go on-line 'n order any tidle w'thout leaving their homes!
>
> *Also 1:* **dot bombed** *n.* a person who worked for a *dot com* company but lost his or her job when the company failed.
>
> *Also 2:* **dot commer** *n.* a person who works for a *dot com* (Internet) company.
>
> **NOW YOU DO IT. COMPLETE THE PHRASE ALOUD:**
> I want to own a **dot com** because...

Even More General Workplace Slang & Idioms (Part 3)

dress-down day *n.* a day when employees are allowed to wear casual clothes to the office.

EXAMPLE: Someone should have told Tim that Friday is **dress-down day**. He's wearing a suit when he could be wearing jeans!

TRANSLATION: Someone should have told Tim that Friday is **the day when employees are allowed to wear casual clothes to the office**. He's wearing a suit when he could be wearing jeans!

"REAL SPEAK": Someone should 'ev told Tim th't Friday's **dress-down day**. He's wearing a suit wh'n 'e could be wearing jeans!

NOW YOU DO IT. COMPLETE THE PHRASE ALOUD:
I'm going to wear … on the next **dress-down day**.

give someone a fair shake (to) *exp.* to give someone an equal opportunity to succeed.

EXAMPLE: No matter who you are, my boss **gives everyone a fair shake** at getting promotions.

TRANSLATION: No matter who you are, my boss **gives everyone an equal opportunity** at getting promotions.

"REAL SPEAK": No madder who you are, my boss **gives ev'ryone a fair shake** 'it gedding pr'motions.

NOW YOU DO IT. COMPLETE THE PHRASE ALOUD:
Janet won't **give me a fair shake** because...

go postal (to) *exp.* to become violently angry.

EXAMPLE: I'm feeling so much stress! If I don't take a vacation soon, I'm going to **go postal**!

TRANSLATION: I'm feeling so much stress! If I don't take a vacation soon, I'm going to **become violently angry**!

"REAL SPEAK": I'm feeling so much stress! If I don't take a vacation soon, I'm gonna **go postal**!

Note: This is a humorous expression that comes from a very serious situation where a postal worker shot several other workers out of revenge for getting fired. This event became publicized so quickly, that it only took a short period of time for it to be turned into an expression referring to anyone who becomes violently angry.

Synonym 1: **crack (to)** *exp.*

Synonym 2: **freak out (to)** *exp*

Synonym 3: **lose it (to)** *exp..*

NOW YOU DO IT. COMPLETE THE PHRASE ALOUD:
I'm going to **go postal** if Ned...

THE SLANGMAN GUIDE TO BIZ SPEAK 2

new blood *exp.* new employees with fresh ideas, usually considered a revitalizing force in a company.

EXAMPLE: Our executives haven't thought of any new ideas lately. We need to bring in some **new blood** if we want to stay competitive.

TRANSLATION: Our executives haven't thought of any new ideas lately. We need to bring in some **new employees with fresh ideas** if we want to stay competitive.

"REAL SPEAK": 'Ar execudives haven't thod 'ev any new ideas lately. We need da bring in s'm **new blood** 'ef we wanna stay compedidive.

NOW YOU DO IT. COMPLETE THE PHRASE ALOUD:
Some **new blood** would help us to...

old boys' club *exp.* a group of traditionally-minded executives (typically older Caucasian men) who favor certain types of employees, usually other Caucasian men.

EXAMPLE: Margaret really deserves a promotion, but the **old boys' club** will make sure that she never gets one because she's a woman.

TRANSLATION: Margaret really deserves a promotion, but the **group of traditionally-minded executives who favor other Caucasian men** will make sure that she never gets one because she's a woman.

"REAL SPEAK": Margaret really deserves a pr'motion, b't the **ol' boys' club**'ll make sher th't she never gets one b'cuz she's a woman.

NOW YOU DO IT. COMPLETE THE PHRASE ALOUD:
The **old boys' club** doesn't like Ted because …

polish one's résumé (to) *exp.* to update one's résumé in preparation for looking for a new job.

EXAMPLE: I just heard the company is having financial problems. We had better **polish our résumés**!

TRANSLATION: I just heard the company is having financial problems. We had better **update our résumés**!

"REAL SPEAK": I just heard the comp'ny's having financial problems. We'd bedder **polish 'ar résumés**!

NOW YOU DO IT. COMPLETE THE PHRASE ALOUD:
… is **polishing her résumé** because she thinks she's going to get fired.

LET'S PRACTICE!

READING

CD-A: TRACK 14

A. WHAT DOES IT MEAN?

Choose the correct definition of the words in boldface.

1. **dinosaur:**
   ❏ someone or something outdated
   ❏ someone or something dangerous

2. **to go postal:**
   ❏ to go to the Post Office
   ❏ to become violently angry

3. **new blood:**
   ❏ a bleeding employee
   ❏ a new employee

4. **to do the lion's share of the work:**
   ❏ to work like an animal
   ❏ to do most of the work

5. **to give someone a fair shake:**
   ❏ to give someone an equal opportunity to succeed
   ❏ to give someone a strong handshake

6. **old boys' club:**
   ❏ a group of traditionally-minded executives
   ❏ a group of innovative executives

7. **corporate culture:**
   ❏ a company's ethnic employees
   ❏ a company's mood

8. **dress-down day:**
   ❏ a day when employees are allowed to wear casual clothes
   ❏ a day when employees must wear suits

9. **to polish one's résumé:**
   ❏ to translate one's résumé into a Slavic language
   ❏ to update one's résumé

10. **dot com:**
   ❏ an Internet company
   ❏ a specialized factory that makes dresses with a specific pattern

B. COMPLETE THE FAIRY TALE

Fill in the blanks by choosing the correct words from the list at the bottom of the page.

CD–A: TRACK 15

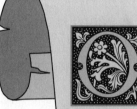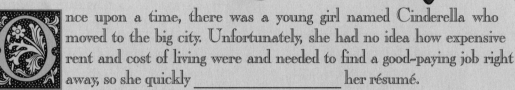

Once upon a time, there was a young girl named Cinderella who moved to the big city. Unfortunately, she had no idea how expensive rent and cost of living were and needed to find a good-paying job right away, so she quickly _____ her résumé.

The next morning, Cinderella got her first job interview with a dot _____. Just as she was ready to leave, she stopped suddenly, looked down at her clothes, and began to cry. "I can't go to a job interview dressed in these old clothes," she thought. "And I can't afford to buy new ones!"

Oh, she was so sad! But suddenly a voice from behind her said, "I'll help you dress for your interview. What's a Fairy Godmother for?" Cinderella could hardly believe her eyes! "Now. Let's get you dressed. What's the corporate _____ of the office?" asked the Fairy Godmother. Cinderella had no idea. "Well, since today is Friday, it's probably a _____ day, so let's put you into a silk top and slacks." With that, the Fairy Godmother waved her magic wand and Cinderella was instantly dressed in a beautiful gown! But the Fairy Godmother added, "Just remember to come back before sunset or your clothes will suddenly disappear." "I'll remember," said Cinderella.

When she arrived at her interview, she knew right away that it was an _____ club and that she may not be given a fair _____ at the interview. They told her that she would have to do the _____ share of the work using an old _____ of a computer. In fact, it made the last marketing manager go _____ and quit! But that didn't scare Cinderella. After a long interview, the executives still weren't convinced that she would be the right person for the job.

Tired and losing hope, Cinderella forgot about the time and the sun was starting to set. In an instant, her clothes disappeared! The executives were clearly stunned. Then, after a moment, they all said at the same time, "You're hired! It'll be good to get some new _____ in here!" And with her new salary, Cinderella could finally afford to live on the upper east side in a charming converted brownstone.

BLOOD	**CULTURE**	**DRESS-DOWN**	**OLD BOYS'**	**POSTAL**
COM	**DINOSAUR**	**LION'S**	**POLISHED**	**SHAKE**

C. CONTEXT EXERCISE
Look at the phrase in the left column, then find the best match in the right column. Write the appropriate letter in the box.

CD-A: TRACK 16

1. It's so unfair! The executives of this company only promote Caucasian men.

2. Jenny does more work than everyone else in the department.

3. We haven't developed a new product in months. We need some new ideas!

4. My computer is so old!

5. Don't you hate wearing suits to the office every day?

6. I love my company! We have a picnic every month and a room where we can sleep if we're tired during the day.

7. Internet companies pay their employees a lot of money because they don't have a lot of operating costs.

8. The boss never listens to Bonnie's ideas just because she's shy.

9. Don can't handle the stress of his job. He always looks so angry and constantly screams at everyone!

10. If you don't like working here, you should find a new job.

A. He's not **giving her a fair shake**!

B. I know. It's a **dinosaur**. I don't know how you can do your work on it.

C. It's an **old boys' club**. If you're a minority, you won't get promoted.

D. I know what you mean. I'm afraid if he doesn't take a vacation soon, he'll **go postal**!

E. You're right! We should hire some **new blood**.

F. That may be true, but **dot coms** aren't stable. You could lose your job at any time.

G. You're right. I'll start **polishing my résumé** tonight!

H. She must be tired of **doing the lion's share of the work**.

I. I'm jealous! Your **corporate culture** sounds like fun!

J. Definitely! We need a **dress-down day**, so we can all wear jeans.

D. COMPLETE THE PHRASE

Complete the phrase by choosing the appropriate words from the list below.

CLUB	**FAIR**
COM	**NEW**
CULTURE	**POLISH**
DINOSAURS	**POSTAL**
DOWN	**SHARE**

Cheryl: I love my new job! We have a **dress-_____ day** every Friday, free lunch once a

week, and most important, there's no favoritism. Everyone **gets a _____**

shake. That's why the company has such a great **corporate _____**.

Laura: You're really lucky! My company is very different. It's an **old boys' _____** where

there's absolutely no respect for women. The women **do the lion's _____ of**

the work and don't make much money. Sometimes I feel if I don't get out of there,

I'm going to **go _____**!

Cheryl: Your executives sound like **_____**! You should **_____ your résumé** and

come to work for my **dot _____**. We always need **_____ blood**.

THE SLANGMAN FILES

Even More General Workplace Slang & Idioms (P-Z)

pass the buck (to) *exp.* to give an unwanted responsibility to another person.

> **EXAMPLE:** Maureen didn't have time to write the report, so she **passed the buck** to me. Now I need to work late tonight!
>
> **TRANSLATION:** Maureen didn't have time to write the report, so she **gave the unwanted responsibility** to me. Now I need to work late tonight!
>
> **"REAL SPEAK":** Maureen didn' 'ave time da write the r'port, so she **passed the buck** ta me. Now I need da work late tanight!
>
> *Also:* **dodge the bullet (to)** *exp.* to avoid the blame for something.

pay something lip service (to) *exp.* to officially agree with something despite doubts.

> **EXAMPLE:** I don't like our new business plan but I had to **pay it lip service** or the boss would have gotten angry at me.
>
> **TRANSLATION:** I don't like our new business plan but I had to **officially agree with it despite my doubts** or the boss would have gotten angry at me.
>
> **"REAL SPEAK":** I don't like 'ar new bizness plan b'd I had da **pay it lip service** 'er the boss would 'a gotten angry 'it me.

peanuts *n.* a very small amount of money.

> **EXAMPLE:** I'm tired of making **peanuts**! I need to find a new job.
>
> **TRANSLATION:** I'm tired of making **a very small amount of money**! I need to find a new job.
>
> **"REAL SPEAK":** I'm tired 'a making **peanuts**! I need da find a new job.

peon *n.* an unimportant person, usually a low-level employee.

> **EXAMPLE:** I wish the executives would keep us **peons** informed. We're the ones who keep this company running!

> **TRANSLATION:** I wish the executives would keep us **unimportant, low-level employees** informed. We're the ones who keep this company running!
>
> **"REAL SPEAK":** I wish the execudives would keep us **peons** informed. W'r the ones 'oo keep th's comp'ny running!
>
> *Synonym 1:* **grunt** *n.*
>
> *Synonym 2:* **little people** *pl.n.*
>
> *Synonym 3:* **nobody** *n.*

pigeonhole someone (to) *v.* to assign someone a certain responsibility indefinitely.

> **EXAMPLE:** Beth started filing her first week here, and now she's been **pigeonholed**!
>
> **TRANSLATION:** Beth started filing her first week here, and now she's been **assigned to do it indefinitely**!

THE SLANGMAN GUIDE TO BIZ SPEAK 2

"REAL SPEAK": Beth starded filing 'er first week here, an' now she's been **pigeonholed**!

pissing contest *n.* an intense argument motivated by ego.

EXAMPLE: I wish Harold and Anne would decide on a new business plan. At this point, it's just a **pissing contest**.

TRANSLATION: I wish Harold and Anne would decide on a new business plan. At this point, it's just an **intense argument motivated by ego**.

"REAL SPEAK": I wish Harold 'n Anne would decide on a new bizness plan. At this point, it's just a **pissing contest**.

Note: The verb *to piss* is a slang synonym for "to urinate" and is considered somewhat vulgar.

play devil's advocate (to) *exp.* to take the opposite side of an argument for the purpose of exploring the discussion more fully.

EXAMPLE: I like your proposed plan, but allow me to **play devil's advocate**. What if you can't finish in time?

TRANSLATION: I like your proposed plan, but allow me to **take the opposite side of the argument for the purpose of exploring the discussion more fully**. What if you can't finish in time?

"REAL SPEAK": I like yer pr'posed plan, b'd allow me da play **devil's adva'cat**. Whad 'ef ya can't finish 'n time?

play it safe (to) *exp.* to make decisions that minimize risk.

EXAMPLE: Isabelle is a great executive except that she always **plays it safe**. Sometimes you need to take chances.

TRANSLATION: Isabelle is a great executive except that she always **makes decisions that minimize risk**. Sometimes you need to take chances.

"REAL SPEAK": Isabelle's a grade execudive except th't she ahweez **plays it safe**. Sometimes ya need da take chances.

prove oneself (to) *exp.* to display one's skills and abilities.

EXAMPLE: Poor Herbert! He got fired before he had a chance to **prove himself**.

TRANSLATION: Poor Herbert! He got fired before he had a chance to **display his skills and abilities**.

"REAL SPEAK": Poor Herbert! He got fired b'fore 'e had a chance ta **prove 'imself**.

pull something out of thin air (to) *exp.* to fabricate something, often facts.

EXAMPLE: Did you hear Victor in that meeting? When the boss asked him for a financial report, he **pulled** the numbers **out of thin air** because he hadn't done any research!

TRANSLATION: Did you hear Victor in that meeting? When the boss asked him for a financial report, he **fabricated** the numbers because he hadn't done any research!

"REAL SPEAK": Did 'ju hear Victer 'n that meeding? When the boss ast 'im fer a financial r'port, he **pulled** those numbers **outta thin air** b'cuz 'e hadn't done any research!

puppet *n.* a person controlled by someone else.

> **EXAMPLE:** Steven is such a **puppet**! He does whatever Trevor tells him to do, and Trevor isn't even his supervisor!

> **TRANSLATION:** Steven is such a **person controlled by someone else**! He does whatever Trevor tells him to do, and Trevor isn't even his supervisor!

> **"REAL SPEAK":** Steve's such a **puppet**! He does whadever Tever tells 'im da do, an' 'e isn' even 'is superviser!

> *Synonym 1:* **henchman** *n.*

> *Synonym 2:* **lackey** *n.*

> *Synonym 3:* **patsy** *n.*

> *Synonym 4:* **tool** *n.*

push the envelope (to) *exp.* to exceed the limits of what is normally done; to be innovative.

> **EXAMPLE:** Our normal advertising strategy doesn't seem to be working. We need to **push the envelope** and come up with something totally new.

> **TRANSLATION:** Our normal advertising strategy doesn't seem to be working. We need to **exceed the limits of what is normally done** and come up with something totally new.

> **"REAL SPEAK":** 'Ar normal advertising stradegy doesn' seem da be working. We need da **push the envelope** 'n come up w'th something todally new.

put something on the back burner (to) *exp.* to postpone something indefinitely.

> **EXAMPLE:** We need to **put this project on the back burner** because we don't have enough money to continue it.

> **TRANSLATION:** We need to **postpone this project indefinitely** because we don't have enough money to continue it.

> **"REAL SPEAK":** We need da **put this project on the back burner** b'cuz we don'ave anuf money da continue it.

put the cart before the horse (to) *exp.* to focus on an issue in the incorrect order by putting something first that should be second.

> **EXAMPLE:** Don't **put the cart before the horse**! We need to earn money before we can discuss how to spend it.

> **TRANSLATION:** Don't **focus on the issue in the incorrect order**! We need to earn money before we can discuss how to spend it.

> **"REAL SPEAK":** Don't **put the cart b'fore the horse**! We need da earn money b'fore we c'n discuss how da spend it.

rip someone a new one (to) *exp.* to yell at someone.

> **EXAMPLE:** If Naomi is late for work again, the boss is going to **rip her a new one**!

> **TRANSLATION:** If Naomi is late for work again, the boss is going to **yell at her**!

> **"REAL SPEAK":** If Naomi's late fer work again, the boss 'ez gonna **rip 'er a new one**!

> *Note:* This is a euphemistic variation of the expression *to rip someone a new asshole*, which is certainly vulgar, yet popular.

red flag *n.* a warning sign.

> **EXAMPLE:** The fact that Jessie was late to her interview was a big **red flag**. We should never have hired her.

> **TRANSLATION:** The fact that Jessie was late to her interview was a big **warning sign**. We should never have hired her.

> **"REAL SPEAK":** The fact th't Jessie w'z late to 'er in'erview w'z a big **red flag**. We should never 'ev hired 'er.

rep *abbrev.* an abbreviation for "representative."

> **EXAMPLE:** I got promoted! I'm the new sales **rep** for the company!

> **TRANSLATION:** I got promoted! I'm the new sales **representative** for the company!

> **"REAL SPEAK":** I got pr'moded! I'm the new sales **rep** fer the comp'ny!

revamp (to) *v.* to update and improve.

> **EXAMPLE:** This is last year's report! You'll need to completely **revamp** it before the meeting.

> **TRANSLATION:** This is last year's report! You'll need to completely **update and improve** it before the meeting.

> **"REAL SPEAK":** This 'ez last year's r'port! You'll need da completely **revamp** it b'fore the meeding.

save someone's neck (to) *exp.* to rescue someone from a difficult situation.

> **EXAMPLE:** I **saved your neck** today. You were late to work, but I told the boss you were at a doctor's appointment.

> **TRANSLATION:** I **rescued you from a difficult situation** today. You were late to work, but I told the boss you were at a doctor's appointment.

> **"REAL SPEAK":** I **saved jer neck** ta'day. You were late ta work, b'd I told the boss you were ad a docter's appointment.

search on something (to) *v.* to use the Internet to find information on something.

> **EXAMPLE:** We need more information on our competitor. Go **search on it** and let me know what you find.

> **TRANSLATION:** We need more information on our competitor. Go **use the Internet to find information on it** and let me know what you discover.

> **"REAL SPEAK":** We need more infermation on 'ar c'mpedider. Go **search on it** 'n lemme know what cha find.

send someone packing (to) *exp.* to fire someone.

> **EXAMPLE:** If you aren't prepared for the next meeting, the boss is going to **send you packing**!

> **TRANSLATION:** If you aren't prepared for the next meeting, the boss is going to **fire you**!

> **"REAL SPEAK":** If ya aren't pr'pared fer the next meeding, the boss 'ez gonna **sen' 'ju packing**!

small talk *n.* casual conversation.

> **EXAMPLE:** I don't know the new president well. We shared some **small talk** during lunch, but that's all.

> **TRANSLATION:** I don't know the new president well. We shared some **casual conversation** during lunch, but that's all.

> **"REAL SPEAK":** I dunno the new president well. We shared s'm **small talk** during lunch, b't that's all.

snail mail *n.* traditional mail sent through the Post Office (which takes much longer to deliver than email).

> **EXAMPLE:** I haven't received the invoice yet, but **snail mail** usually takes a week to get here.

TRANSLATION: I haven't received the invoice yet, but **traditional mail sent through the Post Office** usually takes a week to get here.

"REAL SPEAK": I haven't received the invoice yet, b't **snail mail** ujally takes a week ta get here.

sell someone down the river (to) *exp.* to betray a trusted friend or co-worker.

EXAMPLE: We didn't make enough money this month, so Jane **sold me down the river** and told the boss it was my fault!

TRANSLATION: We didn't make enough money this month, so Jane **betrayed me** and told the boss it was my fault!

"REAL SPEAK": We didn' make anuf money th's month, so Jane **sold me down the river** 'n told the boss it's my fault!

Synonym: **stab someone in the back (to)** *exp.*

something needs work *exp.* said of something that is not successful without further effort.

EXAMPLE: This report **needs work**. Where's the section on our past performance?

TRANSLATION: This report **is not successful without further effort**. Where's the section on our past performance?

"REAL SPEAK": This r'port **needs work**. Where's the section on 'ar past performance?

Starbucks *n.* (short for *Starbucks Coffee Company*) • **1.** a popular coffee seller • **2.** coffee from Starbucks.

EXAMPLE 1: I always buy coffee from **Starbucks** in the morning before I go to work.

TRANSLATION: I always buy coffee from **a popular coffee seller** in the morning before I go to work.

"REAL SPEAK": I ahweez buy coffee fr'm **Starbucks** 'n the morning b'fore I go da work.

EXAMPLE 2: We have fifteen minutes before the meeting. Let's get some **Starbucks**.

TRANSLATION: We have fifteen minutes before the meeting. Let's get some **coffee**.

"REAL SPEAK": We 'ave fifteen minutes b'fore the meeding. Let's get s'm **Starbucks**.

Note: *Starbucks* is a popular place to buy coffee as well as an extremely popular location for casual meetings of business associates and friends. Today there are so many *Starbucks* locations that you'll probably see one within your first five minutes of being in the United States!

start-up company *n.* a business that has recently begun operation.

EXAMPLE: The Publishers' Network is a **start-up company** but its investors think it's going to make a lot of money within the next few years.

TRANSLATION: The Publishers' Network is a **business that has recently begun operation** but its investors think it's going to make a lot of money within the next few years.

"REAL SPEAK": The Publishers' Network is a **stard-up comp'ny** b'd its investers think it's gonna make a lodda money within the nex' few years.

steal someone's thunder (to) *exp.* to take credit for another person's contribution.

> **EXAMPLE:** I worked all night finishing the report, but George **stole my thunder** and now he's getting a raise!

> **TRANSLATION:** I worked all night finishing the report, but George **took credit for my contribution** and now he's getting a raise!

> **"REAL SPEAK":** I worked all night finishing the r'port, b't George **stole my thunder** 'n now 'e's gedding a raise!

streamline something (to) *exp.* to make something more efficient.

> **EXAMPLE:** We need to **streamline this project**. There are too many people involved and it's taking too long!

> **TRANSLATION:** We need to **make this project more efficient**. There are too many people involved and it's taking too long!

> **"REAL SPEAK":** We need da **streamline th's project**. There 'er too many people involved 'n it's taking too long!

sweat bullets (to) *exp.* to be extremely nervous.

> **EXAMPLE:** I'm **sweating bullets** about this interview. I really need this job!

> **TRANSLATION:** I'm **extremely nervous** about this interview. I really need this job!

> **"REAL SPEAK":** I'm **swedding bullets** about th's in'erview. I really need th's job!

sweat shop *n.* a company that demands an unreasonable amount of work from its employees, usually in unfavorable work conditions.

> **EXAMPLE:** This place is a **sweat shop**! We have to work a lot of hours and they won't let us take breaks!

> **TRANSLATION:** This place is a **company that demands an unreasonable amount of work from its employees**! We have to work a lot of hours and they won't let us take breaks!

> **"REAL SPEAK":** This place 'ez a **sweat shop**! We hafta work a lod 'ev hours 'n they won't led us take breaks!

take a bath on something (to) *exp.* to lose a lot of money due to a particular venture.

> **EXAMPLE:** The company really **took a bath on** our new marketing plan. We spent a huge sum of money but got little response.

> **TRANSLATION:** The company really **lost a lot of money due to** our new marketing plan. We spent a huge sum of money but got little response.

> **"REAL SPEAK":** The comp'ny really **took a bath on** 'ar new markeding plan. We spen' a huge sum 'a money b't got liddle r'sponse.

take no prisoners (to) *exp.* to pursue one's objectives by any means necessary.

> **EXAMPLE:** We need to finish this project by June, so **take no prisoners**!

> **TRANSLATION:** We need to finish this project by June, so **pursue our objectives by any means necessary**!

> **"REAL SPEAK":** We need da finish th's project by June, so **take no pris'ners**!

take the high road (to) *exp.* to pursue one's objectives in a dignified and respectable way.

> **EXAMPLE:** I know I should **take the high road**, but I'm tempted to lie in order to win the argument.
>
> **TRANSLATION:** I know I should **pursue my objectives in a dignified and respectable way**, but I'm tempted to lie in order to win the argument.
>
> **"REAL SPEAK":** I know I should **take the high road**, b'd I'm tempted da lie 'n order da win the argument.

tech geek *n.* a person especially good at technical tasks, often lacking social skills.

> **EXAMPLE:** If you're having computer problems, talk to Ernie, our **tech geek**. He may be a little strange, but he can fix anything!

> **TRANSLATION:** If you're having computer problems, talk to Ernie, our **specialist who is good at technical tasks**. He may be a little strange, but he can fix anything!
>
> **"REAL SPEAK":** If y'r having c'mpuder problems, talk ta Ernie, 'ar **tech geek**. He may be a liddle strange, b'd 'e c'n fix anything!

think outside the box (to) *exp.* to approach a problem in a creative, non-traditional way.

> **EXAMPLE:** I like Nathan. He can **think outside the box** when the typical solutions don't work.
>
> **TRANSLATION:** I like Nathan. He can **approach a problem in a creative, non-traditional way** when the typical solutions don't work.
>
> **"REAL SPEAK":** I like Nathan. He c'n **think outside the box** when the typical solutions don't work.

throw something against the wall and see if it sticks (to) *exp.* to try something and see if it is successful.

> **EXAMPLE:** We can't just guess which plan will work. We need to **throw them against the wall and see if they stick**.
>
> **TRANSLATION:** We can't just guess which plan will work. We need to **try them and see if they're successful**.
>
> **"REAL SPEAK":** We can't jus' guess which plan'll work. We need da **throw 'em agains' the wall 'n see 'ef they stick**.

twenty-four seven *adj.* all the time; constantly • (lit.): twenty-four hours a day, seven days a week.

> **EXAMPLE:** Our store is open for business **twenty-four seven**.
>
> **TRANSLATION:** Our store is open for business **all the time**.
>
> **"REAL SPEAK":** 'Ar store's open fer bizness **twen'y-four seven**.
>
> *Variation:* Also seen as *24/7*.

up (to be) *adv.* to be functioning.

> **EXAMPLE:** Is our website **up**? I keep getting an error when I try to access it.
>
> **TRANSLATION:** Is our website **functioning**? I keep getting an error when I try to access it.
>
> **"REAL SPEAK":** Is 'ar webside **up**? I keep gedding 'n error when I try da access it.
>
> *Synonym:* **up and running** *exp.*

used car salesman *n.* an untrustworthy person who resorts to dishonest sales methods, like a stereotypical used car salesman.

> **EXAMPLE:** Fred is such a **used car salesman**. He lied to that customer in order to make a sale!

> **TRANSLATION:** Fred is such an **untrustworthy person who resorts to dishonest sales methods**. He lied to that customer in order to make a sale!

> **"REAL SPEAK":** Fred's such a **used car salesman**. He lied da that custamer 'n order da make a sale!

wow someone (to) *v.* to impress someone.

> **EXAMPLE:** I really **wowed** the boss with my report. He offered me a raise after he read it!

> **TRANSLATION:** I really **impressed** the boss with my report. He offered me a raise after he read it!

> **"REAL SPEAK":** I really **wowed** the boss w'th my r'port. He offered me a raise after 'e read it!

yes man *exp.* a person who always agrees with his/her superiors in order to gain their favor.

> **EXAMPLE:** Pauline is a **yes man**. Even when Mike suggests something stupid, she tell him he's brilliant!

> **TRANSLATION:** Pauline is a **person who always agrees with her superiors**. Even when Mike suggests something stupid, she tells him he's brilliant!

> **"REAL SPEAK":** Pauline's a **yes man**. Ev'n when Mike suggests something stupid, she tells him he's brilliant!

> *Note:* This is a strange one! Although this expression is *yes* **man**, it applies to a woman as well! Some people may try to adjust the expression to *yes woman* or *yes person*, hoping to make it more politically correct.

LESSON 4

BILL REINVENTS THE WHEEL

"Bureaucratese"

THIS LESSON FEATURES **12** NEW SLANG WORDS & IDIOMS

LET'S WARM UP!

MATCH THE PICTURES

As a fun way to get started, see if you can guess the meaning of the new slang words and expressions on the opposite page by using the pictures below and following the context of the sentences.

"Bureaucratese" Slang & Jargon

1. If this project is a success, I'll get promoted. If it fails, I'll get fired. It's worth **the whole ball of wax**!
   ☐ a large wax ball
   ☐ everything

2. If we don't finish this report by the **drop-dead date**, we're all in big trouble!
   ☐ the latest date by which it must be completed
   ☐ date we die

3. Ted is very high up in the **chain of command**. Everyone reports directly to him.
   ☐ army
   ☐ hierarchy of company executives

4. Alison isn't qualified to answer that question. We need to ask one of the **higher-ups**.
   ☐ executives
   ☐ people standing on chairs

5. The mistake I made is going to create a **situation** unless we fix it immediately!
   ☐ furry monster
   ☐ very big problem

6. Martin is a **whistle-blower**! He told the boss that I was late for work yesterday.
   ☐ referee
   ☐ informant

7. I'm tired of being the **low man on the totem pole**. I need a promotion or a new job!
   ☐ native American Indian
   ☐ person with the least power

8. Johnson spent six hours **reinventing the wheel**. He should have asked someone first!
   ☐ solving a problem that has already been solved
   ☐ manufacturing tires

9. If you understand the **big picture**, you'll understand the company's decisions.
   ☐ large image of our logo
   ☐ overall strategy

10. Rhonda tried to solve the problem, but she just **opened a whole new can of worms**.
    ☐ created a large new problem
    ☐ opened a can of spoiled food

11. I need to **interface** with Tony. He's supposed to work on the project, but he missed today's meeting.
    ☐ use a computer
    ☐ talk

12. I want a promotion but I hate all the **red tape** involved.
    ☐ official forms and procedures
    ☐ physical tests

"Bureaucratese" Slang & Jargon

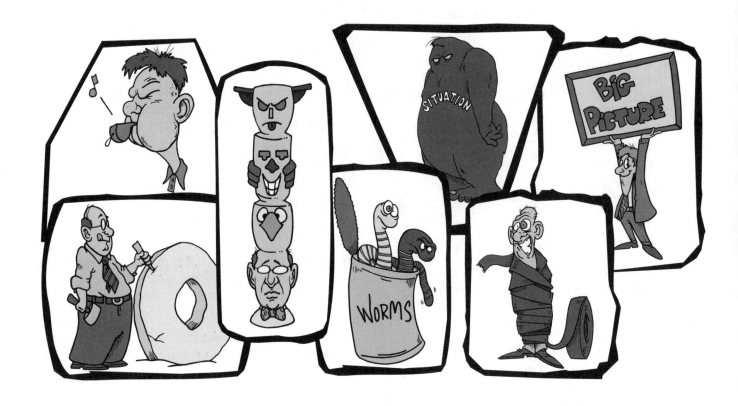

LET'S TALK!

A. DIALOGUE USING SLANG & IDIOMS

The words introduced on the first two pages are used in the dialogue below. See if you can understand the conversation. *Note:* The translation of the words in boldface is on the right-hand page.

CD-A: TRACK 18

Alex: I don't like working with Bill. He's always **reinventing the wheel** because he doesn't see the **big picture**. If we keep working like this, we'll never meet the **drop-dead date**. Maybe I should ask someone in the **chain of command** if I can get him replaced. I know I'd have to go through a lot of **red tape** to make it happen, but I think it would be worth it.

Nicole: Don't be a **whistle-blower**! To the **higher-ups**, you're **the low man on the totem pole**. If you go to them, you could lose **the whole ball of wax**. Do you want to cause a **situation**?

Alex: No, you're right. It could **open a whole new can of worms**. I'll just **interface** with Bill and try to find a solution.

"Bureaucratese" Slang & Jargon

B. DIALOGUE TRANSLATED INTO STANDARD ENGLISH

LET'S SEE HOW MUCH YOU REMEMBER!
Just for fun, move around in random order to the words and
expressions in boldface below. See if you can remember their
slang equivalents without looking at the left-hand page!

Alex: I don't like working with Bill. He's always **spending time on problems that have already been solved** because he doesn't see the **overall strategy**. If we keep working like this, we'll never meet the **latest date by which our task must be completed**. Maybe I should ask someone in the **official ranking of personnel by position** if I can get him replaced. I know I'd have to go through a lot of **official forms and procedures** to make it happen, but I think it would be worth it.

Nicole: Don't be an **informant**! To the **executives** you're **in a job position with the least power**. If you go to them, you could lose **everything**. Do you want to cause a **a very big problem**?

Alex: No, you're right. It could **create a large new problem**. I'll just **talk** with Bill and try to find a solution.

"Bureaucratese" Slang & Jargon

C. DIALOGUE USING "REAL SPEAK"

The dialogue below demonstrates how the slang conversation on the previous page would *really* be spoken by native speakers!

CD-A: TRACK 18

Alex: I don't like working with Bill. He's always **reinven(t)ing the wheel** b'cuz 'e doesn' see the **big picture**. If we keep working like this, we'll never meet the **drop-dead date**. Maybe I should ask someone in the **chain 'a command** if I c'n ged 'im replaced. I know I'd hafta go through a lodda **red tape** ta make it happen, b'd I think it'd be worth it.

Nicole: Don't be a **whistle-blower**! Ta the **higher-ups**, y'r **the low man on the todem pole**. If ya go da them, ya could lose **the whole ball 'a wax**. Ya wanna cause a **situation**?

Alex: No, y'r right. It could **open a whole new can 'a worms**. A'll just **in(t)erface** with Bill 'n try da find a salution.

LET'S LEARN!

VOCABULARY

The following words and expressions were used in the previous dialogues. Let's take a closer look at what they mean.

CD-A: TRACK 19

big picture *n.* the overall strategy.

EXAMPLE: Before I can help your company with its advertising, I need to understand the **big picture**. What are you trying to accomplish?

TRANSLATION: Before I can help your company with its advertising, I need to understand the **overall strategy**. What are you trying to accomplish?

"REAL SPEAK": B'fore I c'n help yer comp'ny w'th its advertising, I need da understan' the **big picture**. Whad 'er ya trying ta accomplish?

NOW YOU DO IT. COMPLETE THE PHRASE ALOUD:
Carrie needs to understand the **big picture** instead of...

chain of command *exp.* the official ranking of company personnel by position.

EXAMPLE: You should follow the **chain of command** and complain to your boss before you talk to her superior.

TRANSLATION: You should follow the **official ranking of company personnel by position** and complain to your boss before you talk to her superior.

"REAL SPEAK": You should follow the **chain 'a command** 'n c'mplain ta yer boss b'fore ya talk to 'er saperier.

Synonym: **pecking order** *n.*

NOW YOU DO IT. COMPLETE THE PHRASE ALOUD:
I'm going up the **chain of command** because...!

drop-dead date *n.* the absolute latest date by which a task must be completed.

EXAMPLE: This Friday is our **drop-dead date** to get this project finished. If we don't, we could all get fired!

TRANSLATION: This Friday is **the absolute latest date we have** to get this project finished. If we don't, we could all get fired!

"REAL SPEAK": This Friday's 'ar **drop-dead date** ta get th's project finished. If we don't, we could all get fired!

Synonym 1: **deadline** *n.*

Synonym 2: **due date** *n.*

NOW YOU DO IT. COMPLETE THE PHRASE ALOUD:

The **drop-dead date** is Friday, so we need to finish...

higher-up *n.* an executive; one who has a rank, position, or status superior to others.

EXAMPLE: Did you hear all the suggestions Heather made in the meeting? The **higher-ups** didn't look very happy to be evaluated by a new employee!

TRANSLATION: Did you hear all the suggestions Heather made in the meeting? The **executives** didn't look very happy to be evaluated by a new employee!

"REAL SPEAK": Did 'ja hear all the suggestions Heather made 'n the meeding? The **higher-ups** didn' look very happy da be evaluaded by a new employee!

NOW YOU DO IT. COMPLETE THE PHRASE ALOUD:

The **higher-ups** are upset with me because I...

interface (to) *v.* to talk.

EXAMPLE: There's a problem with this report. I need to **interface** with Jesse and find out what happened.

TRANSLATION: There's a problem with this report. I need to **talk** with Jesse and find out what happened.

"REAL SPEAK": There's a problem w'th this r'port. I need da **in(t)erface** w'th Jesse 'n find out what happened.

NOW YOU DO IT. COMPLETE THE PHRASE ALOUD:

Let's **interface** today so we can discuss...

"Bureaucratese" Slang & Jargon

low man on the totem pole (to be) *exp.* to hold the job with the least power.

EXAMPLE:
I hate **being low man on the totem pole**. Everyone can tell me what to do, and I have to do it.

TRANSLATION:
I hate **holding the job with the least power**. Everyone can tell me what to do, and I have to do it.

"REAL SPEAK":
I hate **being low man on the todem pole**. Ev'ryone c'n tell me what ta do, 'n I hafta do it.

Note:
Oddly enough, this expression is also used in reference to a woman. However, a non-gender-specific (or politically correct) version is, *to be low on the totem pole*.

NOW YOU DO IT. COMPLETE THE PHRASE ALOUD:
John is **low man on the totem pole**, so tell him to...

open a [whole new] can of worms (to) *exp.* to create a large new problem.

EXAMPLE:
Our company was growing so quickly, that our old office became way too small to work in. So, we moved to a bigger space downtown. Unfortunately, that **opened a whole new can of worms**. We just found out that the new office has major electrical problems!

TRANSLATION:
Our company was growing so quickly, that our old office became way too small to work in. So, we moved to a bigger space downtown. Unfortunately, that **created a large new problem**. We just found out that the new office has major electrical problems!

"REAL SPEAK":
'Ar comp'ny w'z growing so quickly, th'd 'ar old office b'came way too small da work in. So, we moved to a bigger space downtown. Unfortunately, thad **opened a whole new can 'a worms**. We jus' found out th't the new office has majer electrical problems!

NOW YOU DO IT. COMPLETE THE PHRASE ALOUD:
If we ... it will **open a whole new can of worms**!

red tape *n.* official forms and complicated procedures that must be followed in order to get approval for something.

EXAMPLE:
You wouldn't believe all the **red tape** I had to go through just to order more ink for the printer!

TRANSLATION:
You wouldn't believe all the **official forms and complicated procedures** I had to go through just to order more ink for the printer!

"REAL SPEAK":
Ya wouldn' b'lieve all the **red tape** I had da go through jus' ta order more ink fer the prin(t)er!

NOW YOU DO IT. COMPLETE THE PHRASE ALOUD:
I have to go through a lot of **red tape** if I want to...

reinvent the wheel (to) *exp.* to spend time on a problem that has already been solved.

EXAMPLE: Before you start your project, you should read Valerie's report on that topic, so you don't **reinvent the wheel**.

TRANSLATION: Before you start your project, you should read Valerie's report on that topic, so you don't **spend time on a problem that has already been solved**.

"REAL SPEAK": B'fore ya start cher project, ya should read Valerie's r'pord on that topic, so ya don't **reinvent the wheel**.

NOW YOU DO IT. COMPLETE THE PHRASE ALOUD:
Don't **reinvent the wheel**! Sally already...

situation *n.* a very big problem.

EXAMPLE: Carl got so angry with our clients in the meeting this morning that he almost caused a **situation**.

TRANSLATION: Carl got so angry with our clients in the meeting this morning that he almost caused a **very big problem**.

"REAL SPEAK": Carl got so angry w'th 'ar clients 'n the meeding th's morning thad 'e almos' caused a **situation**.

NOW YOU DO IT: COMPLETE THE PHRASE ALOUD:
If you don't ... there's going to be a **situation** here.

whistle-blower *n.* an informant.

EXAMPLE: I've never been a **whistle-blower**. I'd rather stay quiet, even if I see someone doing something wrong.

TRANSLATION: I've never been an **informant**. I'd rather stay quiet, even if I see someone doing something wrong.

"REAL SPEAK": I've never been a **whistle-blower**. I'd rather stay quied, even if I see someone doing something wrong.

Synonym 1: **rat** *n.*
Also 1: **rat on someone (to)** *exp.* to report someone.
Also 2: **rat someone out (to)** *exp.* to report someone.
Synonym 2: **snitch** *n.*

NOW YOU DO IT. COMPLETE THE PHRASE ALOUD:
Tony's a **whistle-blower**! He told the boss that I ...

whole ball of wax (the) *n.* everything.

EXAMPLE: If we don't finish this project by Monday, it could cost us **the whole ball of wax**. The client may fire us.

TRANSLATION: If we don't finish this project by Monday, it could cost us **everything**. The client may fire us.

"REAL SPEAK": If we don' finish th's project by Monday, it could cost us **the whole ball 'a wax**. The client may fire us.

NOW YOU DO IT. COMPLETE THE PHRASE ALOUD:
Charlie gambled **the whole ball of wax** on...

"Bureaucratese" Slang & Jargon

LET'S PRACTICE!

CD-A: TRACK 20

A. CHOOSE THE RIGHT WORD
Underline the word that best completes the phrase.

1. When you're the low man on the (**May**, **totem**, **flag**) pole, anyone can tell you what to do and you have to do it.

2. I need to hire someone to help me immediately, but there's so much (**yellow**, **blue**, **red**) tape. It's going to take me a week just to complete all of the paperwork!

3. Bob is a whistle-(**singer**, **blower**, **dancer**)! I came in late this morning and he told the boss.

4. If you don't understand the (**huge**, **large**, **big**) picture, you shouldn't be working on this project.

5. If you invite Heather to the meeting, you'll be opening a whole new can of (**worms**, **horses**, **elephants**). She'll try to take control of the project.

6. Walter is high up in the (**chain**, **ladder**, **rope**) of command, so we have to do what he tells us.

7. Where's Maria? We need to (**interweave**, **interface**, **interlace**) about yesterday's meeting.

8. If the client doesn't like our ideas, we're going to lose the whole ball of (**lint**, **tar**, **wax**).

9. Don't reinvent the (**wheel**, **tire**, **circle**). Sarah already solved this problem.

10. Don't lose your temper. If you yell at Jenkins, you're going to cause a (**scenario**, **situation**, **scenery**).

11. Before we spend money on a new computer, we should ask one of the higher-(**downs**, **overs**, **ups**) for permission.

12. The boss gave me an extra day to get this project finished, but that's the (**drop**, **drip**, **droop**)-dead date!

B. MATCH THE COLUMN

Match the words in boldface with their meaning in the right column. Write the letter of the definition in the box.
Note: Not all the answers will be used.

1. Keep working! The **drop-dead date** is tomorrow!

2. I hate **red tape**! We'll never finish this paperwork in just one day!

3. I've explained to Harry a dozen times that we can't work on the project without him, but he still arrives late every day. I think it's time to go up the **chain of command** and talk to Harry's boss.

4. I know you don't like Bonnie, but if you fire her, she'll probably sue the company for sexual discrimination. You may be **opening a whole new can of worms**!

5. I'm going to ask one of the **higher-ups** if I can hire an assistant. I need help getting my work done!

6. You should never cause a **situation** by arguing with a client during a meeting.

7. Craig is a **whistle-blower**. If he sees anyone doing something wrong, he reports it to the boss!

8. Let's **interface** after lunch and discuss our strategy for the meeting.

9. Janine took a chance on this project, but she lost **the whole ball of wax**. The client fired her for not following their instructions.

10. I don't want to **reinvent the wheel**. Find out what work has already been done on this problem.

11. Since Bob is the **low man on the totem pole**, he has to do the lion's share of the research.

12. I'm confused about this project. What's the **big picture**?

A. talk

B. working all night

C. executives

D. person with the least powerful position in a company

E. overall strategy

F. absolute latest date by which a task must be completed

G. go to lunch

H. everything

I. creating a large new problem

J. solve a problem that's already been solved

K. big problem

L. informant

M. nothing

N. official forms and procedures

O. day a project starts

P. hierarchy of executives

C. CROSSWORD PUZZLE

Fill in the crossword puzzle by choosing the correct word from the list below.
Note: Not all the words are used.

CD-A: TRACK 22

BLOOD	PAPERWORK
BOSS	PEANUTS
COMPLETED	POWER
DANCING	PROBLEM
DRIVEN	SOLVED
EXECUTIVE	STARTED
EVERYTHING	STRATEGY
GENERAL	SUPERIOR
MONSTER	TALKING
MOVIE	TAPE
NOTHING	WAX

ACROSS

11. When you **interface** with people, you are ____ to them.

20. The **drop-dead date** is the absolute latest date by which a task can be ____.

26. A **higher-up** is another name for an ____.

31. If you understand the **big picture**, you undertand the company's overall ____.

35. If you went up the **chain of command**, you spoke with someone who has a ____ position in the company.

DOWN

2.   **Red tape** usually involves a lot of ____.

12. When you **reinvent the wheel**, you are solving a problem that has already been ____.

16. If you've caused a **situation**, you've created a very large ____.

21. If you risk the **whole ball of wax**, you are risking ____.

30. A **whistle-blower** tells the ____ when you've done something wrong.

CROSSWORD PUZZLE

"Bureaucratese" Slang & Jargon

FROM THE SLANGMAN FILES

More "Bureaucratese"

Conducting any kind of business with the United States government is certainly **non-trivial** (*difficult*) because of all the **red tape** (*complicated procedures*). But the **root cause** (*main cause*) of many people's frustration is all the **buzzwords** (*jargon*) that are encountered along the way. Once you're **up-to-speed** (*familiar*) with the words in the following list, you'll find that working with the government is certainly **doable** (*possible*)!

above-board *adj.* honest and legal.

> **EXAMPLE:** Thomas hired his sister, but it was totally **above-board**. She had to go through the same process as the other applicants.

> **TRANSLATION:** Thomas hired his sister, but it was totally **honest and legal**. She had to go through the same process as the other applicants.

> **"REAL SPEAK":** Thomas hired 'is sister, b'd it w'z todally **above-board**. She had da go through the same process 'ez the other applic'nts.

action item *n.* a task, usually assigned as a result of a meeting.

> **EXAMPLE:** I still have three **action items** to finish before Friday!

> **TRANSLATION:** I still have three **tasks** to finish before Friday!

> **"REAL SPEAK":** I still 'ave three **action idems** ta finish b'fore Friday!

bandwidth *n.* extra time.

> **EXAMPLE:** I don't have enough **bandwidth** to meet with you until next week.

> **TRANSLATION:** I don't have enough **extra time** to meet with you until next week.

> **"REAL SPEAK":** I don'ave anuf **bandwi'th** ta meet w'th you 'til nex' week.

> *Note:* This comes from the Internet term which describes the amount of data that can be passed to or from one's website.

bargaining chip *n.* leverage.

> **EXAMPLE:** I know Ron arrived to work late yesterday. That's my **bargaining chip** if he tries to yell at me for missing today's meeting.

> **TRANSLATION:** I know Ron arrived to work late yesterday. That's my **leverage** if he tries to yell at me for missing today's meeting.

> **"REAL SPEAK":** I know Ron arrived ta work late yesterday. That's my **bargaining chip** 'ef 'e tries da yell 'it me fer missing taday's meeding.

bean counter *n.* a person in charge of a company's finances, especially an accountant.

> **EXAMPLE:** I want to buy new desks for my team, but the **bean counters** will never allow it.

THE SLANGMAN GUIDE TO BIZ SPEAK 2

TRANSLATION: I want to buy new desks for my team, but the **people in charge of the company's finances** will never allow it.

"REAL SPEAK": I wanna buy new desks fer my team, b't the **bean coun'ers**'ll never allow it.

bells and whistles *exp.* interesting features.

EXAMPLE: I think the product is fine, but Allison wants to add more **bells and whistles**.

TRANSLATION: I think the product is fine, but Allison wants to add more **interesting features**.

"REAL SPEAK": I think the produc's fine, b'd Allison wants ta add more **bells 'n whistles**.

blacklist (to) *v.* to classify someone as a person who should not be permitted to join certain groups.

EXAMPLE: Ever since Randal was arrested for stealing, he's been **black-listed**. He can't get a job anywhere.

TRANSLATION: Ever since Randal was arrested for stealing, he's been **classified as a person who should not be hired**. He can't get a job anywhere.

"REAL SPEAK": Ever since Randal w'z arrested fer stealing, he's been **black-listed**. He can't ged a job anywhere.

buzzword *n.* popular business jargon.

EXAMPLE: When you go on your job interview, make sure to us a lot of **buzzwords**. They'll think you have more experience than you really have!

TRANSLATION: When you go on your job interview, make sure to us a lot of **popular business jargon**. They'll think you have more experience than you really have!

"REAL SPEAK": When ya go on yer job in'erview, make sher da us a lod 'ev **buzzwords**. They'll think ya have more experience th'n ya really have!

competitive landscape *n.* the full range of competitors.

EXAMPLE: Before we decide on the price of our new product, we need to examine the **competitive landscape**.

TRANSLATION: Before we decide on the price of our new product, we need to examine the **full range of competitors**.

"REAL SPEAK": B'fore we decided on the price 'ev 'ar new product, we need da examine the **compedidive lan'scape**.

cook the books (to) *exp.* to falsify records.

EXAMPLE: At my last company, they used to **cook the books** in order to reach our sales goals each month!

TRANSLATION: At my last company, they used to **falsify records** in order to reach our sales goals each month!

"REAL SPEAK": At my las' comp'ny, they usta **cook the books** 'n order da reach 'ar sales goals each month!

cost-prohibitive *adj.* too expensive.

EXAMPLE: We wanted to go to London for the conference, but it's **cost-prohibitive**.

TRANSLATION: We wanted to go to London for the conference, but it's **too expensive**.

> **"REAL SPEAK":** We wan'ed da go da London fer the conf'rence, b'd it's **cost-prohibidive**.

crack the whip (to) *exp.* to force someone to work harder.

> **EXAMPLE:** The boss has really been **cracking the whip** lately. She wants this project finished as soon as possible!
>
> **TRANSLATION:** The boss has really been **forcing us to work harder** lately. She wants this project finished as soon as possible!
>
> **"REAL SPEAK":** The boss 'ez really been **cracking the whip** lately. She wants th's project finished 'ez soon 'ez possible!

deliverable *n.* a specific task to be completed.

> **EXAMPLE:** I understand the overall scope of the project, but what are the **deliverables**?
>
> **TRANSLATION:** I understand the overall scope of the project, but what are the **specific tasks to be completed**?
>
> **"REAL SPEAK":** I understand the overall scope 'a the project, b't what 'er the **deliverables**?

do a one-eighty (to) *exp.* to change one's mind completely.

> **EXAMPLE:** Pamela **did a one-eighty**. She used to favor Mark for the position, but now she prefers Ted.
>
> **TRANSLATION:** Pamela **changed her mind completely**. She used to favor Mark for the position, but now she prefers Ted.
>
> **"REAL SPEAK":** Pamela **did a one-aidy**. She usta faver Mark fer the pasition, b't now she pr'fers Ted.
>
> *Note:* This refers to 180 degrees, which is halfway around a circle in geometry.
>
> *Synonym:* **do an about face (to)** *exp.* (from military slang).

doable *adj.* possible to achieve.

> **EXAMPLE:** This next project will be difficult, but it's **doable**.
>
> **TRANSLATION:** This next project will be difficult, but it's **possible to achieve**.
>
> **"REAL SPEAK":** Th's nex' project'll be difficult, b'd it's **doable**.

drill down on something (to) *exp.* to discuss something in detail.

> **EXAMPLE:** Let's **drill down on the financial issues** since cost is the most important factor.
>
> **TRANSLATION:** Let's **discuss the financial issues in detail** since cost is the most important factor.
>
> **"REAL SPEAK":** Let's **drill down on the f'nancial issues** since cost 'ez the most important facter.

earmark (to) *v.* to reserve.

> **EXAMPLE:** I wanted to use the money for raises, but it's been **earmarked** for investment.
>
> **TRANSLATION:** I wanted to use the money for raises, but it's been **reserved** for investment.
>
> **"REAL SPEAK":** I wan'ed da use the money fer raises, b'd it's been **earmarked** fer investment.

etched in stone (to be [not]) *exp.* to be (not) unchangeable.

> **EXAMPLE:** The procedure is **not etched in stone**. We're willing to consider other options.

"Bureaucratese" Slang & Jargon

TRANSLATION: The procedure is **not unchangeable**. We're willing to consider other options.

"REAL SPEAK": The pr'cedure isn' **etched 'n stone**. W'r willing da c'nsider other options.

feedback *n.* reaction.

EXAMPLE: Please read this report and give me your **feedback**. I want to improve it but I don't know how.

TRANSLATION: Please read this report and give me your **reaction**. I want to improve it but I don't know how.

"REAL SPEAK": Please read th's r'port 'n gimme yer **feedback**. I wanna improve it b'd I don't know how.

figure-head *n.* a person who appears to be in charge but who has little power.

EXAMPLE: Marcus may be the president, but he's just a **figure-head**. His brother Brad actually makes all the decisions.

TRANSLATION: Marcus may be the president, but he's just a **person who appears to be in charge but who has little power**. His brother Brad actually makes all the decisions.

"REAL SPEAK": Marcus may be the president, b'd 'e's just a **figure-head**. His brother Brad akshelly makes all the decisions.

give something the once over (to) *exp.* to look at something briefly.

EXAMPLE: I don't have time to read your report carefully, but I can **give it the once over** before my next meeting.

TRANSLATION: I don't have time to read your report carefully, but I can **look at it briefly** before my next meeting.

"REAL SPEAK": I don'ave time da read jer r'port carefully, b'd I c'n **give it the once over** b'fore my nex' meeding.

glass ceiling *n.* a discriminatory barrier that prevents women and minorities from rising to positions of power within a company.

EXAMPLE: Olivia is really talented. If it weren't for the **glass ceiling** at this company, she'd be a vice president by now!

TRANSLATION: Olivia is really talented. If it weren't for the **discriminatory barrier that prevents women from rising to positions of power** at this company, she'd be a vice president by now!

"REAL SPEAK": Olivia's really talented. If it weren't fer the **glass ceiling** 'it th's comp'ny, she'd be a vice presid'nt by now!

golden parachute *n.* a favorable severance agreement, usually just for executives.

EXAMPLE: Evan doesn't care if he's fired. He has a **golden parachute**, so he'll get a lot of money.

TRANSLATION: Evan doesn't care if he's fired. He has a **favorable severance agreement**, so he'll get a lot of money.

"REAL SPEAK": Evan doesn' care 'ef 'e's fired. He 'as a **gold'n parachute**.

Note: *Severance* refers to the money an employee receives when terminated from a company.

hands-off *adj.* uninvolved.

EXAMPLE: Harold is a **hands-off** manager. He lets me do what I want as long as I meet my project goals.

TRANSLATION: Harold is an **uninvolved** manager. He lets me do what I want as long as I meet my project goals.

"REAL SPEAK": Harold's a **hanzs-off** manager. He lets me do wh'd I wan' 'ez long 'ez I meet my project goals.

Also: **hands-off policy** *n.* a policy where a manager or boss does not get directly involved in the duties of an employee.

"Bureaucratese" Slang & Jargon

in the trenches (to be) *exp.* (from military jargon) to be working closely on a project.

> **EXAMPLE:** The executives would really understand our problems better if they spent more time **in the trenches** with us.
>
> **TRANSLATION:** The executives would really understand our problems better if they spent more time **working closely on projects** with us.
>
> **"REAL SPEAK":** The execudives 'ed really understand 'ar problems bedder 'ef they spent more time **'n the trenches** w'th us.

infrastructure *n.* the basic framework.

> **EXAMPLE:** The **infrastructure** of this company needs improvement. We're losing more money every month!
>
> **TRANSLATION:** The **basic framework** of this company needs improvement. We're losing more money every month!
>
> **"REAL SPEAK":** The **infrastructure** 'a th's comp'ny needs improvement. W'r losing more money ev'ry month!

ivory tower *n.* a state of mind where one is preoccupied with abstract concepts rather than practical everyday business.

> **EXAMPLE:** The executives are all living in an **ivory tower**. They have no idea how the company actually functions!
>
> **TRANSLATION:** The executives are all living in a **state of mind where they are preoccupied with abstract concepts rather than practical everyday business**. They have no idea how the company actually functions!
>
> **"REAL SPEAK":** The executives 'er all living in 'n **iv'ry tower**. They 'ave no idea how the comp'ny akshelly functions!

low-hanging fruit *exp.* money that is easy to acquire.

> **EXAMPLE:** We need more money, and we need it quickly! How can we get the **low-hanging fruit**?

> **TRANSLATION:** We need more money, and we need it quickly! How can we get the **money that is easy to acquire**?
>
> **"REAL SPEAK":** We need more money, 'n we need it quickly! How c'n we get the **low-hanging fruit**?

mission-critical *adj.* essential for the success of the project.

> **EXAMPLE:** Getting this report approved is **mission-critical**! We can't do anything else until then.
>
> **TRANSLATION:** Getting this report approved is **essential for the success of the project**! We can't do anything else until then.
>
> **"REAL SPEAK":** Gedding th's r'pord approved 'ez **mission-cridic'l**! We can't do anything else 'til then.

non-trivial task *n.* a task that requires significant effort to complete.

> **EXAMPLE:** I'll need more than fifteen minutes to fix your computer. It's a **non-trivial task**!
>
> **TRANSLATION:** I'll need more than fifteen minutes to fix your computer. It's a **task that requires significant effort to complete**!

"REAL SPEAK": I'll need more th'n fifteen minutes ta fix yer c'mpuder. It's a **non-trivial task**!

offline *n.* • **1.** (Internet jargon) not connected to the Internet • **2.** after the current meeting.

EXAMPLE 1: I haven't read the email you sent yet. I have been **offline** since this morning.

TRANSLATION: I haven't read the email you sent yet. I have **not been connected to the Internet** since this morning.

"REAL SPEAK": I haven't read the email ya sent yet. I've been **offline** s'nce th's morning.

EXAMPLE 2: We don't have time to discuss last month's report in this meeting. We'll have to do that **offline**.

TRANSLATION: We don't have time to discuss last month's report in this meeting. We'll have to do that **after the current meeting**.

"REAL SPEAK": We don'ave time da discuss las' munt's r'pord 'n th's meeding. We'll hafta do thad **offline**.

paradigm shift *n.* a change in basic concept.

EXAMPLE: We could try selling our products on the Internet, but we don't have the personnel to accommodate that kind of **paradigm shift**.

TRANSLATION: We could try selling our products on the Internet, but we don't have the personnel to accommodate that kind of **change in basic concept**.

"REAL SPEAK": We could try selling 'ar produc's on the In'ernet, b't we don'ave the personnel da accommadate that kind 'a **paradigm shift**.

pencil someone in (to) *exp.* to set a tentative date and time to meet with someone.

EXAMPLE: You want to talk? I think I have an hour available next Tuesday. I'll **pencil you in**.

TRANSLATION: You want to talk? I think I have an hour available next Tuesday. I'll **set a tentative date and time to meet with you**.

"REAL SPEAK": You wanna talk? I think I 'ave 'n hour available nex' Tuesday. A'll **pencil ya in**.

Note: Assistants sometimes write in pencil so that the appointment can be easily changed if necessary. Now it refers to any tentative appointment, regardless of how it's recorded.

phase out (to) *v.* to discontinue gradually.

EXAMPLE: We used to give out bonuses at Christmas, but we're **phasing out** that practice since we don't have much money.

TRANSLATION: We used to give out bonuses at Christmas, but we're **gradually discontinuing** that practice since we don't have much money.

"REAL SPEAK": We usta give out bonuses 'it Chris'mas, b't w'r **phasing out** that practice since we don't have much money.

reskill (to) *v.* to retrain.

EXAMPLE: Next week, I'm being transferred to the sales department because they're low on personnel. I'm being **reskilled** tomorrow because I don't know a thing about sales.

"Bureaucratese" Slang & Jargon

TRANSLATION: Next week, I'm being transferred to the sales department because they're low on personnel. I'm being **retrained** tomorrow because I don't know a thing about sales.

"REAL SPEAK": Nex' week, I'm being transferred ta the sales department b'cuz'air low on personnel. I'm being **reskilled** tamorrow b'cuz I don't know a thing about sales.

revenue-driven *adj.* said of a project whose only purpose is to make money.

EXAMPLE: This project is **revenue-driven**. That's why it's extremely important for the company's success.

TRANSLATION: This project's **only purpose is to make money**. That's why it's extremely important for the company's success.

"REAL SPEAK": This projec's **revenue-driven**. That's why it's extremely important fer the comp'ny's success.

robust *adj.* full of attractive characteristics.

EXAMPLE: Our new products are expensive but **robust**. I'm sure they'll sell well.

TRANSLATION: Our new products are expensive but **full of attractive characteristics**. I'm sure they'll sell well.

"REAL SPEAK": 'Ar new produc's 'er expensive b't **robust**. I'm sher they'll sell well.

role *n.* function, responsibility.

EXAMPLE: I would interview Robert, but that's not the **role** I perform for the company.

TRANSLATION: I would interview Robert, but that's not the **function** I perform for the company.

"REAL SPEAK": I'd in'erview Robert, b't that's not the **role** I perform fer the comp'ny.

root cause *n.* the reason behind the entire problem.

EXAMPLE: We can fix the computers after they break, but we still don't know the **root cause** of why they keep malfunctioning.

TRANSLATION: We can fix the computers after they break, but we still don't know the **reason behind the entire problem** of why they keep malfunctioning.

"REAL SPEAK": We c'n fix the c'mpuders after they break, b't we still don't know the **root cause** 'ev why they keep malfunctioning.

sacred cow *n.* an indisputable ideal.

EXAMPLE: Good customer service is the **sacred cow** of this company. We can't compromise that for any reason!

TRANSLATION: Good customer service is the **indisputable ideal** of this company. We can't compromise that for any reason!

"REAL SPEAK": Good custamer service 'ez the **sacred cow** 'a this comp'ny. We can't compr'mise that fer any reason!

scalable *adj.* easily expandable.

EXAMPLE: Our solution isn't **scalable**. If the company gets much bigger, we won't be able to function.

TRANSLATION: Our solution isn't **easily expandable**. If the company gets much bigger, we won't be able to function.

"REAL SPEAK": 'Ar salution isn't **scalable**. If the comp'ny gets much bigger, we won't be able da function.

spearhead (to) *v.* to lead.

EXAMPLE: I want Gretchen to **spearhead** the team. She has many years of experience.

TRANSLATION: I want Gretchen to **lead** the team. She has many years of experience.

"REAL SPEAK": I want Gretchen da **spearhead** the team. She 'as many years 'ev experience.

Synonym: **head up (to)** *v.*

take something under advisement (to)

exp. to consider something, usually without the intention to act on it.

EXAMPLE: We have heard your complaints and will **take them under advisement**.

TRANSLATION: We have heard your complaints and will **consider them**.

"REAL SPEAK": We've heard jer c'mplaints 'n will **take th'm under advisement**.

task force *n.* a temporary committee created to accomplish a specific duty.

EXAMPLE: We need to assemble a **task force** to organize the company Christmas party.

TRANSLATION: We need to assemble a **temporary committee** to organize the company Christmas party.

"REAL SPEAK": We need da assemble a **task force** ta organize the comp'ny Chris'mas pardy.

turnkey *adj.* easy-to-implement.

EXAMPLE: We don't have much time, so we need to find a **turnkey** solution to the problem.

TRANSLATION: We don't have much time, so we need to find an **easy-to-implement** solution to the problem.

"REAL SPEAK": We don'ave much time, so we need da find a **turnkey** solution ta the problem.

up-to-speed *exp.* at a sufficient level of understanding.

EXAMPLE: Rita just started working here. It will take her at least a month to be **up-to-speed** on this project.

TRANSLATION: Rita just started working here. It will take her at least a month to be **at a sufficient level of understanding** on this project.

"REAL SPEAK": Rita jus' starded working here. Id'll take 'er 'it least a month ta be **up-ta-speed** on th's project.

value-add *n.* something which provides an additional benefit at no cost.

EXAMPLE: We're offering free technical assistance as a **value-add** to the product.

TRANSLATION: We're offering free technical assistance as **something which provides additional benefit at no cost** to the product.

"REAL SPEAK": W'r off'ring free technical assistance as a **value-add** ta the product.

TRACEY DEFENDS THE THIRD WORLD

Globalization Slang & Jargon

THIS LESSON FEATURES 12 NEW SLANG WORDS & IDIOMS

LET'S WARM UP!

MATCH THE PICTURES

As a fun way to get started, see if you can guess the meaning of the new slang words and expressions on the opposite page by using the pictures below and following the context of the sentences.

1. In the United States, many people enjoy a high **standard of living**.
   Definition: *"temperature"*
   ☐ True ☐ False

2. **Deregulation** makes international commerce cheaper and easier.
   Definition: *"reduced governmental control"*
   ☐ True ☐ False

3. **Globalization** is bringing the people of the world closer together.
   Definition: *"photographs of the world"*
   ☐ True ☐ False

4. People in the **Third World** don't have the most recent technology and medicine.
   Definition: *"poor countries of the world"*
   ☐ True ☐ False

5. The idea that the world is a **global village** makes nations less selfish.
   Definition: *"single community"*
   ☐ *True* ☐ *False*

6. The introduction of a universal Eurpoean unit of currency will increase Europe's **boundary erosion**.
   Definition: *"loss of soil due to heavy rains"*
   ☐ True ☐ False

7. The United States and Canada are part of the **Global North**, but Mexico is not.
   Definition: *"countries that speak English"*
   ☐ True ☐ False

8. Some rich countries are in favor of **free trade** because it will make them richer.
   Definition: *"commerce without trade barriers"*
   ☐ True ☐ False

9. Import tax is an example of a **trade barrier** because it restricts international trade.
   Definition: *"brick wall"*
   ☐ True ☐ False

10. **Multinational corporations** like to make money in many different countries.
    Definition: *"company's with a foreign president"*
    ☐ True ☐ False

11. Concern over the environment is a **transcultural** issue. It affects us all!
    Definition: *"small"*
    ☐ True ☐ False

12. The **WTO** regulates trade between nations.
    Definition: *"Western Tennis Organization"*
    ☐ True ☐ False

Globalization Slang & Jargon

LET'S TALK!

A. DIALOGUE USING SLANG & IDIOMS

The words introduced on the first two pages are used in the dialogue below. See if you can understand the conversation. *Note:* The translation of the words in boldface is on the right-hand page.

CD–A: TRACK 23

Alan: I think the **WTO** has the right idea. In this era of **globalization**, we need to promote **free trade** through **deregulation**. Reducing **trade barriers** will raise the **standard of living** in the **Third World**.

Tracey: I disagree. The **multinational corporations** of the **global North** will just continue to grow richer, and **boundary erosion** will increase. We're a **global village** now, so we have to consider the **transcultural** implications of every new policy.

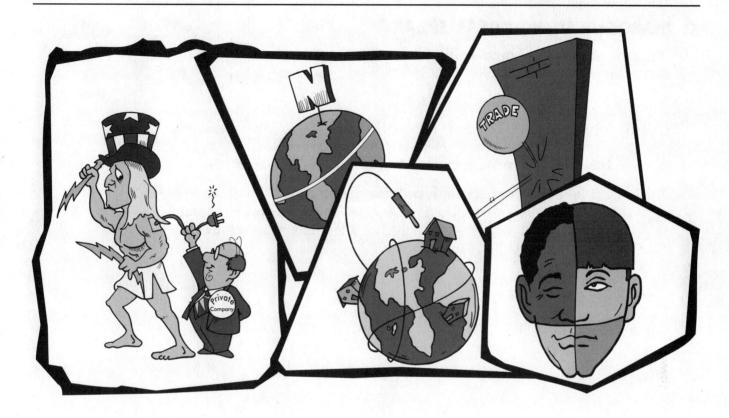

B. DIALOGUE TRANSLATED INTO STANDARD ENGLISH

LET'S SEE HOW MUCH YOU REMEMBER!
Just for fun, move around in random order to the words and expressions in boldface below. See if you can remember their slang equivalents without looking at the left-hand page!

Alan: I think the **World Trade Organization** has the right idea. In this era of **the increase of human interaction across the world**, we need to promote **commerce without trade or tax barriers** through **a decrease in government control**. Reducing **rules that restrict international trade** will raise the **level of material comfort** in the **underdeveloped countries of the world**.

Tracey: I disagree. The **corporations that operate in multiple countries** of the **world's wealthy industrialized countries** will just continue to grow richer, and **the collapse of the distinction between territories** will increase. We're a **single community composed of the entire world and its inhabitants** now, so we have to consider the implications **concerning all human cultures** of every new policy.

C. DIALOGUE USING "REAL SPEAK"

The dialogue below demonstrates how the slang conversation on the previous page would *really* be spoken by native speakers!

CD-A: TRACK 23

Alan: I think the **W-T-O** has the ride idea. In this era 'ev **globelization**, we need da pr'mote **free trade** through **deregulation**. Reducing **trade barriers**'ll raise the **standard 'a living** in the **Third World**.

Tracey: I disagree. The **multinational corperations** 'a the **globel North**'ll jus' continue da grow richer, an' **bound'ry erosion**'ll increase. W'r a **globel village** now, so we hafta consider the **transcultural** implications 'ev ev'ry new policy.

LET'S LEARN!

VOCABULARY

The following words and expressions were used in the previous dialogues. Let's take a closer look at what they mean.

CD-A: TRACK 24

boundary erosion *n.* a collapse of the political, social, and/or legal distinctions between territories.

EXAMPLE: The **boundary erosion** between the United States and Canada is increasing every year. Sometimes Americans can cross the border without passports!

TRANSLATION: The **collapse of the political, social, and legal distinctions** between the United States and Canada is increasing every year. Sometimes Americans can cross the border without passports!

"REAL SPEAK": The **bound'ry erosion** b'tween the Unided States 'n Canada's increasing ev'ry year. Sometimes Americans c'n cross the border w'thout passports!

NOW YOU DO IT. COMPLETE THE PHRASE ALOUD:
There's been significant **boundary erosion** between Mexico and ...

deregulation *n.* a decrease in government control.

> **EXAMPLE:** After the **deregulation** of electrical power in California, private companies were able to offer power to the state's residents.

> **TRANSLATION:** After the **decrease in government control** of electrical power in California, private companies were able to offer power to the state's residents.

> **"REAL SPEAK":** After the **deregulation** 'ev electrical power 'n California, private comp'nies were able da offer power da the state's residents.

> **NOW YOU DO IT. COMPLETE THE PHRASE ALOUD:**
> I wish… would undergo **deregulation**.

free trade *n.* commerce without trade or tax barriers which makes it easier and less expensive for countries to do business together.

> **EXAMPLE:** I'm a supporter of **free trade**. I'm tired of the world's governments telling everyone what to do!

> **TRANSLATION:** I'm a supporter of **commerce without trade or tax barriers**. I'm tired of the world's governments telling everyone what to do!

> **"REAL SPEAK":** I'm a supporder 'ev **free trade**. I'm tired 'a the world's gover'ments telling ev'ryone what ta do!

> **NOW YOU DO IT. COMPLETE THE PHRASE ALOUD:**
> If we had **free trade**, it would be a lot easier and less expensive for us to get… from Cuba.

Global North *n.* the world's wealthy, industrialized countries.

> **EXAMPLE:** I've heard Mexico is really beautiful, but I like living in the **Global North** where I can easily buy all of the newest electronics.

> **TRANSLATION:** I've heard Mexico is really beautiful, but I like living in the **world's wealthy industrialized countries** where I can easily buy all of the newest electronics.

> **"REAL SPEAK":** I've heard Mexico's really beaudiful, b'd I like living in the **Global North** where I c'n easily buy all 'a the newest electronics.

> *Synonym:* **First World** *n.*

> **NOW YOU DO IT. COMPLETE THE PHRASE ALOUD:**
> In the **Global North** it's easy to get …

global village *n.* a single community composed of the entire world and its inhabitants.

EXAMPLE: I never used to worry about the poor in other countries, but now I realize that we live in a **global village** and it's wrong not to care.

TRANSLATION: I never used to worry about the poor in other countries, but now I realize that we live in a **single community composed of the entire world and its inhabitants** and it's wrong not to care.

"REAL SPEAK": I never usta worry about the poor 'n other countries, b't now I re'lize th't we live 'n a **global village** an' it's wrong not ta care.

NOW YOU DO IT. COMPLETE THE PHRASE ALOUD:
Even … is part of the **global village**.

globalization *n.* the increase of human interaction around the world, which stimulates new economic, political, technological, societal, and cultural developments.

EXAMPLE: The Internet has really contributed to **globalization**. Now I have friends in countries I'd never even heard of before!

TRANSLATION: The Internet has really contributed to **the increase of human interaction around the world**. Now I have friends in countries I'd never even heard of before!

"REAL SPEAK": The In(t)ernet's really c'ntribuded ta **globalization**. Now I 'ave friends 'n countries I'd never even heard 'ev b'fore!

NOW YOU DO IT. COMPLETE THE PHRASE ALOUD:
Globalization is bringing people closer together. The other day I received an email from someone in …

multinational corporation *n.* (also called an *MNC*) a corporation that operates in multiple countries.

EXAMPLE: Every year there are more and more **multinational corporations**. I even ate at a McDonald's in Germany last month!

TRANSLATION: Every year there are more and more **corporations that operate in multiple countries**. I even ate at a McDonald's in Germany last month!

"REAL SPEAK": Ev'ry year there 'er more 'n more **multinational corperations**. I even ade 'id a McDonald's 'n Germany las' month!

NOW YOU DO IT. COMPLETE THE PHRASE ALOUD:
… is a **multinational corporation**.

Globalization Slang & Jargon

standard of living *exp.* a level of material comfort, usually measured by the goods, services, and luxuries that we are able to enjoy.

EXAMPLE: I'm accustomed to a high **standard of living**. I don't know how I would function without my computer or my car!

TRANSLATION: I'm accustomed to a high **level of material comfort**. I don't know how I would function without my computer or my car!

"REAL SPEAK": I'm accustom' ta a high **standard 'ev living**. I dunno how I'd function w'thout my c'mpuder 'r my car!

NOW YOU DO IT. COMPLETE THE PHRASE ALOUD:
We have a high **standard of living** because we have...

Third World *n.* underdeveloped countries of the world, especially those not associated with Communist countries.

EXAMPLE: The **Third World** produces a lot of pollution because they don't have enough money to invest in new, cleaner technologies.

TRANSLATION: The **underdeveloped countries of the world** produce a lot of pollution because they don't have enough money to invest in new, cleaner technologies.

"REAL SPEAK": The **Third World** pr'duces a lodda pallution b'cuz they don'ave anuf money da invest 'n new, cleaner technoligies.

NOW YOU DO IT. COMPLETE THE PHRASE ALOUD::
... is part of the **Third World**.

trade barrier *n.* a rule that restricts international trade.

EXAMPLE: I want to ship my products to India, but there are too many **trade barriers**!

TRANSLATION: I want to ship my products to India, but there are too many **rules that restrict international trade**!

"REAL SPEAK": I wanna ship my produc's ta India, b't there 'er too many **trade barriers**!

NOW YOU DO IT. COMPLETE THE PHRASE ALOUD:
An example of a **trade barrier** might be ...

transcultural *adj.* said of something that concerns all cultures.

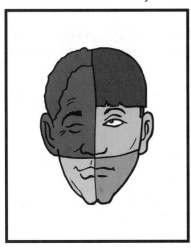

EXAMPLE: Food and shelter are **transcultural** ideals. Everybody needs a safe place to sleep and enough food to eat!

TRANSLATION: Food and shelter are ideals that **concern all cultures**. Everybody needs a safe place to sleep and enough food to eat!

"REAL SPEAK": Food 'n shelter 'er **transcultural** ideals. Ev'rybody needs a safe place ta sleep an' anuf food da eat!

NOW YOU DO IT: COMPLETE THE PHRASE ALOUD:
The idea of... is **transcultural** because it affects everyone.

WTO *abbrev.* (a common abbreviation for "World Trade Organization") an organization which enforces global rules of trade between nations.

EXAMPLE: The **WTO** gives money to developing nations. Unfortunately these nations sometimes spend that money on factories and other industries that hurt the environment.

TRANSLATION: The **World Trade Organization, the organization which enforces global rules of trade between nations**, gives money to developing nations. Unfortunately these nations sometimes spend that money on factories and other industries that hurt the environment.

"REAL SPEAK": The **W-T-O** gives money ta developing nations. Unfortunately these nations sometimes spend that money on factories and other industries that hurt the environment.

Note: If you would like more information on the WTO, please visit http://www.wto.org.

NOW YOU DO IT. COMPLETE THE PHRASE ALOUD:
I want to work for the **WTO** because...

LET'S PRACTICE!

WRITING

CD-A: TRACK 25

A. I KNOW THE ANSWER, BUT WHAT'S THE QUESTION?

Read the answer and place a check next to the correct question.

1.

The answer is...

Yes, it's a multinational corporation.

Questions:

☐ Does your company offer good salaries?

☐ Does your company sell computers?

☐ Does your company operate in America and Mexico?

2.

The answer is...

Because I enjoy a high standard of living.

Questions:

☐ Why is it so important to you to make a lot of money?

☐ Why do you always leave work early?

☐ Why did you fire Bob?

3.

The answer is...

Yes, it's part of the Global North.

Questions:

☐ Does America welcome immigrants?

☐ Is England a wealthy country?

☐ Is Kenya hosting the Olympics?

4.

The answer is...

Yes, I work for the WTO.

Questions:

☐ Do you work for the World Tariff Organization?

☐ Do you work for the World Trade Organization?

☐ Do you work for the Wide Trade Organization?

5.

The answer is...

Because of the trade barriers.

Questions:

☐ Why does it cost so much to ship items to India?

☐ Why is so hard to travel to Europe?

☐ Why don't we give more money to the poor?

6.

The answer is...

Not at all. Boundary erosion has made it easy.

Questions:

☐ Is it difficult to learn this computer program?

☐ Is it difficult to travel within the United States?

☐ Is it difficult to travel from America to Canada?

B. FIND YOUR PERFECT MATCH

Write the number of the slang term or idiom from Column A next to its matching picture in Column B as well as next to the matching definition in Column C.

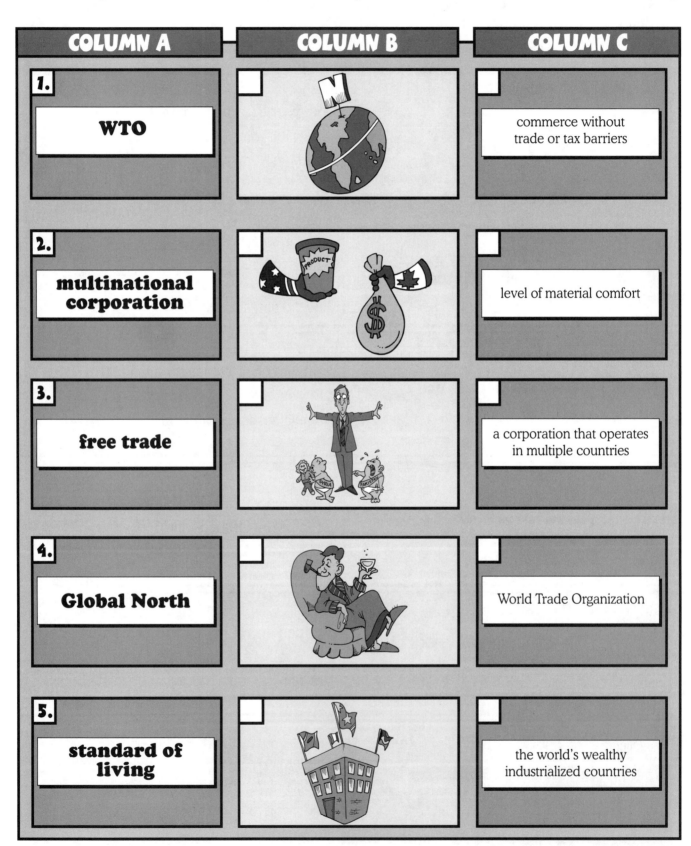

COLUMN A	COLUMN B	COLUMN C
1. WTO		commerce without trade or tax barriers
2. multinational corporation		level of material comfort
3. free trade		a corporation that operates in multiple countries
4. Global North		World Trade Organization
5. standard of living		the world's wealthy industrialized countries

Globalization Slang & Jargon

C. IMAGINE THAT...

Someone has presented you with a situation as seen below. Respond to each situation aloud by making a complete sentence using one of the groups of words below. Use each group only once.

✔ boundary erosion ✔ global village	✔ transcultural ✔ globalization	✔ Third World ✔ WTO
✔ trade barrier ✔ deregulation	✔ Global North ✔ standard of living	✔ free trade ✔ multinational corporation

IMAGINE THAT...

1. You live in a poor country.

IMAGINE THAT...

2. You want to start selling your products in another country.

IMAGINE THAT...

3. You want to drive from the United States to Canada.

IMAGINE THAT...

4. You're organizing an event for people of many different nations.

IMAGINE THAT...

5. You live in a wealthy country.

IMAGINE THAT...

6. You work for a company with offices in six different countries.

Globalization Slang & Jargon

D. YOU'RE THE AUTHOR
Complete the dialogue using the words below.

CD-A: TRACK 27

BARRIERS	**FREE**	**THIRD**
CORPORATIONS	**GLOBALIZATION**	**TRANSCULTURAL**
DEREGULATION	**NORTH**	**VILLAGE**
EROSION	**STANDARD**	**WTO**

Chandler: If we remove all the trade _____ to international trade, then the rich countries

of the Global _____ are just going to get richer.

Rachel: Yes, but the _____ of trade will also help the poor countries of the

_____ World, at least that's what the _____ has been saying.

Chandler: I think _____ trade is definitely a good thing. As boundary _____

increases, the world is becoming more of a global _____. We should encourage

this _____ as much as possible.

Rachel: Yes, but poverty should be a _____ concern. I want everyone to have a better

_____ of living, not just the rich multinational _____.

Globalization Slang & Jargon

FROM THE SLANGMAN FILES

More Globalization Slang & Jargon

There's no doubt about it. As our world becomes smaller and smaller due to globalization, a new vocabulary is emerging. For the linguist, this is an exciting time as our dictionaries are being updated at lightning speed in order to stay current with the changes. For the native speaker of English, and especially the nonnative speaker, hearing so many new terms can certainly be intimidating. The following list is sure to make your first encounter with these terms a lot easier!

commodification *n.* the increasing trend of services (instead of physical objects) being traded for money.

> **EXAMPLE:** Did you know you can pay someone to buy clothes for you? I love **commodification**!
>
> **TRANSLATION:** Did you know you can pay someone to buy clothes for you? I love **the increasing trend of services being traded for money**!
>
> **"REAL SPEAK":** Did ja know ya c'n pay someone da buy cloz for ya? I love **commodification**!

Common Market *n.* a coalition of European nations, formed to facilitate trade and cooperation.

> **EXAMPLE:** As the **Common Market** expands, it will be easier to travel through Europe. We'll be able to use the same currency regardless of what country we're in!
>
> **TRANSLATION:** As the **coalition of European nations** expands, it will be easier to travel through Europe. We'll be able to use the same currency regardless of what country we're in!
>
> **"REAL SPEAK":** As the **Common Marked** expands, id'll be easier da travel through Europe. We'll be able da use the same currency regardless 'ev what country w'r in!
>
> *Synonym:* **The European Economic Community** (or *EEC*) *n.*

decentralization *n.* the transfer of power from a higher to a lower administrative level of government.

> **EXAMPLE:** State-level officials are usually in favor of **decentralization** because it gives them more control over their own states.
>
> **TRANSLATION:** State-level officials are usually in favor of **the transfer of power from a higher to a lower administrative level of government** because it gives them more control over their own states.
>
> **"REAL SPEAK":** State-level afficials 'er ujally 'n favor 'ev **decentralization** b'cuz it gives th'm more control over their own states.

economies of scale *pl.n.* reductions in cost of production due to a large number of items produced.

> **EXAMPLE:** **Economies of scale** help big companies more than small ones. Big companies have the money to make larger quantities of products, and therefore larger profits.
>
> **TRANSLATION:** **Reductions in cost of production due to a large number of items produced** help big companies more than small ones. Big companies have the money to make larger quantities of products, and therefore larger profits.

"REAL SPEAK": **Econamies 'ev scale** help big comp'nies more th'n small ones. Big comp'nies have the money da make larger quan'idies 'ev produc's, 'n therefore larger profits.

European Union *n.* (commonly shorted to *EU*) a coalition of European countries whose purpose is to unify various social, political, and economic policies across its member nations. Previously known as the "European Community."

EXAMPLE: Countries that want to join the **European Union** must agree to obey all its laws.

TRANSLATION: Countries that want to join the **coalition of European countries whose purpose is to unify various social, political, and economic policies across its member nations** must agree to obey all its laws.

"REAL SPEAK": Countries th't wanna join the **EU** must agree do obey all its laws.

Note: For more information visit http://europa.eu.int.

First World *n.* the industrialized non-Communist countries of the world.

EXAMPLE: The United States has been a leader of the **First World** for a long time.

TRANSLATION: The United States has been a leader of the **industrialized non-Communist countries of the world** for a long time.

"REAL SPEAK": The Unided States 'ez been a leader 'ev the **First World** fer a long time.

free port *n.* a port available to all traders in which imported goods may be held while awaiting re-export, without the need to pay fees.

EXAMPLE: If the world had more **free ports**, it would be cheaper to buy items from all over the world!

TRANSLATION: If the world had more **ports available to all traders in which imported goods may be held while awaiting re-export, without the need to pay fees**, it would be cheaper to buy items from all over the world!

"REAL SPEAK": If the world had more **free ports**, it'd be cheaper da buy idems fr'm all over the world!

GATS *n.* (**G**eneral **A**greement on **T**rade in **S**ervices) an agreement whose purpose is to remove all restrictions that apply to trade in services (where services are actions, not physical objects).

EXAMPLE: Because of the **GATS**, any government ruling that affects services can be challenged.

TRANSLATION: Because of the **General Agreement on Trade in Services, an agreement whose purpose is to remove all restrictions to trade in services**, any government ruling that affects services can be challenged.

"REAL SPEAK": B'cuz 'a the **GATS**, any gover'ment ruling th'd affec's services c'n be challenged.

Globalization Slang & Jargon

GATT *n.* (**G**eneral **A**greement on **T**ariffs and **T**rade) an agreement whose purpose was to reduce trade restrictions among the participants — replaced by the World Trade Organization in 1995.

> **EXAMPLE:** Nations that participated in the **GATT** agreed to trade with each other using the same standards, without favoring one nation over another.

> **TRANSLATION:** Nations that participated in the **General Agreement on Tariffs and Trade, an agreement whose purpose was to reduce trade restrictions**, agreed to trade with each other using the same standards, without favoring one nation over another.

> **"REAL SPEAK":** Nations th't perticipaded in the **GATT** agreed da trade w'th each other using the same standerds, w'thout favering one nation over another.

Global Exchange *n.* a human rights organization dedicated to promoting environmental, political, and social justice around the world.

> **EXAMPLE:** Whenever I hear about a group of people being treated unfairly, I inform the **Global Exchange**. They know how to help!

> **TRANSLATION:** Whenever I hear about a group of people being treated unfairly, I inform the **human rights organization dedicated to promoting environmental, political, and social justice around the world**. They know how to help!

> **"REAL SPEAK":** Wh'never I hear 'aboud a group 'a people being treeded unfairly, I inform the **Global Exchange**. They know how da help!

> *Note:* For more information, visit http://www.globalexchange.org.

Global South *n.* the world's poor countries.

> **EXAMPLE:** I use the Internet every day, but some people in the **Global South** don't even have telephones yet!

> **TRANSLATION:** I use the Internet every day, but some people in **the world's poor countries** don't even have telephones yet!

> **"REAL SPEAK":** I use the In'ernet ev'ry day, b't some people 'n the **Global South** don' even have telephones yet!

global warming *n.* the speculation that the world's temperature is increasing each year due to various factors.

> **EXAMPLE:** If **global warming** is true, then the polar glaciers will start to melt, and cities along the coast will be flooded!

> **TRANSLATION:** If **the speculation that the world's temperature is increasing each year** is true, then the polar glaciers will start to melt, and cities along the coast will be flooded!

> **"REAL SPEAK":** If **global warming** 'ez true, then the poler glaciers start ta melt, an' cidies along the coast'll be flooded!

GNP *n.* (**G**ross **N**ational **P**roduct) the total market value of all the goods and services produced by a country during a specified period.

> **EXAMPLE:** Non-industrialized countries have a much lower **GNP** than countries with lots of factories.

> **TRANSLATION:** Non-industrialized countries have a much lower **Gross National Product, the total market value of all the goods and services produced**, than countries with lots of factories.

> **"REAL SPEAK":** Non-industrialized countries have a much lower **G-N-P** th'n countries w'th lots 'ev fact'ries.

Globalization Slang & Jargon

grassroots *n.* having to do with the general public or the average person.

> **EXAMPLE:** Nelson isn't well liked in Washington, D.C., but the **grassroots** love him!
>
> **TRANSLATION:** Nelson isn't well liked in Washington, D.C., but the **general public** loves him!
>
> **"REAL SPEAK":** Nelson isn't well liked 'n Washington, D-C, b't the **grassroots** love 'im!

hard currency *n.* a currency that is stable and acceptable for international transactions.

> **EXAMPLE:** Gold is a good example of **hard currency**. It's accepted all around the world.
>
> **TRANSLATION:** Gold is a good example of **a currency that is stable and acceptable for international transactions**. It's accepted all around the world.
>
> **"REAL SPEAK":** Gold's a good example 'ev **hard currency**. It's accepted all aroun' the world.

IMF *n.* (International Monetary Fund) an organization that encourages international monetary cooperation, promotes economic growth, and loans money to poor countries.

> **EXAMPLE:** If a poor country can't pay another country for goods it has purchased, it can usually borrow money from the **IMF**.
>
> **TRANSLATION:** If a poor country can't pay another country for goods it has purchased, it can usually borrow money from the **International Monetary Fund**.
>
> **"REAL SPEAK":** If a poor country can't pay another country fer goods it's purchased, it c'n ujally borrow money fr'm the **I-M-F**.
>
> *Note:* For more information, visit http://www.imf.org.

intellectual property *n.* the ownership of ideas and legal control over the representation of those ideas.

> **EXAMPLE:** Laverne invented a new kind of car while working for her last company. She claims that the invention is her **intellectual property**, but the company disagrees.
>
> **TRANSLATION:** Laverne invented a new kind of car while working for her last company. She claims that the invention is her **idea and that she legally controls it**, but the company disagrees.
>
> **"REAL SPEAK":** Laverne inven'ed a new kinda car while working for 'er las' comp'ny. She claims the invention's her **intellectual properdy**, b't the comp'ny disagrees.

inter-cultural *adj.* relating to, involving, or representing different cultures.

> **EXAMPLE:** Making country borders easier to cross will have **inter-cultural** consequences as regional distinctions start disappearing.
>
> **TRANSLATION:** Making country borders easier to cross will have consequences **involving different cultures** as regional distinctions start disappearing.
>
> **"REAL SPEAK":** Making country borders easier da cross'll have **in(t)er-cultural** consequences 'ez regional distinctions start disappearing.

LDC *n.* (Less-Developed Country or Least-Developed Country) an undeveloped country with limited natural resources and a poor supply of skilled workers.

> **EXAMPLE:** Jerry went to work in an **LDC** in South America. They need skilled architects and it's very inexpensive to live there.
>
> **TRANSLATION:** Jerry went to work in a **less-developed country** in South America. They need skilled architects and it's very inexpensive to live there.

"REAL SPEAK": Jerry went ta work in 'n **L-D-C** 'n South America. They need skilled architec's an' it's very inexpensive ta live there.

liberalization *n.* the act of making a regulation less strict or more *liberal*.

EXAMPLE: Many people think the **liberalization** of trade regulations will help the whole world. If it's easier to trade across country borders, many countries will grow rich very quickly.

TRANSLATION: Many people think the **act of making** trade regulations **more liberal** will help the whole world. If it's easier to trade across country borders, many countries will grow rich very quickly.

"REAL SPEAK": Many people think the **lib'ralization** 'ev trade regulations'll help the whole world. If it's easier da trade across country borders, many countries'll grow rich very quickly.

MAI *n.* (**M**ultilateral **A**greement on **I**nvestment) a trade agreement designed to eliminate almost all barriers to international trade by increasing the rights of foreign corporations operating domestically.

EXAMPLE: If the **MAI** is adopted, American corporations will receive equal or better treatment than their local competition when they operate in foreign countries.

TRANSLATION: If the **Multilateral Agreement on Investment** is adopted, American corporations will receive equal or better treatment than their local competition when they operate in foreign countries.

"REAL SPEAK": If the **M-A-I's** adopted, American corperations'll receive equal 'er bedder treatment th'n their local competition when they operade in foreign countries.

member nation *n.* a country that belongs to a specific organization.

EXAMPLE: Only the **member nations** are obligated to abide by the organization's rules.

TRANSLATION: Only the **countries that belong to a specific organization** are obligated to abide by the organization's rules.

"REAL SPEAK": Only the **member nations** 'er obligaded ta abide by the organization's rules.

MFN *n.* (**M**ost-**F**avored **N**ation) a foreign country which is granted the most favorable terms in its international trade with another country.

EXAMPLE: Some agreements require poor countries to be treated as **MFNs** in order to receive the same trading benefits as richer countries.

TRANSLATION: Some agreements require poor countries to be treated as **Most-Favored Nations** in order to receive the same trading benefits as richer countries.

"REAL SPEAK": Some agreements require poor countries ta be treaded 'ez **M-F-Ns** 'n order da receive the same trading benefits 'ez richer countries.

multilateral *adj.* involving many nations.

EXAMPLE: I support laws that limit nuclear weapon production, but unless they're **multilateral** laws, they'll have little effect on the world in general.

TRANSLATION: I support laws that limit nuclear weapon production, but unless they're laws **involving many nations**, they'll have little effect on the world in general.

"REAL SPEAK": I support laws th't limit nuclear weapon praduction, b'd unless they're **multiladeral** laws, they'll have liddle effect on the world 'n general.

NAFTA *n.* (**N**orth **A**merican **F**ree **T**rade **A**greement) an agreement between the United States, Canada and Mexico to remove many of the trade barriers between the three countries.

> **EXAMPLE:** Ever since President Clinton introduced **NAFTA**, our publishing company has been able to sell books easily to Canada and Mexico.

> **TRANSLATION:** Ever since President Clinton introduced **North American Free Trade Agreement**, our publishing company has been able to sell books easily to Canada and Mexico.

> **"REAL SPEAK":** Ever since President Clinton intraduced **nafta**, 'ar publishing comp'ny's been able da sell books easily da Canada 'n Mexico.

NIC *n.* (**N**ewly **I**ndustrialized **C**ountry) a country that is developing rapidly.

> **EXAMPLE:** There are many international laws concerning countries on the verge of technological revolution. In order to encourage development, environmental restrictions are sometimes lighter for these **NICs**.

> **TRANSLATION:** There are many international laws concerning countries on the verge of technological revolution. In order to encourage development, environmental restrictions are sometimes lighter for these **Newly Industrialized Countries**.

> **"REAL SPEAK":** There 'er many in(t)ernational laws concerning countries on the verge 'ev technalogical revolution. In order ta encourage development, enviro'men(t)al restrictions 'er sometimes lider fer these **N-I-Cs**.

> *Also:* **NIE** *n.* (**N**ewly **I**ndustrialized **E**conomy)

OECD *n.* (**O**rganization for **E**conomic **C**ooperation and **D**evelopment) a group of industrialized nations who meet to discuss and coordinate international, economic, and social policies.

> **EXAMPLE:** The **OECD** produces a lot of reports involving economics, statistics, and advice for developing countries.

> **TRANSLATION:** The **Organization for Economic Cooperation and Development** produces a lot of reports involving economics, statistics, and advice for developing countries.

> **"REAL SPEAK":** The **O-E-C-D** pr'duces a lodda r'ports involving ecanomics, statistics, an' advice fer developing countries.

> *Note:* For more information, visit http://www.oecd.org.

OPEC *n.* (**O**rganization of **P**etroleum-**E**xporting **C**ountries – pronounced: *oh-pek*) a group of petroleum-producing nations that attempts to influence the supply and price of oil.

> **EXAMPLE:** When oil prices rise drastically, it's usually the decision of **OPEC**, since they control over 40% of the world's oil production.

TRANSLATION: When oil prices rise drastically, it's usually the decision of **the Organization of Petroleum-Exporting Countries**, since they control over 40% of the world's oil production.

"REAL SPEAK": When oil prices rise drastic'ly, it's ujally the decision 'ev **oh-pek**, since they c'ntrol over fordy percen' 'a the world's oil pr'duction.

Note: For more information, visit http://www.opec.org.

private sector *n.* the business community.

EXAMPLE: If Senator Smith doesn't keep the **private sector** happy, he won't get enough donations to win his next election.

TRANSLATION: If Senator Smith doesn't keep the **business community** happy, he won't get enough donations to win his next election.

"REAL SPEAK": If Senader Smith doesn' keep the **private secter** happy, he won't ged anuf donations ta win 'is next alection.

privatization *n.* refers to an industry's change from governmental or public control to private enterprise.

EXAMPLE: Because of the **privatization** of jails in the United States, convicted prisoners can be sent to privately controlled prisons which are operated for profit, just like regular businesses.

TRANSLATION: Because of the **change** of jails **from governmental control to private enterprise** in the United States, convicted prisoners can be sent to privately controlled prisons which are operated for profit, just like regular businesses.

"REAL SPEAK": B'cuz 'a the **privadization** 'ev jails 'n the Unided States, convicted pris'ners c'n be sen' ta privately c'ntrolled prisons which 'er operaded fer profit, jus' like reguler bizness.

Also: **public sector** *n.* the government, the people.

protectionism *n.* advocating that the government impose political barriers to international trade in order to protect domestic producers from their foreign competition.

EXAMPLE: **Protectionism** helps some companies by making it harder for their foreign competitors to sell their goods domestically.

TRANSLATION: **Advocating that the government impose political barriers to international trade** helps some companies by making it harder for their foreign competitors to sell their goods domestically.

"REAL SPEAK": **Protectionism** helps some comp'nies by making it harder fer their foreign compediders ta sell their goods damestic'ly.

SAP *n.* (**S**tructural **A**djustment **P**rogram) a special program which makes countries eligible to receive money from the **IMF** (*p. 95*), if they agree to reform their economies by lowering spending, privatizing industry, and opening their countries to foreign investment and trade.

EXAMPLE: A poor country must agree to follow **SAPs** in order to receive money from the *IMF*.

TRANSLATION: A poor country must agree to follow **Structural Adjustment Programs** in order to receive money from the *IMF*.

"REAL SPEAK": A poor country must agree da follow **saps** 'n order da receive money fr'm the *I-M-F*.

soft currency *n.* a currency that cannot be easily converted into gold or other foreign currency.

EXAMPLE: Money from small countries is **soft currency** which is why it's not accepted around the world.

TRANSLATION: Money from small countries is **currency that cannot be easily converted into gold or other foreign currency** which is why it's not accepted around the world.

"REAL SPEAK": Money fr'm small countries 'ez **soft currency**, so it's nod accepted aroun' the world.

sphere *n.* an area of influence, such as political, economic, geographical, or cultural.

EXAMPLE: The United States is one of the most powerful countries in the world, so it is active in many **spheres**.

TRANSLATION: The United States is one of the most powerful countries in the world, so it is active in many **areas of influence**.

"REAL SPEAK": The Unided States 'ez one 'a the most powerful countries 'n the world, so it's active 'n many **spheres**.

TBT Agreement *n.* (**T**echnical **B**arriers to **T**rade) an agreement that tries to ensure that regulations, standards, testing, and certification procedures do not create unnecessary obstacles to international trade.

EXAMPLE: Countries can create whatever rules they want in order to control the importing and exporting of merchandise. The **TBT Agreement** tries to keep international trade successful despite these rules.

TRANSLATION: Countries can create whatever rules they want in order to control the importing and exporting of merchandise. The **Technical Barriers to Trade Agreement** tries to keep international trade successful despite these rules.

"REAL SPEAK": Countries c'n create whadever rules they want 'n order da c'ntrol the impording 'n exporting 'ev merchandise. The **T-B-T Agreement** tries da keep in(t)ernational trade successful despite these rules.

transnational *adj.* (also referred to as a **TNC**) involving more than one nation.

EXAMPLE: I work for a **transnational** company. Our main office is in the United States, but we have other offices in Germany, South Africa, and Brazil.

TRANSLATION: I work for a company **involving more than one nation**. Our main office is in the United States, but we have other offices in Germany, South Africa, and Brazil.

"REAL SPEAK": I work fer a **transnational** comp'ny. 'Ar main office 'ez in the Unided States, b't we 'ave other offices 'n Germany, South Africa, an' Brazil.

TRIPS Agreement *n.* (**T**rade-**R**elated aspects of **I**ntellectual **P**roperty **R**ights) an agreement which insures *intellectual property (see p. 95)* rights for corporations and industries.

EXAMPLE: The **TRIPS Agreement** was created to promote technical innovation by both protecting the inventor and encouraging the transfer of the new technology to the public.

TRANSLATION: The **Trade-Related aspects of Intellectual Property Rights Agreement** was created to promote technical innovation by both protecting the inventor and encouraging the transfer of the new technology to the public.

"REAL SPEAK": The **TRIPS agreement** w'z creaded da pr'mote technical innavation by both pr'tecting the inven(t)er an' encouraging the transfer 'ev the new technolagy ta the public.

World Bank *n.* an agency which grants low-cost, long-term loans to poor countries for infrastructure projects (such as drinking water systems, irrigation systems, etc.)

EXAMPLE: If a country is suffering from a drought, the **World Bank** might be able to help it build a better irrigation system.

TRANSLATION: If a country is suffering from a drought, the **World Bank, an agency which grants low-cost, long-term loans to poor countries**, might be able to help it build a better irrigation system.

"REAL SPEAK": If a country's suff'ring fr'm a drought, the **World Bank** might be able da help it build a bedder irrigation system.

Note: For more information, visit http://www.worldbank.org.

Political Slang & Jargon

THIS LESSON FEATURES 14 NEW SLANG WORDS & IDIOMS

LET'S WARM UP!

MATCH THE PICTURES

As a fun way to get started, see if you can guess the meaning of the new slang words and expressions on the opposite page by using the pictures below and following the context of the sentences.

1. I'm tired of your **middle-of-the-road** approach. You need stronger opinions!
   - ❏ politically neutral
   - ❏ reckless

2. The **incumbent** has been in office for five years. It's time for a change!
   - ❏ politician currently in office
   - ❏ Democratic candidate

3. All new proposals must be approved by **Capitol Hill**.
   - ❏ Mr. Hill
   - ❏ congress

4. I don't know how Senator Brown feels about gun control. She always **waffles** on difficult issues.
   - ❏ vague and misleading
   - ❏ cook breakfast

5. Carol's family is very **right wing**. They don't believe in birth control.
   - ❏ liberal
   - ❏ conservative

6. Smith talks a lot, but I can't determine his **platform**!
   - ❏ principles
   - ❏ style

7. The **polls** open at six in the morning. I want to be the first to vote in my city!
   - ❏ stores
   - ❏ voting locations

8. Fuller doesn't have a chance. Her opponent has the election **wrapped up**!
   - ❏ hidden
   - ❏ won

9. Hanson should spend less time **mudslinging** and more time talking about his plans if he's elected.
   - ❏ criticizing his opponent
   - ❏ throwing mud

10. The election is over and Gruber **won by a landslide**!
    - ❏ won because of a disaster
    - ❏ won by an overwhelming number of votes

11. Meisner **took a stand** on abortion and lost the election!
    - ❏ stood through a debate
    - ❏ defended his beliefs

12. I like Murphy's **running mate**. He's smart and friendly.
    - ❏ political partner
    - ❏ jogging companion

13. Thomson's a **lame duck**. He lost the election and is wasting his last two months in office.
    - ❏ politican who has no reason to work hard
    - ❏ politician with a broken leg

14. I voted for Brown, but I don't think he's going to win the **race**! He doesn't seem to be very popular.
    - ❏ marathon
    - ❏ election

LET'S TALK!

A. DIALOGUE USING SLANG & IDIOMS

The words introduced on the first two pages are used in the dialogue below. See if you can understand the conversation. Note: The translation of the words in boldface is on the right-hand page.

CD-B: TRACK 1

David: The new election **poll** predicts that Jane will **win by a landslide**. I like her, but her **running mate**, Philip, is too **middle-of-the-road**. He needs to **take a stand** on more issues instead of **waffling**.

Al: I think the **incumbent**, Carolyn, has the election **wrapped up**. Some people at **Capitol Hill** say she's a **lame duck**, but I think they're just **mudslinging**. Her **platform** is more **right wing** than Jane's. She'll win the **race** for sure!

B. DIALOGUE TRANSLATED INTO STANDARD ENGLISH

LET'S SEE HOW MUCH YOU REMEMBER!
Just for fun, move around in random order to the words and
expressions in boldface below. See if you can remember their
slang equivalents without looking at the left-hand page!

David: The new election **survey** predicts that Jane will **win by an overwhelming number of votes**. I like her, but her **political partner in the election**, Philip, is too **politically neutral**. He needs to **defend his positions** on more issues instead of **being vague and misleading**.

Al: I think the **politician currently in office**, Carolyn, has the election **won**. Some people at **the Senate and House of Representatives** say she's an **official who has no reason to perform well because she won't be re-elected**, but I think they're just **criticizing their opponent**. Her **publicly-stated principles** are more **politically conservative** than Jane's. She'll win the **election** for sure!

Political Slang & Jargon

C. DIALOGUE USING "REAL SPEAK"

The dialogue below demonstrates how the slang conversation on the previous page would *really* be spoken by native speakers!

CD-B: TRACK 1

David: The new election **poll** predic's th't Jane'll **win by a lan'slide**. I like 'er, bud 'er **running mate**, Philip, is too **middle-'a-the-road**. He needs da **take a stand** on more issues instead 'a **waffling**.

Al: I think the **incumb'nt**, Caralyn, has the election **wrapped up**. Some people 'it **Capid'l Hill** say she's a **lame duck**, b'd I think they're jus' **mudslinging**. Her **platform**'s more **right wing** th'n Jane's. She'll win the **race** fer sher!

LET'S LEARN!

VOCABULARY

The following words and expressions were used in the previous dialogues. Let's take a closer look at what they mean.

CD-B: TRACK 2

Capitol Hill *n.* • **1.** Congress; the politicians of the United States Senate and House of Representatives • **2.** the building where Congress meets, which is located on a hill in Washington, D.C.

EXAMPLE 1:	I disagree with most of the laws that come from **Capitol Hill**. Those people don't understand what it's like to be an average American!
TRANSLATION:	I disagree with most of the laws that come from **Congress**. Those people don't understand what it's like to be an average American!
"REAL SPEAK":	I disagree w'th mosta the laws th't come fr'm **Capidol Hill**. Those people don' understand what it's like ta be 'n av'rage American!
EXAMPLE 2:	I have to go to **Capitol Hill** and present my ideas. I hope they're accepted!
TRANSLATION:	I have to go to **the building where Congress meets** and present my ideas. I hope they're accepted!
"REAL SPEAK":	I hafta go da **Capidol Hill** 'n pr'sent my ideas. I hope they're accepted!

Variation: **the Hill** *n.*

NOW YOU DO IT:
(use "**Capitol Hill**" in a sentence)

incumbent • **1.** *n.* the politician currently in office • **2.** *adj.* currently in office.

EXAMPLE 1:	Burke is the **incumbent** in this election. He's done a lot for our state in the last few years, so he'll be difficult to beat.
TRANSLATION:	Burke is the **politician currently in office** in this election. He's done a lot for our state in the last few years, so he'll be difficult to beat.
"REAL SPEAK":	Burke's the **incumbent** 'n th's election. He's done a lot fer 'ar state 'n the las' few years, so he'll be difficult ta beat.
EXAMPLE 2:	Cole is the **incumbent** governor. He's doing a great job!
TRANSLATION:	Cole is the **current** governor. He's doing a great job!
"REAL SPEAK":	Cole's the **incumbent** gov'ner. He's doing a great job!

NOW YOU DO IT:
(use "**incumbent**" in a sentence)

lame duck *n.* an official who has no reason to perform well because he or she didn't get re-elected for the next term.

EXAMPLE:	Hanson didn't win the election, so now he's a **lame duck**. Nothing will get accomplished in the next few months!
TRANSLATION:	Hanson didn't win the election, so now he's an **official who has no reason to perform well because he didn't get re-elected for the next term**. Nothing will get accomplished in the next few months!
"REAL SPEAK":	Hanson didn' win the alection, so now 'e's a **lame duck**. Nothing'll ged accomplished 'n the nex' few munts!
Note:	The presidential elections occur in November, but the new president doesn't start until the following January. During this time, the president is often referred to as a *lame duck president*.

NOW YOU DO IT:
(use "**lame duck**" in a sentence)

middle-of-the-road *adj.* politically neutral.

EXAMPLE:	I don't like arguing about politics. That's why I've adopted a **middle-of-the-road** attitude.
TRANSLATION:	I don't like arguing about politics. That's why I've adopted a **politically neutral** attitude.
"REAL SPEAK":	I don' like arguing about politics. That's why I've adoped a **middle-'a-the-road** additude.
Synonym:	**walk the fence (to)** *exp.* to remain neutral regarding an issue; not to choose a side.

NOW YOU DO IT:
(use "**middle-of-the-road**" in a sentence)

mudslinging *n.* criticizing an opponent, sometimes unfairly.

> **EXAMPLE:** The candidates for this election are spending more time **mudslinging** than talking about the issues!
>
> **TRANSLATION:** The candidates for this election are spending more time **criticizing their opponents** than talking about the issues!
>
> **"REAL SPEAK":** The can'idates fer this alection 'er spending more time **mudslinging** th'n talking about the issues!
>
> *Variation:* **mudslinger** *n.* a person who criticizes a candidate, sometimes unfairly.
>
> **NOW YOU DO IT:**
> (use "**mudslinging**" in a sentence)

platform *n.* publicly-stated principles, such as positions on abortion, gun-control, and the death penalty.

> **EXAMPLE:** I don't agree with Wilson's opinions on taxation and unemployment. I agree with Clinton's **platform** more.
>
> **TRANSLATION:** I don't agree with Wilson's opinions on taxation and unemployment. I agree with Clinton's **publicly-stated principles** more.
>
> **"REAL SPEAK":** I don' agree w'th Wilson's apinions on taxation 'n unemployment. I agree w'th Clinton's **platform** more.
>
> **NOW YOU DO IT:**
> (use "**platform**" in a sentence)

poll *n.* • **1.** *n.* survey • **2.** *n.pl.* (*the polls*) the place where voting takes place.

> **EXAMPLE 1:** I took a **poll** of the voters before the election, so I could assess my chances of winning.
>
> **TRANSLATION:** I took a **survey** of the voters before the election, so I could assess my chances of winning.
>
> **"REAL SPEAK":** I took a **poll** 'a the voders b'fore the alection, so I could assess my chances 'ev winning.
>
> **EXAMPLE 2:** I have to hurry! The **polls** close at six o'clock and I really want to vote!
>
> **TRANSLATION:** I have to hurry! The **place where voting takes place** closes at six o'clock and I really want to vote!
>
> **"REAL SPEAK":** I hafta hurry! The **polls** close 'it six a'clock 'n I really wanna vote!
>
> *Also:* **poll (to)** *v.* to survey.
>
> **NOW YOU DO IT:**
> (use "**poll**" in a sentence)

race *n.* an election (when used in reference to politics).

EXAMPLE: I really want Sarah Felt to win the **race**. She will be a much better president than Scott Stevens!

TRANSLATION: I really want Sarah Felt to win the **election**. She will be a much better president than Scott Stevens!

"REAL SPEAK": I really want Sarah Felt ta win the **race**. She'll be a much bedder president th'n Scott Stevens!

Note: Many expressions coming from horse racing can be used in reference to political races as well. For example, *to be neck and neck* ("to be tied in the race"), *to pull ahead* ("to start to win"), *to be still at the starting gate* (said of a politician who hasn't even started the race), *to be in the home stretch* (said of an election where all the votes are close to being counted), *to be a long shot* ("to be unlikey to win"), *etc.*

NOW YOU DO IT:
(use "**race**" in a sentence)

---

right wing • **1.** *adj.* politically conservative • **2.** *n.* the conservative faction of a group.

EXAMPLE 1: Dilley is way too **right wing** for me. I'm going to vote for Nash whose views are much more liberal.

TRANSLATION: Dilley is way too **politically conservative** for me. I'm going to vote for Nash whose views are much more liberal.

"REAL SPEAK": Dilley's way too **right wing** fer me. I'm gonna vote fer Nash whose views 'er much more lib'ral.

EXAMPLE 2: The **right wing** of the Republican party is in favor of the death penalty.

TRANSLATION: The **conservative faction** of the Republican party is in favor of the death penalty.

"REAL SPEAK": The **right wing** 'a the Republican pardy's in faver 'a the death penalty.

Variation: **right-winger** *n.* one who is politically conservative.

Antonym: **left wing** • see *p. 120.*

NOW YOU DO IT:
(use "**right wing**" in a sentence)

---

running mate *n.* the candidate who is running for the lesser of two closely related political offices.

EXAMPLE: Reese is running for president and Jones is his **running mate**. I think Jones would make a great vice president!

TRANSLATION: Reese is running for president and Jones is his **political partner**. I think Jones would make a great vice president!

"REAL SPEAK": Reese 'ez running fer president an' Jones 'ez **running mate**. I think Jones 'ed make a great vice president!

NOW YOU DO IT:
(use "**running mate**" in a sentence)

Political Slang & Jargon

take a stand (to) *exp.* to defend one's opinion regardless of the opposition.

EXAMPLE: I admire Franklin for **taking a stand** on the abortion issue. He will receive a lot of criticism for his views!

TRANSLATION: I admire Franklin for **defending his position** on the abortion issue. He will receive a lot of criticism for his views!

"REAL SPEAK": I admire Franklin fer **taking a stand** on the abortion issue. He'll receive a lodda cridicism fer 'is views!

Variation: **stand one's ground (to)** *exp.* to remain firm in one's belief or position.

NOW YOU DO IT:
(use "**take a stand**" in a sentence)

waffle (to) *v.* • **1.** to avoid an issue, to be vague and misleading • **2.** to change one's position on an issue frequently.

EXAMPLE 1: I asked Francine how she feels about abortion, but she always stalls or changes the subject. I hate it when she **waffles**!

TRANSLATION: I asked Francine how she feels about abortion, but she always stalls or changes the subject. I hate it when she **evades an issue**!

"REAL SPEAK": I ast Francine how she feels aboud abortion, b't she ahweez stalls 'er changes the subject. I hate it when she **waffles**!

EXAMPLE 2: Sanders keeps **waffling** on the issue of taxes. Yesterday he promised to cut taxes, and today he said he'll have to raise them!

TRANSLATION: Sanders keeps **changing his position** on the issue of taxes. Yesterday he promised to cut taxes, and today he said he'll have to raise them!

"REAL SPEAK": Sanders keeps **waffling** on the issue 'ev taxes. Yesterday 'e promise' ta cut taxes, an' taday 'e said 'e'll hafta raise 'em!

Synonym 1: **dodge the issue (to)** *exp.* to avoid discussing an issue.

Synonym 2: **hem and haw (to)** *exp.* to avoid discussing an issue by stalling.

NOW YOU DO IT:
(use "**waffle**" in a sentence)

win by a landslide (to) *exp.* to win by an overwhelming number of votes.

EXAMPLE: Everybody loves our candidate. He's going to **win by a landslide**!

TRANSLATION: Everybody loves our candidate. He's going to **win by an overwhelming number of votes**!

"REAL SPEAK": Ev'rybody loves 'ar can'idit. He's gonna **win by a lan'slide**!

Variation: **landslide** *n.* an overwhelming victory.

NOW YOU DO IT:

(use "**win by a landslide**" in a sentence)

wrap up (to) *v.* • **1.** to win • **2.** to finish.

EXAMPLE 1: If Patricia Wrede does well in the debate, she will have this election **wrapped up**!

TRANSLATION: If Patricia Wrede does well in the debate, she will have this election **won**!

"REAL SPEAK": If Patricia Wrede does well 'n the debate, she'll have this alection **wrapped up**!

EXAMPLE 2: I'm tired. Let's **wrap up** this report and go home.

TRANSLATION: I'm tired. Let's **finish** this report and go home.

"REAL SPEAK": I'm tired. Let's **wrap up** this r'port 'n go home.

Synonym: **all sewn up (to be)** *exp.* to be completed successfully.

NOW YOU DO IT:

(use "**wrap up**" in a sentence)

LET'S PRACTICE!

A. THE UNFINISHED CONVERSATION

Read the conversations, then fill in the last line with your own words in response to what you've just read. Make sure to use the suggested words in your response. Your response can be in the form of a question or statement.

WRITING

CD-B: TRACK 3

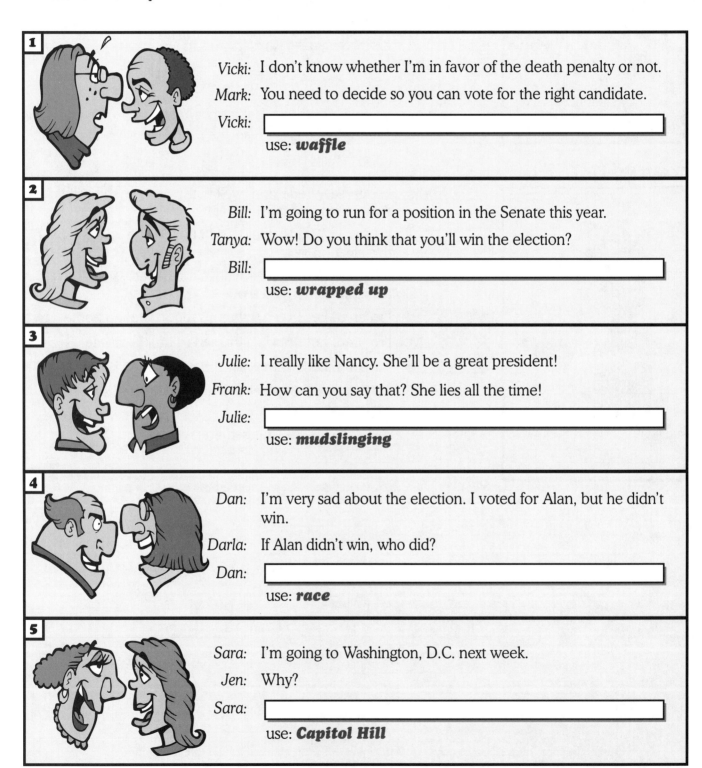

1

Vicki: I don't know whether I'm in favor of the death penalty or not.

Mark: You need to decide so you can vote for the right candidate.

Vicki:

use: ***waffle***

2

Bill: I'm going to run for a position in the Senate this year.

Tanya: Wow! Do you think that you'll win the election?

Bill:

use: ***wrapped up***

3

Julie: I really like Nancy. She'll be a great president!

Frank: How can you say that? She lies all the time!

Julie:

use: ***mudslinging***

4

Dan: I'm very sad about the election. I voted for Alan, but he didn't win.

Darla: If Alan didn't win, who did?

Dan:

use: ***race***

5

Sara: I'm going to Washington, D.C. next week.

Jen: Why?

Sara:

use: ***Capitol Hill***

Political Slang & Jargon

B. CHOOSE THE RIGHT WORD
Underline the words that best complete the phrase.

1. If I'm going to run for president, I need to find a (**jogging**, **running**, **skipping**) mate to be my political partner.

2. Before we can announce our candidate for the election, we need to decide on her (**boardwalk**, **basement**, **platform**)!

3. Every time Hunter is asked a question, he (**waffles**, **pancakes**, **omelettes**)! He never gives a direct answer about anything.

4. The people on Capitol (**Mound**, **Slope**, **Hill**) spend too much time arguing with each other instead of deciding on issues that affect our lives!

5. Everyone said Julie Kramer would win by a (**storm**, **landslide**, **landfill**), but she actually lost the election.

6. If Herb doesn't win the election for governor, he's going to be a lame (**cat**, **buck**, **duck**) until he's replaced. Nothing will get done until the new governor takes over.

7. I wanted to vote today, but I couldn't get to the (**pools**, **polls**, **poles**) before they closed.

8. Mertz is too right (**wing**, **beak**, **claw**) to win the election. He doesn't even believe in birth control.

9. McCracken criticizes her opponents too much. She needs to stop (**dirt throwing**, **line dancing**, **mudslinging**)!

10. Devon Darrant has the advantage because he's the (**incumbent**, **incompetent**, **cucumber**). He already knows how to do the job.

11. I've taken a firm (**sit**, **stand**, **jump**) on the issue of gun control. I don't think anyone should have guns in the home. It's just too dangerous.

12. The Republican candidate is too middle-of-the-(**street**, **avenue**, **road**). If he wants to win the election, he'll have to take a more conservative position.

C. COMPLETE THE STORY

Use the illustrations to help you fill in the blanks with the
correct slang terms from the list below.

CD-B: TRACK 5

CAPITOL HILL	MUDSLING	RIGHT WING	WIN BY A LANDSLIDE
INCUMBENT	PLATFORM	RUNNING MATE	WRAPPED UP
LAME DUCK	POLLS	TOOK A STAND	
MIDDLE-OF-THE-ROAD	RACE	WAFFLES	

Hello! I'm a candidate for president, and I hope you'll vote for me! I spent ten years on

_____ where I _____ on many important issues.

My _____ is a _____ politician with a strong

_____ . My opponent is the _____ . I don't like to

_____ , but you should know that he _____

on most issues and usually takes a _____ approach. When he loses

the election, I'm sure he'll be a _____ until I start. I have this election

_____ , but please go to the _____ on election

day and vote for me in this presidential _____ . We'll definitely

_____ !

Political Slang & Jargon

D. CREATE YOUR OWN SENTENCE

Read Person A's questions aloud using the suggested words to create your answer for Person B.

PERSON A	PERSON B

1.	How does your candidate feel about gun control?	[use: **middle-of-the-road**]
2.	Heather hasn't been doing much as our Mayor since she lost her re-election.	[use: **lame duck**]
3.	Barbara is really conservative!	[use: **right wing**]
4.	Who is Everett going to chose as his vice presidential candidate?	[use: **running mate**]
5.	I think Quinn is going to win the election.	[use: **wrapped up**]
6.	I need to decide if I'm in favor of the death penalty.	[use: **take a stand**]
7.	Raymond has been our Senator for four years already. Do you think he'll be re-elected?	[use: **incumbent**]
8.	Both Paul and Monica want to be our next Governor.	[use: **race**]
9.	I want to vote, but I don't know where to go!	[use: **polls**]
10.	Did Louise win the election by a large amount?	[use: **won by a landslide**]

Political Slang & Jargon

More Political Slang & Jargon

During election time, politicians and **carpetbaggers** (*politicians who try to get elected in cities where they don't live*) **press the flesh** (*shake hands with the public*) as they go **stumping** (*making political speeches*) from state to state. But why is it so difficult to understand what their **platform** (*political position*) is? The answer is simple. They all tend to speak in **political babble** (*political slang*) — a jargon incomprehensible to many native speakers of English as well... Until now!

absentee ballot *n.* a ballot marked and mailed in advance by a voter who cannot be at his/her assigned voting place on election day.

> **EXAMPLE:** I'll be in Spain during the election, but I'm filling out an **absentee ballot**. I wouldn't miss voting in this election for anything!

> **TRANSLATION:** I'll be in Spain during the election, but I'm filling out a **ballot which I'm allowed to mark and mail in advance if I can't be at my assigned voting place on election day**. I wouldn't miss voting in this election for anything!

> **"REAL SPEAK":** A'll be 'n Spain during the alection, b'd I'm filling oud 'n **absentee ballot**. I wouldn' miss voding 'n th's alection fer anything!

bill *n.* a proposal for a new law.

> **EXAMPLE:** I want Ted's **bill** to be accepted. It would result in a law to lower taxes for the working class!

> **TRANSLATION:** I want Ted's **proposal for a new law** to be accepted. It would result in a law to lower taxes for the working class!

> **"REAL SPEAK":** I want Ted's **bill** da be accepted. It'd result 'n a law da lower taxes fer the working class.

bipartisan *adj.* supported by both major political parties, the Democrats and the Republicans.

> **EXAMPLE:** Olivia is a **bipartisan** candidate for the Supreme Court. Everyone thinks she'll make a great judge!

> **TRANSLATION:** Olivia is a candidate **supported by both major political parties** for the Supreme Court. Everyone thinks she'll make a great judge!

> **"REAL SPEAK":** Olivia's a **bipardisan** can'idit fer the Supreme Court. Ev'ryone thinks she'll make a great judge!

bleeding heart *n.* a derogatory term for a person who is excessively sympathetic toward underprivileged people; anyone extremely liberal.

> **EXAMPLE:** Henrietta is a **bleeding heart**. She donates most of her money to charities for the poor.

> **TRANSLATION:** Henrietta is a **person excessively sympathetic toward underprivileged people**. She donates most of her money to charities for the poor.

> **"REAL SPEAK":** Henriedda's a **bleeding heart**! She donates most 'ev 'er money da charities fer the poor.

bloc *n.* a group united by a commonality such as age, race, belief, religion, etc.

> **EXAMPLE:** The women's **bloc** favors candidate Reynolds because he's promising to reduce taxes for working mothers.

> **TRANSLATION:** The women's **group** favors candidate Reynolds because he's promising to reduce taxes for working mothers.

> **"REAL SPEAK":** The women's **bloc** favors can'idit Reynolds b'cuz 'e's promising ta reduce taxes fer working mothers.

campaign (to) *v.* to engage in a crusade to get votes.

> **EXAMPLE:** I'm going to **campaign** for president next year!

> **TRANSLATION:** I'm going to **engage in a crusade to get votes** for president next year!

> **"REAL SPEAK":** I'm gonna **campaign** fer president next year!

> *Also:* **campaign trail** *n.* the physical and political path one takes when trying to be elected, including publicity efforts, traveling, etc.

carpetbagger *n.* a politician who arrogantly seeks success in a new city where he/she is not even a resident.

> **EXAMPLE:** Since our governor died, we've had a lot of **carpetbaggers** that are hoping to take his place.

> **TRANSLATION:** Since our governor died, we've had a lot of **politicians arrogantly seeking success in a new city where they are not even a resident** that are hoping to take his place.

> **"REAL SPEAK":** Since 'ar gov'ner died, we've had a lodda **carpetbaggers** that 'er hoping da take 'is place.

caucus *n.* • **1.** a group of people with similar political beliefs and goals • **2.** a meeting.

> **EXAMPLE 1:** The proposed changes to retirement funding aren't popular with the elderly **caucus**.

> **TRANSLATION:** The proposed changes to retirement funding aren't popular with the elderly **group**.

> **"REAL SPEAK":** The pr'pose' changes ta retirement funding aren't populer w'th the elderly **caucus**.

> **EXAMPLE 2:** The morning **caucus** has been postponed until the afternoon, so that everyone can be there.

> **TRANSLATION:** The morning **meeting** has been postponed until the afternoon, so that everyone can be there.

> **"REAL SPEAK":** The morning **caucus** 'ez been postpone' 'till the afdernoon, so that ev'ryone c'n be there.

chad *n.* the small circular or retangular piece of paper that is punched out of a ballot, indicating a vote.

> **EXAMPLE:** In Florida, the presidential election was affected by **chads**. If the piece of paper was not completely removed from the voting sheet, the vote was not counted.

> **TRANSLATION:** In Florida, the presidential election was affected by **the small circular or rectangular piece of paper that is punched out of a ballot, indicating a vote**. If the piece of paper was not completely removed from the voting sheet, the vote was not counted.

"REAL SPEAK": In Florida, the presidential alection w'z affec'ded by **chads**. If the piece 'a paper wasn' completely removed from the voding sheet, the vote wasn' coun(t)ed.

Note: Most Americans didn't know this word until the presidential election of 2000, where the winner of the election was determined by hand-counted votes in Florida. The process lasted several weeks and the word *chad* became so frequently used that it quickly became a regular part of American's everyday vocabulary.

demagoguery *n.* the use of popular prejudices and misleading claims to gain political power.

EXAMPLE: Candidate Williamson's **demagoguery** is winning him more supporters, but I wish he would just be honest!

TRANSLATION: Candidate Williamson's **use of popular prejudices and misleading claims to gain political power** is winning him more supporters, but I wish he would just be honest!

"REAL SPEAK": Can'idit Williamson's **demagoguery**'s winning 'im more sapporters, b'd I wish 'e'd jus' be honest!

electoral college *n.* a group of officials who, after the vote for president and vice-president, inform Washington D.C. of the winner in their particular state.

EXAMPLE: Although Gore had more actual votes, the **electoral college** cast more votes for Bush, so Bush was elected.

TRANSLATION: Although Gore had more actual votes, the **group of delegates who, after the vote for president and vice-president, inform Washington D.C. of the winner in their particular state** cast more votes for Bush, so Bush was elected.

"REAL SPEAK": Although Gore had more actual votes, the **electeral college** cast more votes fer Bush, so Bush w'z alected.

filibuster • **1.** *v.* to speak for a long time in order to prevent legislative activity • **2.** *n.* a tactic used to delay or prevent legislative activity.

EXAMPLE 1: The Vice President always **filibusters** about his extensive charity work in order to avoid the real issues.

TRANSLATION: The Vice President always **speaks for a long time** about his extensive charity work in order to avoid the real issues.

"REAL SPEAK": The Vice President ahweez **filibusters** 'bout 'is extensive charidy work 'n order to avoid the real issues.

EXAMPLE 2: The Vice President started his **filibuster** by talking about his extensive charity work.

TRANSLATION: The Vice President started his **delaying tactic** by talking about his extensive charity work.

"REAL SPEAK": The Vice President starded 'is **filibuster** by talking about 'is extensive charidy work.

Political Slang & Jargon

floor *n.* the main area of the Senate or House of Representatives where debating and voting occurs.

> EXAMPLE: The **floor** was chaotic yesterday as the Senators debated the proposed tax law.
>
> TRANSLATION: The **main area of the Senate** was chaotic yesterday as the Senators debated the proposed tax law.
>
> "REAL SPEAK": The **floor** w'z chaotic yesterday 'ez the Senaders debated the pr'pose' tax law.
>
> *Also:* **have the floor (to)** *exp.* to have permission to speak, usually granted by the chairperson • *Mr. Chairman, may I have the* **floor**? *I have new information I'd like to share with everyone;* Mr. Chairman, may I have **permission to speak**? I have new information I'd like to share with everyone.

freshman *n. & adj.* an official serving his or her first term in office.

> EXAMPLE: Senator Davenport is a **freshman**, so no one expects her to get a lot done until she's had more experience.
>
> TRANSLATION: Senator Davenport is an **official serving her first term in office**, so no one expects her to get a lot done until she's had more experience.
>
> "REAL SPEAK": Senader Davenport's a **freshm'n**, so no one expec's 'er da ged a lot done 'til she's had more experience.
>
> *Note:* For years, the term *freshman* has been used to refer to a student in his/her first year in school. However, since this term contains the word "man," feminists created the more politically correct, or non-gender specific term, *frosh*. Although *frosh* is commonly used in schools, *freshman* is still used in political jargon.

gag rule *n.* a ruling that forbids anyone from revealing information presented during an official meeting or hearing.

> EXAMPLE: I really want to tell you what happened in the court case, but the judge issued a **gag rule**.
>
> TRANSLATION: I really want to tell you what happened in the court case, but the judge issued a **ruling that forbids anyone from revealing information presented during the hearing**.
>
> "REAL SPEAK": I really wanna tell ya what happened in the court case, b't the judge issued a **gag rule**.
>
> *Note:* A gag is something put into a person's mouth (usually some sort of handkerchief) to prevent speaking.

glad-hand (to) *v.* to be excessively friendly by shaking hands with people in order to gain political favor.

> EXAMPLE: I hate seeing candidates **glad-handing** on the news. It's just another way that they're manipulating voters.
>
> TRANSLATION: I hate seeing candidates **being excessively friendly by shaking hands with people in order to gain political favor** on the news. It's just another way that they're manipulating voters.
>
> "REAL SPEAK": I hate seeing can'idits **glad-handing** on the news. It's just another way th't they're m'nipulading voders.

GOP *abbrev.* (an abbreviation for *Grand Old Party*) the Republican Party, one of the two major political parties in the United States.

> EXAMPLE: I thought Wilbur was a Democrat, but he's in the **GOP**.
>
> TRANSLATION: I thought Wilbur was a Democrat, but he's in the **Republican Party**.
>
> "REAL SPEAK": I thought Wilbur w'z a Demacrat, b'd 'e's 'n the **G-O-P**.

Note: Beginning with political cartoons in the 1800s, the elephant has symbolized the Republicans and the donkey has symbolized the Democrats. Democrats think the elephant is stupid, pompous, and conservative but Republicans consider it dignified, strong, and intelligent. Republicans think the donkey is stubborn, silly, and ridiculous whereas the Democrats claim it is humble, smart, courageous, and lovable.

grandstand (to) *v.* to try excessively to impress an audience through speech or action.

> **EXAMPLE:** I was enjoying the debate until one of the candidates started **grandstanding**. She just wouldn't stop talking!
>
> **TRANSLATION:** I was enjoying the debate until one of the candidates started **trying excessively to impress the audience**. She just wouldn't stop talking!
>
> **"REAL SPEAK":** I w'z enjoying the debate 'til one 'a the can'idits starded **gran'standing**. She jus' wouldn' stop talking!

heartland *n.* a politically vital region of a nation which is primarily in the mid-west (Ohio, Illinois, etc.).

> **EXAMPLE:** Bradley did well with voters in New York City and Los Angeles, but he did poorly in the **heartland**.
>
> **TRANSLATION:** Bradley did well with voters in New York City and Los Angeles, but he did poorly in the **politically vital region of America which is primarily the Midwest.**
>
> **"REAL SPEAK":** Bradley did well w'th voders 'n New York Cidy 'n Los Angeles, b'd 'e did poorly in the **heartland**.

hold office (to) *exp.* to be responsible for the duties of a political position.

> **EXAMPLE:** Siegal has only been **holding office** for a week and he's already made some important changes to our city.
>
> **TRANSLATION:** Siegal has only been **in his political position** for a week and he's already made some important changes to our city.
>
> **"REAL SPEAK":** Siegal's only b'n **holding office** fer a week 'n 'e's ahready made s'm important changes ta 'ar cidy.

> *Synonym:* **in office (to be)** *exp.*

in the running *exp.* said of someone who is doing well enough to be considered a contender.

> **EXAMPLE:** I wanted Malcolm to win the election, but he's made too many mistakes. I don't think he's **in the running** anymore.

> **TRANSLATION:** I wanted Malcolm to win the election, but he's made too many mistakes. I don't think he's **doing well enough to be considered a contender** anymore.
>
> **"REAL SPEAK":** I wan'ed Malc'm da win the alection, b'd 'e's made too many mistakes. I don't think 'e's **'n the running** anymore.

inauguration *n.* the official induction of a politician into a position.

> **EXAMPLE:** A newly elected official can't make any political decisions until after his or her **inauguration**.

Political Slang & Jargon

TRANSLATION: A newly elected official can't make any political decisions until after his or her **official induction into a position**.

"REAL SPEAK": A newly alected afficial can't make any polidical decisions until after his 'r her **inauguration**.

junket *n.* a political business trip.

EXAMPLE: The Senator is going on a **junket** to survey the flood damage in Pennsylvania.

TRANSLATION: The Senator is going on a **political business trip** to survey the flood damage in Pennsylvania.

"REAL SPEAK": The Senader's going on a **junket** ta survey the flood damage 'n Pennsylvania.

left wing • **1.** *adj.* politically liberal • **2.** *n.* the liberal faction of a group.

EXAMPLE 1: Your ideas may be a little too **left wing** for this community. Try to take a more conservative position and you'll be sure to make a good impression.

TRANSLATION: Your ideas may be a little too **politically liberal** for this community. Try to take a more conservative position and you'll be sure to make a good impression.

"REAL SPEAK": Yer ideas may be a liddle too **left wing** fer this communidy. Try da take a more conservadive pasition an' you'll be sher da make a good impression.

EXAMPLE 2: The **left wing** of animal protection groups don't want animals killed for any reason, even medical research.

TRANSLATION: The **liberal faction** of animal protection groups don't want animals killed for any reason, even medical research.

"REAL SPEAK": The **left wing** 'ev animal pr'tection groups don't wan' animals killed fer any reason, even medical research.

lobby *n.* a group of people trying to influence legislators in favor of a specific cause.

EXAMPLE: The endangered animals **lobby** is gaining power every year. More and more animals are being protected by new laws.

TRANSLATION: **The group of people trying to influence legislators in favor of** endangered animals is gaining power every year. More and more animals are being protected by new laws.

"REAL SPEAK": The endangered animals **lobby**'s gaining power ev'ry year. More 'n more animals 'er being pr'tected by new laws.

party *n.* an established political group organized to promote and support its ideology.

EXAMPLE: It's rare for politicians to change **parties**. When they do, they often lose the support of the people who voted for them.

TRANSLATION: It's rare for politicians to change **political groups**. When they do, they often lose the support of the people who voted for them.

"REAL SPEAK": It's rare fer politicians ta change **pardies**. When they do, they often lose the sapport 'a the people 'oo voded for th'm.

Note: In the United States, some of the major political parties are the Democratic, Republican, Independent, Libertarian, and Green (environmental) parties.

plank *n.* one of the many principles that form a political position or *platform (see p. 107)*.

> **EXAMPLE:** Gary is in favor of relaxing gun control laws. That's not a very popular **plank**, so it's going to hurt his chances of winning the election.
>
> **TRANSLATION:** Gary is in favor of relaxing gun control laws. That's not a very popular **principle**, so it's going to hurt his chances of winning the election.
>
> **"REAL SPEAK":** Gary's 'n faver 'ev relaxing gun control laws. That's nod a very popular **plank**, so it's gonna hurd 'is chances 'ev winning the alection.
>
> *Note:* The term *platform* refers to a structure made of wooden *planks* on top of which a political candidate makes speeches.

prop *abbrev.* (an abbreviation for *proposition*) a proposed law presented directly to the voting public.

> **EXAMPLE:** I voted against **prop** 15. I think the politicians are trying to trick us into accepting a tax increase!
>
> **TRANSLATION:** I voted against **the proposed law** 15. I think the politicians are trying to trick us into accepting a tax increase!
>
> **"REAL SPEAK":** I voded against **prop** fifteen. I think the politicians 'er trying da trick us inta acceping a tax increase!

pork barrel *n.* a government project designed to gain public favor by creating jobs and other benefits.

> **EXAMPLE:** The mayor hates spending money, but when he's trying to get re-elected, he loves **pork barrels** like education programs.

> **TRANSLATION:** The mayor hates spending money, but when he's trying to get re-alected, he loves **government projects designed to gain public favor** like education programs.
>
> **"REAL SPEAK":** The mair hates spending money, b't when 'e'z trying da get re-elected, he loves **pork barrels** like edjacation programs.

press the flesh (to) *exp.* to shake hands and meet the public.

> **EXAMPLE:** I don't have time for lunch! I need to **press the flesh** if I want to win the election in two months.

> **TRANSLATION:** I don't have time for lunch! I need to **shake hands and meet the public** if I want to win the election in two months.
>
> **"REAL SPEAK":** I don'ave time fer lunch! I need da **press the flesh** if I wanna win the alection 'n two munts.

primary *n.* a preliminary election in which the registered voters of a political party nominate candidates for office.

> **EXAMPLE:** I think Eleanor would make a great president, but I don't think she'll win the Democratic **primary**.

TRANSLATION: I think Eleanor would make a great president, but I don't think she'll win the Democratic **preliminary election**.

"REAL SPEAK": I think Eleanor 'ed make a great president, b'd I don't think she'll win the Demacradic **primary**.

ramrod (to) *v.* to force the acceptance of a piece of legislation.

EXAMPLE: The president has vowed to **ramrod** the bill if he gets any resistance.

TRANSLATION: The president has vowed to **force the acceptance of** the bill if he gets any resistance.

"REAL SPEAK": The president's vowed da **ramrod** the bill 'ef 'e gets any resist'nce.

returns *n.* election results.

EXAMPLE: Everyone has voted, so now we just need to wait for the **returns**.

TRANSLATION: Everyone has voted, so now we just need to wait for the **election results**.

"REAL SPEAK": Ev'ryone's voded, so now we jus' need da wait fer the **returns**.

ride one's coattails (to) *exp.* to gain success for oneself by exploiting the success of another.

EXAMPLE: Some people say President George W. Bush was just **riding his father's coattails**, and that he didn't deserve to be president.

TRANSLATION: Some people say President George W. Bush was just **gaining success for himself by exploiting the success of his father**, and that he didn't deserve to be president.

"REAL SPEAK": Some people say President George W. Bush w'z jus' **riding 'is father's coattails**, an' thad 'e didn' deserve da be president.

run for office (to) *exp.* to compete for an elected position in the government.

EXAMPLE: This country is a mess! I should **run for office** myself, just so there's at least one smart person in control!

TRANSLATION: This country is a mess! I should **compete for an elected position in the government** myself, just so there's at least one smart person in control!

"REAL SPEAK": This country's a mess! I should **run fer office** myself, jus' so there's 'it least one smart person in c'ntrol!

shoo-in *n.* one that has a sure chance of being chosen.

EXAMPLE: Palmer is a **shoo-in** to win the presidency. He's the best!

TRANSLATION: Palmer **has a sure chance of being chosen** to win the presidency. He's the best!

"REAL SPEAK": Palmer's a **shoo-in** da win the presidency. He's the best!

spin doctor *n.* a spokesperson (for a political candidate) who tries to minimize the effects of negative publicity.

EXAMPLE: Edward did terribly in that debate, but if you listen to his **spin doctors**, he won it easily!

GOOD PRESS

TRANSLATION: Edward did terribly in that debate, but if you listen to his **spokespeople**, he won it easily!

"REAL SPEAK": Edwerd did terr'bly 'n that debate, b'd if ya listen to 'is **spin dockders**, he won id easily!

Note: *Spin doctors* are supposed to be experts at "spinning" or "changing the spin of" bad publicity into good publicity.

Also: **spin (to)** *v.* to minimize the effects of negative publicity by turning bad news into good news.

stump (to) *v.* to travel from town to town making political speeches.

EXAMPLE: I like it when candidates go **stumping** because there's a good chance they'll stop here and I'll get to meet them.

TRANSLATION: I like it when candidates go **traveling from town to town making speeches** because there's a good chance they'll stop here and I'll get to meet them.

"REAL SPEAK": I like it wh'n can'idits go **stumping** b'cuz there's a good chance they'll stop here 'n a'll get ta meet th'm.

Note: This term refers to a time when politicians made speeches while standing on top of a tree stump.

sweep (to) *v.* to win an overwhelming victory in a contest.

EXAMPLE: David **swept** the election despite some early problems.

TRANSLATION: David **won** the election **by an overwhelming victory** despite some early problems.

"REAL SPEAK": David **swept** the alection despite s'm early problems.

table an issue (to) *exp.* to postpone consideration of an issue.

EXAMPLE: We can't make a decision without more information, so let's **table this issue** for now.

TRANSLATION: We can't make a decision without more information, so let's **postpone consideration of this issue** for now.

"REAL SPEAK": We can't make a decision w'thout more infermation, so let's **table this issue** fer now.

term *n.* a period of time that is assigned to a person to hold a particular office.

EXAMPLE: Gregory has already been in office for two **terms**. It's time for a change.

TRANSLATION: Gregory has already been in office for two **assigned periods of time**. It's time for a change.

"REAL SPEAK": Greg'ry's ahready had two **terms** 'n office. It's time fer a change.

throw one's hat in the ring (to) *exp.* to agree to run for office.

EXAMPLE: I thought Melanie was going to win the election, but now that Jason has **thrown his hat in the ring**, nothing is certain!

TRANSLATION: I thought Melanie was going to win the election, but now that Jason has **agreed to run for office**, nothing is certain!

"REAL SPEAK": I thought Melanie w'z gonna win the alection, b't now th't Jason's **thrown 'is hat 'n the ring**, nothing's certain!

toe the party line (to) *exp.* to agree to the principles promoted by one's political party, regardless of one's personal feelings.

EXAMPLE: Dana disagrees with the Democrats' position on gun control, but she needs to **toe the party line** if she wants to get elected.

TRANSLATION: Dana disagrees with the Democrats' position on gun control, but she needs to **agree to the principles promoted by her political party** if she wants to get elected.

Political Slang & Jargon

"REAL SPEAK": Dana disagrees w'th the Democrats' position on gun c'ntrol, b't she needs ta **toe the pardy line** 'ef she wants ta ged alected.

turnout *n.* attendance.

EXAMPLE: I was hoping for a better **turnout** for the election. Less and less people are voting these days!

TRANSLATION: I was hoping for better **attendance** at the election. Less and less people are voting these days!

"REAL SPEAK": I w'z hoping fer a bedder **turnoud** 'it the alection. Less 'n less people 'er voding these days!

Uncle Sam *n.* the government of the United States of America.

EXAMPLE: You'll get in big trouble if you don't pay your taxes to **Uncle Sam** every year.

TRANSLATION: You'll get in big trouble if you don't pay your taxes to **the government of the United States of America** every year.

"REAL SPEAK": You'll ged in big trouble if ya don't pay yer taxes ta **Uncle Sam** ev'ry year.

veto (to) *v.* to reject, cancel.

EXAMPLE: I hope the president doesn't **veto** this bill. I really want it to pass!

TRANSLATION: I hope the president doesn't **reject** this bill. I really want it to pass!

"REAL SPEAK": I hope the president doesn't **vedo** this bill. I really wan' it ta pass!

KELLY MADE A KILLING!

Stock Market Slang & Jargon

THIS LESSON FEATURES ⑭ NEW SLANG WORDS & IDIOMS

LET'S WARM UP!

MATCH THE PICTURES

As a fun way to get started, see if you can guess the meaning of the new slang words and expressions on the opposite page by using the pictures below and following the context of the sentences.

READING

☐ 1. I have several different stocks in my ***portfolio***.

☐ 2. ***Blue-chip stocks*** are a safe investment.

☐ 3. I want to ***make a killing*** in the stock market so that I can quit my job!

☐ 4. I like to ***day trade***. You can make a lot of money very quickly!

☐ 5. I've been saving money my whole life. My ***nest egg*** is very big!

☐ 6. Ray ***buys and holds*** his stocks. He thinks they'll make more money the longer he keeps them.

☐ 7. After the ***stock split*** I had double the shares at half the price.

☐ 8. All my money is in one stock. I need to ***diversify***!

☐ 9. I'm ***going long***. This stock price will rise someday!

☐ 10. Lee has been ***playing the market*** since he was young.

☐ 11. I bought a ***mutual fund*** instead of individual stocks.

☐ 12. I'm not brave enough to buy stocks that are ***high risk***.

☐ 13. I ***took a beating*** last year. All my investments lost money!

☐ 14. I don't like modern technology, so I don't buy any ***tech stocks***.

A. buy and sell stocks in a single day

B. lost a lot of money

C. make a lot of money

D. stock in technology-based companies

E. stock in well-established companies

F. more likely to fail, but have a better reward for success

G. keeping this stock

H. increase in shares worth less money

I. investment managed by a company

J. collection of investments

K. buying and selling stocks, following trends, etc.

L. entire savings

M. invest money in different places

N. buys stocks and keeps them for a long time

Stock Market Slang & Jargon

LET'S TALK!

A. DIALOGUE USING SLANG & IDIOMS

The words introduced on the first two pages are used in the dialogue below. See if you can understand the conversation. *Note:* The translation of the words in boldface is on the right-hand page.

CD-B: TRACK 7

Sarah: Did you hear about Kelly? She's been **playing the market** for years and just **made a killing** when her **stock split**!

Jeremy: That's great! But I'd never gamble like that. I'd rather **go long** with **blue-chip stocks** or a **mutual fund**. I don't want to spend my **nest egg** on anything **high risk**.

Sarah: It's easy to **take a beating** if you don't **diversify** your **portfolio**. I like to **day trade** with **tech stocks**, but I really should **buy and hold** more often.

B. DIALOGUE TRANSLATED INTO STANDARD ENGLISH

LET'S SEE HOW MUCH YOU REMEMBER!
Just for fun, move around in random order to the words and
expressions in boldface below. See if you can remember their
slang equivalents without looking at the left-hand page!

Sarah: Did you hear about Kelly? She's been **following stock market prices and trends** and just **made a lot of money** when her **number of shares increased with a corresponding decrease in value**.

Jeremy: That's great! But I'd never gamble like that. I'd rather **buy a stock and keep it until its price increases** with **stocks of well-established companies** or an **investment managed by a company**. I don't want to spend my **entire savings** on anything **with an increased risk of failure even if it offers a better reward for success**.

Sarah: It's easy to **suffer a big monetary loss** if you don't **invest your money in several different places** in your **collection of investments**. I like to **buy and sell stocks within a single day** with **stocks in technology-based companies**, but I really should **purchase stocks and keep them for a long time** more often.

C. DIALOGUE USING "REAL SPEAK"

The dialogue below demonstrates how the slang conversation on the previous page would *really* be spoken by native speakers!

CD-B: TRACK 7

Sarah: Didja hear about Kelly? She's been **playing the market** fer years 'n jus' **made a killing** when 'er **stock split**!

Jeremy: That's great! B'd I'd never gamble like that. I'd rather **go long** with **blue-chip stocks** 'er a **mutual fund**. I don't wanna spen' my **nest egg** on anything **high risk**.

Sarah: It's easy da **take a beading** if ya don't **diversify** yer **portfolio**. I like ta **day trade** with **tech stocks**, b'd I really should **buy 'n hold** more often.

LET'S LEARN!

VOCABULARY

The following words and expressions were used in the previous dialogues. Let's take a closer look at what they mean.

CD-B: TRACK 8

blue-chip stock n. stock of a well-established company, usually having a reputation for good management.

EXAMPLE: Pauline only invests in **blue-chip stocks**, but I like to take risks by investing in smaller, newer companies.

TRANSLATION: Pauline only invests in **well-established companies**, but I like to take risks by investing in smaller, newer companies.

"REAL SPEAK": Pauline only inves' in **blue-chip stocks**, b'd I like ta take risks by investing 'n smaller, newer companies.

Also: **blue-chip fund** n. a *mutual fund (see p. 132)* with its money allocated to various *blue-chip stocks.*

NOW YOU DO IT:
(use "**blue-chip stock**" in a sentence)

buy and hold (to) *exp.* to purchase stocks and keep them for a long time.

EXAMPLE: Every time my stock goes up, I want to sell it, but I'm trying to **buy and hold**. Over several years, the stock should go up much more than it does in just a day or a week.

TRANSLATION: Every time my stock goes up, I want to sell it, but I'm trying to **purchase stocks and keep them for a long time**. Over several years, the stock should go up much more than it does in just a day or a week.

"REAL SPEAK": Ev'ry time my stock goes up, I wanna sell it, b'd I'm trying da **buy 'n hold**. Over sev'ral years, the stock should go up much more th'n it does 'n justa day 'er a week.

NOW YOU DO IT:

(use "**buy and hold**" in a sentence)

day trade (to) *exp.* to buy and sell stocks within a single day in order to make fast profit.

EXAMPLE: Wally likes to **day trade**. He watches the stock reports all day so he can buy or sell right away if a good price appears.

TRANSLATION: Wally likes to **buy and sell stocks within a single day in order to make fast profit**. He watches the stock reports all day so he can buy or sell right away if a good price appears.

"REAL SPEAK": Wally likes ta **day trade**. He watches the stock reports all day so 'e c'n buy 'er sell ride away if a good price appears.

Also: **day trader** *n.* a person who day trades.

NOW YOU DO IT:

(use "**day trade**" in a sentence)

diversify (to) *v.* to invest one's money in several different places which minimizes risk (in case one of the places loses money).

EXAMPLE: My father lost all his money because he didn't **diversify**. If he had invested his money in several places, he'd still have some of it!

TRANSLATION: My father lost all his money because he didn't **invest his money in several different places which minimizes risk**. If he had invested his money in several places, he'd still have some of it!

"REAL SPEAK": My father lost all 'is money b'cuz 'e didn't **diversify**. If 'e'd invested 'is money 'n sev'ral places, he'd still have some 'ev it!

NOW YOU DO IT:

(use "**diversify**" in a sentence)

---

go long (to) *exp.* to buy a stock and keep it until its price increases.

EXAMPLE: I think you should **go long** if you think the company will become more successful over time.

TRANSLATION: I think you should **buy a stock and keep it** if you think the company will become more successful over time.

"REAL SPEAK": I think you should **go long** if ya think the comp'ny'll b'come more successful over time.

NOW YOU DO IT:
(use "**go long**" in a sentence)

high risk *adj.* something which has an increased risk of failure but offers a better reward for success.

EXAMPLE: I like to buy **high risk** stocks. If just one of those companies succeeds, I could be rich!

TRANSLATION: I like to buy stocks **which have an increased risk of failure but offer a better reward for success**. If just one of those companies succeeds, I could be rich!

"REAL SPEAK": I like ta buy **high risk** stocks. If jus' one 'a those comp'nies succeeds, I could be rich!

Antonym: **low risk** *adj.*

NOW YOU DO IT:
(use "**high risk**" in a sentence)

make a killing (to) *exp.* to make a lot of money buying and selling stocks.

EXAMPLE: If I keep investing money and researching stocks, someday I will **make a killing** and buy a big house!

TRANSLATION: If I keep investing money and researching stocks, someday I will **make a lot of money buying and selling stocks** and buy a big house!

"REAL SPEAK": If I keep invesding money 'n researching stocks, someday a'll **make a killing** 'n buy a big house!

NOW YOU DO IT:
(use "**make a killing**" in a sentence)

mutual fund *n.* an investment managed by a company that collects people's money and invests the total amount in a variety of places.

EXAMPLE: I don't have time to watch the stock market, so I decided to buy a **mutual fund**. I trust the company to invest my money wisely.

TRANSLATION: I don't have time to watch the stock market, so I decided to buy a **investment managed by a company that collects people's money and invests the total amount in a variety of places**. I trust the company to invest my money wisely.

"REAL SPEAK": I don't have time da watch the stock market, so I decided da buy a **muchual fund**. I trust the comp'ny ta invest my money wisely.

NOW YOU DO IT:
(use "**mutual fund**" in a sentence)

nest egg *n.* one's entire savings, usually intended for use in the future.

EXAMPLE: I spent my **nest egg** on that company's stock, and now it's worthless. I lost everything!

TRANSLATION: I spent my **entire savings** on that company's stock, and now it's worthless. I lost everything!

"REAL SPEAK": I spent my **nest egg** on that comp'ny's stock, an' now it's worthless. I lost ev'rything!

NOW YOU DO IT:
(use "**nest egg**" in a sentence)

play the [stock] market (to) *exp.* to buy and sell stocks, follow prices and trends, etc.

EXAMPLE: I don't **play the market**. It seems so complicated and I don't want to lose any money!

TRANSLATION: I don't **buy and sell stocks or follow prices and trends**. It seems so complicated and I don't want to lose any money!

"REAL SPEAK": I don't **play the market**. It seems so complicaded an' I don't wanna lose any money!

Also: **follow the [stock] market (to)** *exp.* to study changes in stock prices and overall trends.

NOW YOU DO IT:
(use "**play the market**" in a sentence)

Stock Market Slang & Jargon

portfolio *n.* the collection of all one's investments, including stocks, bonds, mutual funds, etc.

EXAMPLE: I have purchased a few risky stocks, but my **portfolio** is still very conservative.

TRANSLATION: I have purchased a few risky stocks, but my **collection of investments** is still very conservative.

"REAL SPEAK": I've purchased a few risky stocks, b't my **portfolio**'s still very c'nservadive.

NOW YOU DO IT:
(use "**portfolio**" in a sentence)

stock split *n.* an increase in the number of shares and related decrease in the value of each share.

EXAMPLE: I used to own fifty shares worth ten dollars each. After the **stock split**, I own one hundred shares at twenty-five dollars each.

TRANSLATION: I used to own fifty shares worth ten dollars each. After the **increase in the number of shares and related decrease in the value of each share**, I own one hundred shares at twenty-five dollars each.

"REAL SPEAK": I usta own fifdy shares worth ten dollers each. After the **stock split**, I own a hundred shares 'it twen'y-five dollers each.

Variation: **2-for-1 split** *n.* a *stock split* where you get twice the number of shares at half the price. *2-for-1* describes the ratio of the split. You can also have a *3-for-1* split, etc.

Note: The value of stock is not supposed to be affected by a *stock split*. If you have 10 shares worth $10 each ($10 x 10 = $100), after a *2-for-1 stock split* you have 20 shares at $5 each ($5 x 20 = $100). However, *stock splits* often occur when the stock price is high, so people tend to buy it when the price drops, sometimes causing an increase in the value of the stock.

NOW YOU DO IT:
(use "**stock split**" in a sentence)

take a beating (to) *exp.* to suffer a big monetary loss.

EXAMPLE: I really **took a beating** in the stock market last year. I used to have a lot of money, and now I'm poor!

TRANSLATION: I really **suffered a big monetary loss** in the stock market last year. I used to have a lot of money, and now I'm poor!

"REAL SPEAK": I really **took a beading** 'n the stock market last year. I usta have a lodda money, 'n now I'm poor!

Synonym: **take a [big] hit in the market (to)** *n.* to lose [a lot of] money by investing in the stock market.

NOW YOU DO IT:
(use "**take a beating**" in a sentence)

tech stock *n.* stock in a technology-based company.

EXAMPLE: I heard Malcolm made a million dollars with his **tech stocks** last year! I invested in older, more stable companies and didn't do as well.

TRANSLATION: I heard Malcolm made a million dollars with his **stock in technology-based companies** last year! I invested in older, more stable companies and didn't do as well.

"REAL SPEAK": I heard Malc'm made a million dollers with 'is **tech stocks** last year! I invesded 'n older, more stable comp'nies 'n didn't do 'ez well.

NOW YOU DO IT:

(use "**tech stock**" in a sentence)

LET'S PRACTICE!

A. CREATE YOUR OWN SENTENCES

Read Person A's questions aloud using the suggested words to create your answer for Person B.

SPEAKING

CD-B: TRACK 9

1. **PERSON A:** Did you make a lot of money last year?	**PERSON B:** [**made a killing**] [**tech stocks**] [**day trade**]
2. **PERSON A:** What kind of stock should I buy?	**PERSON B:** [**blue-chip stocks**] [**mutual fund**]
3. **PERSON A:** Should I sell my stock right away?	**PERSON B:** [**buy and hold**] [**stock split**]
4. **PERSON A:** What if I lose all my money?	**PERSON B:** [**nest egg**] [**take a beating**] [**high-risk**]
5. **PERSON A:** How much do you have invested?	**PERSON B:** [**play the market**] [**portfolio**]
6. **PERSON A:** I like this company. Should I buy their stock?	**PERSON B:** [**go long**] [**diversify**]

B. TRUE OR FALSE

Decide if the sentence is true or false.

READING

CD-B: TRACK 10

1. A **mutual fund** is stock in an insurance company.
   ❏ True   ❏ False

2. If something is **high-risk**, it's potentially more dangerous and more rewarding.
   ❏ True   ❏ False

3. If you **take a beating** in the stock market, you've made a lot of money.
   ❏ True   ❏ False

4. If you want to **diversify**, you should buy a lot of one stock.
   ❏ True   ❏ False

5. A **nest egg** refers to money you have saved.
   ❏ True   ❏ False

6. Someone who **plays the market** buys groceries a lot.
   ❏ True   ❏ False

7. A **portfolio** is a collection of rare coins.
   ❏ True   ❏ False

8. Stock in McDonald's is considered a **Tech stock**.
   ❏ True   ❏ False

9. You are **going long** if you buy a stock and keep it for a long time, until its value increases.
   ❏ True   ❏ False

10. If you **make a killing** in the stock market, you have killed someone.
    ❏ True   ❏ False

C. YOU'RE THE AUTHOR
Complete the dialogue using the words below.

BEATING	HOLD
BLUE	KILLING
DAY	LONG
DIVERSIFY	PLAY
EGG	PORTFOLIO
FUNDS	SPLIT
HIGH	TECH

Clarisse: I just took a _____ in the stock market! I lost all of my nest _____ on a

_____-risk _____ stock! I was going to buy and _____ but I

decided to _____ trade instead. What a mistake!

Franklin: Do you have any _____-chip stocks or mutual _____ in your

_____? If you're going to _____ the market, you need to

_____ more. You can make a _____ with a stock _____,

but that only happens when you go _____.

Clarisse: Thanks for the advice!

Stock Market Slang & Jargon

D. CROSSWORD PUZZLE

Fill in the crossword puzzle on the opposite page using the
words from the list.

CD-B: TRACK 12

BEATING	LONG	RISK
CHIP	MARKET	STOCK
DIVERSIFY	MUTUAL	TECH
HOLD	NEST	TRADING
KILLING	PORTFOLIO	

ACROSS

8. I really like computers, so I might buy some _____ stocks.

13. Day _____ is very stressful. You can lose a lot of money in just one day!

17. Companies that manage _____ funds combine money from a lot of investors, so they can buy a larger number of stocks.

25. I took a _____ on that stock. The price of the shares just kept dropping!

29. I love playing the _____! It's exciting to watch all the stock prices go up and down.

33. After the _____ split, I had twice as many shares!

38. I have six different stocks in my _____.

DOWN

3. I have a large _____ egg and I'm ready to invest it all!

7. You should buy that stock and go _____. It'll be worth a lot in a few years.

12. I made a _____ in the stock market last year, so I bought a new car!

24. To be safe, you should _____. If your money is invested in different places, you can't lose everything at once.

28. I heard that stock is high-_____. Don't spend all of your money on it!

34. Companies with blue-_____ stocks are generally well-established.

36. I want to buy and _____, but I'm too impatient. I always sell the next day!

CROSSWORD PUZZLE

More Stock Market Slang & Jargon

If someone at the **Exchange** (*marketplace where stocks are traded*) told you that there is sure to be a **crash** (*a widespread decrease in the value of stocks*) soon and advises you to wait for a **bull market** (*a market which is on a consistent upward trend*) before **executing** (*completing*) your request to buy stocks, you may not know what to do — that is unless you have a good understand of popular stock market slang and jargon.

The following list may not prevent you from ever **going down in flames** (*suffer a huge amount of money*), but it will make understanding the stock market a lot easier!

appreciate *v.* to rise in value.

> **EXAMPLE:** Cars don't usually **appreciate**. They're worth less every year that they're owned.

> **TRANSLATION:** Cars don't usually **rise in value**. They're worth less every year that they're owned.

> **"REAL SPEAK":** Cars don't ujally **appreciate**. They're worth less ev'ry year th't they're owned.

bear *n.* an investor who thinks a stock or the entire stock market will decline.

> **EXAMPLE:** Lyle is a **bear**. He never expects the stock market to go up, at least not for long.

> **TRANSLATION:** Lyle is an **investor who thinks the stock market will decline**. He never expects the stock market to go up, at least not for long.

> **"REAL SPEAK":** Lyle's a **bear**. He never expec's the stock market ta go up, 'it leas' not fer long.

> *Also:* **bear market** *n.* a market which is on a consistent downward trend.

bull *n.* an investor who thinks the stock market will rise.

> **EXAMPLE:** Even though the stock market has been declining lately, I'm still a **bull**. My stock will be worth millions within a few years!

> **TRANSLATION:** Even though the stock market has been declining lately, I'm still an **investor who thinks the stock market will rise**. My stock will be worth millions w'thin a few years!

> **"REAL SPEAK":** Even though the stock market's been declining lately, I'm still a **bull**. My stock'll be worth millions within a few years!

> *Also:* **bull market** *n.* a market which is on a consistent upward trend.

burned (to be) *n.* to suffer a loss of money.

> **EXAMPLE:** Steven was **burned** last year when his company closed. He had a lot of stock and now it's worthless!

TRANSLATION: Steven **suffered a loss of money** last year when his company closed. He had a lot of stock and now it's worthless!

"REAL SPEAK": Steven w'z **burned** last year when 'is comp'ny closed. He had a lodda stock 'n now it's worthless!

buy low (to) *exp.* to purchase stocks at a low price.

EXAMPLE: If you manage to **buy low**, you can make a quick profit when the stock returns to its normal price.

TRANSLATION: If you manage to **purchase a stock at a low price**, you can make a quick profit when the stock returns to its normal price.

"REAL SPEAK": If ya manage ta **buy low**, you c'n make a quick profit when the stock returns to its normal price.

capital *n.* available money.

EXAMPLE: I would love to buy more stocks, but I just don't have the **capital**!

TRANSLATION: I would love to buy more stocks, but I just don't have the **available money**!

"REAL SPEAK": I'd love da buy more stocks, b'd I jus' don't have the **capid'l**.

capital gain *n.* monetary profit, calculated by the difference between the sale price of a stock and its original cost.

EXAMPLE: Toby made a lot of money in the stock market, but forgot to report his **capital gains** to the government. Now he's in big trouble!

TRANSLATION: Toby made a lot of money in the stock market, but forgot to report his **monetary profit** to the government. Now he's in big trouble!

"REAL SPEAK": Toby made a lodda money in the stock market, b't fergot ta repord 'is **capidal gains** ta the gover'ment. Now 'e's 'n big trouble!

capital loss *n.* monetary loss, calculated by the difference between the sale price of a stock and its original cost.

EXAMPLE: I had a bad year in the stock market, but the **capital loss** will help to decrease the amount of taxes I have to pay.

TRANSLATION: I had a bad year in the stock market, but the **monetary loss** will help to decrease the amount of taxes I have to pay.

"REAL SPEAK": I had a bad year 'n the stock market, b't the **capid'l loss**'ll help ta decrease the amount 'ev taxes I hafta pay.

corner a market (to) *exp.* to purchase enough of the available supply of something (such as stocks, merchandise, gasoline, etc.) in order to manipulate its price.

EXAMPLE: Adam **cornered the market** on The Computer Corporation's stock. Whenever someone was selling, he bought. Now he owns more of the company than anyone else!

TRANSLATION: Adam **purchased enough of the available supply of** The Computer Corporation's stock **that he'll be able to manipulate its price**. Whenever someone was selling, he bought. Now he owns more of the company than anyone else!

"REAL SPEAK": Adam **cornered the marked** on The C'mpuder Corperation's stock. Whenever someone w'z selling, he bought. Now 'e owns more 'a the comp'ny th'n anyone else!

crash • **1.** *n.* a large, widespread decrease in the value of stocks. • **2.** *v.* to suffer a large, widespread decrease in the value of stocks.

EXAMPLE 1: The **crash** of 1929 was the start of the Great Depression in American history. Millions of people were financially devastated.

TRANSLATION: The **large, widespread decrease in the value of stocks** in 1929 was the start of the Great Depression in American history. Millions of people were financially devastated.

"REAL SPEAK": The **crash** 'ev nineteen-twen'y-nine w'z the start 'ev the Great Depression in American hist'ry. Millions 'ev people were financially devastaded.

EXAMPLE 2: I think the stock market will continue to rise, but Ted thinks it will **crash** within a year.

TRANSLATION: I think the stock market will continue to rise, but Ted thinks it will **suffer a large, widespread decrease** within a year.

"REAL SPEAK": I think the stock marked'll continue da rise, b't Ted thinks id'll **crash** w'thin a year.

day order *n.* an order to buy or sell stock that automatically expires if it can't be executed on the day it is submitted.

EXAMPLE: I always place **day orders**. If my stock doesn't reach the price I specify by the end of the day, it doesn't get sold.

TRANSLATION: I always place **orders to buy or sell stock that automatically expire if they can't be executed on the day they're submitted**. If my stock doesn't reach the price I specify by the end of the day, it doesn't get sold.

"REAL SPEAK": I ahweez place **day orders**. If my stock doesn't reach the price I specify by the end a' the day, it doesn' get sold.

dividend *n.* a portion of a company's earnings that is distributed to its shareholders in cash or additional stock.

EXAMPLE: Whenever my company's value increases, it pays **dividends** to its shareholders instead of increasing the value of its stock.

TRANSLATION: Whenever my company's value increases, it pays **a portion of the company's earnings** to its shareholders instead of increasing the value of its stock.

"REAL SPEAK": Whenever my comp'ny's value increases, it pays **dividends** to its shareholders instead 'ev increasing the value 'ev its stock.

DOW *abbrev.* an abbreviation of the "Dow Jones Industrial Average," the most widely used indicator of how the country's industrial leaders are performing.

EXAMPLE: The **DOW** has gone down every day for the last three weeks! If the stock market doesn't start performing better, I'll scream!

TRANSLATION: The **Dow Jones Industrial Average** has gone down every day for the last three weeks! If the stock market doesn't start performing better, I'll scream!

"REAL SPEAK": The **DOW**'s gone down ev'ry day fer the las' three weeks! If the stock market doesn' start performing bedder, a'll scream!

due diligence *n.* research one should conduct before buying or selling any particular stock.

EXAMPLE: I really liked Opti Books Company until I performed my **due diligence**. Now I don't think it's a very wise investment.

TRANSLATION: I really liked Opti Books Company until I performed my **research**. Now I don't think it's a very wise investment.

"REAL SPEAK": I really liked Opti Books Comp'ny 'till I peformed my **due diligence**. Now I don't think it's a very wise investment.

Exchange (the) *n.* the marketplace where stocks are traded.

EXAMPLE: **The Exchange** opens at nine o'clock Eastern time every weekday, so you can't buy or sell stocks until then.

TRANSLATION: **The marketplace where stocks are traded** opens at nine o'clock Eastern time every weekday, so you can't buy or sell stocks until then.

"REAL SPEAK": **The Exchange** opens 'it nine a'clock Eastern time ev'ry weekday, so ya can't buy 'er sell stocks 'til then.

execute (to) *v.* to complete a request to purchase stock.

EXAMPLE: I wanted to buy that stock when it cost just two dollars a share, but my agent didn't **execute** my request until it cost four dollars a share!

TRANSLATION: I wanted to buy that stock when it cost just two dollars a share, but my agent didn't **complete** my request until it cost four dollars a share!

"REAL SPEAK": I wan'ed da buy that stock when it cost jus' two dollers a share, b't my agent didn' **execute** my request 'til it cost four dollers a share!

exercise (to) *v.* to implement a *stock option* (see *p. 146*) by buying the stock at a pre-determined price and selling at it at the current price (which is higher) for a profit.

EXAMPLE: I only have two weeks left to **exercise**, but the stock price still hasn't risen above the pre-deter-mined price, so I won't make a profit!

TRANSLATION: I only have two weeks left to **implement my stock option**, but the stock price still hasn't risen above the set price, so I won't make a profit!

"REAL SPEAK": I only 'ave two weeks lef' ta **exercise**, b't the stock price still hasn't risen above the pre-determined price, so I won't make a profit!

fall (to) *v.* to decrease.

EXAMPLE: In 1929, the stock market **fell** so much that many investors lost all their money and killed themselves as a result!

TRANSLATION: In 1929, the stock market **decreased** so much that many investors lost all their money and killed themselves as a result!

"REAL SPEAK": In nineteen-twen'y-nine, the stock market **fell** so much th't many invesders lost all their money 'n killed th'mselves as a result!

Fortune 500 company *n.* one of the 500 largest industrial corporations in the U.S., as published by *Fortune* magazine.

EXAMPLE: I just started working for a **Fortune 500 company**. It's not as personal as working for a smaller company, but it's more stable.

TRANSLATION: I just started working for **one of the 500 largest industrial corporations in the U.S.** It's not as personal as working for a smaller company, but it's more stable.

"REAL SPEAK": I jus' starded working fer a **Fortune five-hundred comp'ny**. It's nod 'ez personal 'ez working fer a smaller comp'ny, b'd it's more stable.

go down in flames (to) *exp.* to suffer a huge loss of money.

EXAMPLE: Every stock I own has decreased in value this year. I'm **going down in flames**!

TRANSLATION: Every stock I own has decreased in value this year. I'm **suffering a huge loss of money**!

"REAL SPEAK": Ev'ry stock I own's decreased 'n value this year. I'm **going down 'n flames**!

go short (to) *exp.* to borrow stock from a brokerage, sell it at a high price, and when the price decreases, buy the same amount of stock and return it to the brokerage (because buying the stock at a low price and selling it at a high price, one can make a profit.)

EXAMPLE: Fred thinks our company is doing terribly. He says I should **go short** in order to make money.

TRANSLATION: Fred thinks our company is doing terribly. He says I should **borrow the stock, sell it, and then buy it after its price decreases** in order to make money.

"REAL SPEAK": Fred thinks 'ar comp'ny's doing terr'bly. He says I should **go short** 'n order da make money.

Synonym: **sell short (to)** *exp.*

hiccup *n.* a brief interruption in the normal increase or decrease of the stock market (much like a hiccup is a brief interruption in the normal breathing pattern of a person).

EXAMPLE: Our company's stock suffered a **hiccup** last month, but is increasing steadily this month.

TRANSLATION: Our company's stock suffered a **brief interruption** last month, but is increasing steadily this month.

"REAL SPEAK": 'Ar comp'ny's stock suffered a **hiccup** las' month, bud is increasing steadily th's month.

insider information *n.* secret information which may affect the price of a stock.

EXAMPLE: Adrian is an executive with a lot of **insider information**. If he ever tells anyone, he could go to jail!

TRANSLATION: Adrian is an executive with a lot of **secret information which may affect the price of the stock**. If he ever tells anyone, he could go to jail!

"REAL SPEAK": Adrian's 'n execudive with a lod 'ev **insider infermation**. If 'e ever tells anyone, he could go da jail!

IPO *abbrev.* (an abbreviation for "Initial Public Offering") a company's first sale of stock to the public.

EXAMPLE: John is hoping to make a lot of money when his company makes its **IPO**. If all goes well, the company's stock price will start to increase immediately.

TRANSLATION: John is hoping to make a lot of money when his company makes its **Initial Public Offering, its first sale of stock to the public**. If all goes well, the company's stock price will start to increase immediately.

"REAL SPEAK": John's hoping da make a lodda money when 'is comp'ny makes its **I-P-O**. If all goes well, the comp'ny's stock price'll start ta increase immediately.

Also: **IPO (to go)** *exp.* to make an Initial Public Offering.

limit order *n.* an order to buy or sell stock at a specified price.

EXAMPLE: I placed a **limit order** on that stock. If it reaches $100 a share, I want to sell!

TRANSLATION: I placed an **order to sell at a specified price** on that stock. If it reaches $100 a share, I want to sell!

"REAL SPEAK": I placed a **limid order** on that stock. If it reaches a hundred dollers a share, I wanna sell!

market (the) *n.* short for "the stock market."

EXAMPLE: I don't follow **the market**. I don't have enough money to invest, so it would be a waste of time.

TRANSLATION: I don't follow **the stock market**. I don't have enough money to invest, so it would be a waste of time.

"REAL SPEAK": I don't follow **the market**. I don'ave anuf money ta invest, so id'd be a waste 'ev time.

market order *n.* an order to buy or sell a stock at the current price.

EXAMPLE: I just made a **market order** for this stock. I don't care if I make a profit. I want the money to buy a new car!

TRANSLATION: I just made an **order to sell at the current price** for this stock. I don't care if I make a profit. I want the money to buy a new car!

"REAL SPEAK": I jus' made a **marked order** fer this stock. I don't care 'ef I make a profit. I want the money da buy a new car!

NASDAQ (the) *abbrev.* (an abbreviation for "National Association of Securities Dealers Automated Quotations System") an indicator of the overall success or failure of about 5,000 technology-based companies, represented by a single number.

EXAMPLE: Jennifer is really knowledgeable about technology, so she usually buys stocks that are part of the **NASDAQ**.

TRANSLATION: Jennifer is really knowledgeable about technology, so she usually buys stocks that are part of the **National Association of Securities Dealers Automated Quotations system**.

"REAL SPEAK": Jennifer's really knowledgeable about technology, so she ujally buys stocks thad 'er pard 'a the **Naz-Dack**.

net worth *n.* the total value of all one's possessions (including money) minus one's debts.

EXAMPLE: I have more money in the bank than Debbie, but she owns a house, so her **net worth** is higher.

TRANSLATION: I have more money in the bank than Debbie, but she owns a house, so the **total value of all her possessions** is higher.

"REAL SPEAK": I 'ave more money 'n the bank th'n Debbie, b't she owns a house, so 'er **net worth** 'ez higher.

penny stocks *n.pl.* stocks that cost very little, often under a dollar.

EXAMPLE: **Penny stocks** are very risky. People buy a lot of them because they are so cheap, but the stocks usually become worthless.

TRANSLATION: **Stocks that cost under a dollar** are very risky. People buy a lot of them because they are so cheap, but the stocks usually become worthless.

"REAL SPEAK": **Penny stocks** 'er very risky. People buy a lod 'ev 'em b'cuz they're so cheap, b't the stocks ujally b'come worthless.

profit margin *n.* a number indicating a company's profitability.

EXAMPLE: Since Natalie started to manage our company, the **profit margin** has doubled! She's doing a great job.

TRANSLATION: Since Natalie started to manage our company, the **percentage of company profitability** has doubled! She's doing a great job.

"REAL SPEAK": Since Nadalie starded da manage 'ar comp'ny, the **profit margin**'s doubled! She's doing a great job.

prospectus n. a report that describes a business enterprise, either proposed or existing.

EXAMPLE: I bought stock in Make Me Millions, Inc., last year, so I get their most recent **prospectus** in the mail every few months.

TRANSLATION: I bought stock in Make Me Millions, Inc., last year, so I get their most recent **report that describes their business enterprise** in the mail every few months.

"REAL SPEAK": I bought stock 'n Make Me Millions, Inc., last year, so I get their most recent **prospectus** 'n the mail ev'ry few munts.

return n. the percentage of money gained or lost for a mutual fund in a specific time period.

EXAMPLE: I had a much better **return** on my mutual fund this year than last year. Last year, I lost almost six percent!

TRANSLATION: I had a much better **percentage of money gained** on my mutual fund this year than last year. Last year, I lost almost six percent!

"REAL SPEAK": I had a much bedder **return** on my mutual fun' this year th'n last year. Last year, I lost almos' six percent!

S&P 500 (the) abbrev. (an abbreviation for "Standard & Poor's 500 Index") an indicator of the performance of 500 important companies.

EXAMPLE: **The S&P 500** fell for the tenth day in a row, indicating a downward trend in the overall market.

TRANSLATION: **The Standard & Poor's 500 Index, an indicator of the performance of 500 important companies**, fell for the tenth day in a row, indicating a downward trend in the overall market.

"REAL SPEAK": **The S-'n-P Five Hundred** fell fer the tenth day 'n a row, indicading a downward trend 'n the overall market.

sell high (to) v. to sell stock at a high price.

EXAMPLE: Everyone wants to **sell high**, but it's hard to know if a stock's price has just hit its peak, or if it's still rising.

TRANSLATION: Everyone wants to **sell stock at a high price**, but it's hard to know if a stock's price has just hit its peak, or if it's still rising.

"REAL SPEAK": Ev'ryone wansta **sell high**, b'd it's hard da know 'ef a stock's price's just hid its peak, or if it's still rising.

share n. individual unit of ownership in a company; a unit of stock.

EXAMPLE: I want to buy **shares** of Profits-R-Us. I really like their products and their president is really smart.

TRANSLATION: I want to buy **units of stock** of Profits-R-Us. I really like their products and their president is really smart.

"REAL SPEAK": I wanna buy **shares** 'ev Profits-R-Us. I really like their produc's an' their president's really smart.

Also: **share-holder** *n.* a person who owns shares in a company.

stock *n.* a group of shares (units of ownership) in a company.

EXAMPLE: I have **stock** in IBM, so I hope it starts making more money!

TRANSLATION: I have **a group of shares** in IBM, so I hope it starts making more money!

"REAL SPEAK": I 'ave **stock** 'n I-B-M, so I hope it starts making more money!

Also 1: **stock broker** *n.* a person who buys and sells stocks for other people.

Also 2: **stock-holder** *n.* a person who owns stock in a company.

stock options *n.pl.* an opportunity given to an employee by a company to buy stock from that company at a pre-determined price, even if the current purchase price is higher.

EXAMPLE: When I was hired, the company gave me **stock options**. I can buy the stock at ten dollars per share whenever I want, and sell it at the current price.

TRANSLATION: When I was hired, the company gave me **the opportunity to buy stock at a pre-determined price**. I can buy the stock at ten dollars per share whenever I want, and sell it at the current price.

"REAL SPEAK": When I w'z hired, the comp'ny gay me **stock options**. I c'n buy the stock 'it ten dollars per share wh'never I want, an' sell id at the current price.

stock symbol *n.* the abbreviation (written in all capitals) by which a company's stock is known on the stock market.

EXAMPLE: Do you know the **stock symbol** for Slangman Publishing? I thought it was S.P.O, but that's Sears Parcel Company.

TRANSLATION: Do you know the **stock market abbreviation** for Slangman Publishing? I thought it was S.P.O., but that's Sears Parcel Company.

"REAL SPEAK": Do ya know the **stock symbol** fer Slangman Publishing? I thod it w'z S-P-O, but that's Sears Parcel Comp'ny.

through the roof (to go) *exp.* to increase a huge amount.

EXAMPLE: I was worried about my stock purchase, but yesterday the price **went through the roof**!

TRANSLATION: I was worried about my stock purchase, but yesterday the price **increased a huge amount**!

"REAL SPEAK": I w'z worried about my stock purchase, b't yesterday the price **went through the roof**!

trade *n.* a transaction in which stock is bought or sold.

EXAMPLE: I only pay ten dollars for each **trade** that I make, but Hannah pays ten percent for each of hers. That's a lot of money when she buys large amounts of stock!

TRANSLATION: I only pay ten dollars for each **transaction** that I make, but Hannah pays ten percent for each of hers. That's a lot of money when she buys large amounts of stock!

"REAL SPEAK": I only pay ten dollars fer each **trade** th'd I make, b't Hannah pays ten percent fer each 'ev hers. That's a lodda money when she buys large amounts 'ev stock!

Stock Market Slang & Jargon

LESSON 8

FRANK TRACKS THE PALLET

Shipping and International Trade Slang & Jargon

THIS LESSON FEATURES **14** NEW SLANG WORDS & IDIOMS

LET'S WARM UP!

MATCH THE PICTURES

As a fun way to get started, see if you can guess the meaning of the new slang words and expressions on the opposite page by using the pictures below and following the context of the sentences.

1. If you're sending that package to another country, you need to attach a **commercial invoice** on the outside.
   Definition: "bill to be paid by customs"
   ☐ True ☐ False

2. If we stack all the boxes on a **pallet**, we can send them all as one shipment.
   Definition: "wooden platform"
   ☐ True ☐ False

3. The **bill of lading** says the transportation company must deliver our products today.
   Definition: "verbal agreement"
   ☐ True ☐ False

4. Our client never received his order. We need to **track** it!
   Definition: "examine"
   ☐ True ☐ False

5. The customer needs the products quickly, so arrange for a **drop shipment**.
   Definition: "delivery where merchandise is dropped from a plane"
   ☐ True ☐ False

6. Let's weigh the crate before it's filled. Then we'll know the **tare weight**.
   Definition: "weight of the contents"
   ☐ True ☐ False

7. **Shrinkwrap** the items together so that they don't slip during transportation.
   Definition: "wrap tightly in plastic"
   ☐ True ☐ False

8. Weigh the crate after it's filled. Then we'll have the **gross weight** of the shipment.
   Definition: "weight of each item"
   ☐ True ☐ False

9. Make sure to pack the dishes in a **container**. We want to make sure they don't break during shipment.
   Definition: "large shipping crate"
   ☐ True ☐ False

10. The truck's **lift gate** broke, so we have to lower the boxes to the ground ourselves.
    Definition: "security gate"
    ☐ True ☐ False

11. Unload the truck at our **dock** in the back of the building.
    Definition: "doctor"
    ☐ True ☐ False

12. I ordered the products **COD** which means I need to pay when the shipment arrives.
    Definition: "collect on delivery"
    ☐ True ☐ False

13. Margaret tried to pay the transportation company when they came to pick up the shipment. She didn't realize the shipment terms were **FOB** warehouse.
    Definition: "free for women"
    ☐ True ☐ False

14. Our **freight forwarder** is helping us ship products to India.
    Definition: "freight train owner"
    ☐ True ☐ False

LET'S TALK!

A. DIALOGUE USING SLANG & IDIOMS

The words introduced on the first two pages are used in the dialogue below. See if you can understand the conversation. *Note:* The translation of the words in boldface is on the right-hand page.

CD-B: TRACK 13

Delia: Where's Kevin? He was supposed to ship a **pallet** of **shrinkwrapped** books **COD** to our customer in Japan **FOB** Los Angeles. The **freight forwarder** just called and said the books never arrived!

Frank: I know. Kevin forgot that our warehouse doesn't have a **dock**, so he didn't ask for a **lift gate**. A different truck had to be scheduled which finally arrived after two days. Then, Kevin realized that he forgot to include three copies of the **commercial invoice** with the **bill of lading**! Even worse, he forgot to subtract the **tare weight** from the **gross weight**, so we're paying to ship the **container**, too!

Delia: Next time, we'll arrange for a **drop shipment**. We can rely on our manufacturer to **track** it if we need to and Kevin won't cost us more money!

Shipping and International Trade Slang & Jargon

B. DIALOGUE TRANSLATED INTO STANDARD ENGLISH

LET'S SEE HOW MUCH YOU REMEMBER!
Just for fun, move around in random order to the words and expressions in boldface below. See if you can remember their slang equivalents without looking at the left-hand page!

Delia: Where's Kevin? He was supposed to ship a **wooden platform** of **tightly plastic-covered** books **"collect on delivery"** to our customer in Japan **free on board, where the buyer pays for transportation costs from** Los Angeles. The **company which prepares documents and arranges deliveries for domestic manufacturers** just called and said the books never arrived!

Frank: I know. Kevin forgot that our warehouse doesn't have an **elevated loading and unloading platform**, so he didn't ask for a **piece of machinery attached to the back of the truck that allows merchandise to be lowered to the ground**. A different truck had to be scheduled which finally arrived after two days. Then, Kevin realized that he forgot to include three copies of the **international document which decribes the shipment and gives the value of each item** with the **document that specifies the terms of the shipping contract**! Even worse, he forgot to subtract the **weight of the empty shipping materials** from the **entire weight of the shipment**, so we're paying to ship the **large shipping receptacle**, too!

Delia: Next time, we'll arrange for the **shipment to be sent directly from our manufacturer to the customer**. We can rely on our manufacturer to **electronically document the shipment's journey to its destination** if we need to and Kevin won't cost us more money!

Shipping and International Trade Slang & Jargon

C. DIALOGUE USING "REAL SPEAK"

The dialogue below demonstrates how the slang conversation on the opposite page would *really* be spoken by native speakers!

CD-B: TRACK 13

Delia: Where's Kevin? He w'z sapposta ship a **pallet** 'a **shrinkwrapped** books **C-O-D** da 'ar custamer 'n Japan **F-O-B** destination. The **freight forwarder** jus' called 'n said the books never arrived!

Frank: I know. Kevin fergot th'd 'ar warehouse doesn' have a **dock**, so 'e didn' ask fer a **lift gate**. A diff'rent truck had da be scheduled which fin'lly arrived after two days. Then, Kevin reelized thad 'e fergot ta include three copies 'a the **commercial invoice** with the **bill 'ev lading**! Even worse, he fergot ta subtract the **tare weight** fr'm the **gross weight**, so w'r paying da ship the **c'ntainer**, too!

Delia: Nex' time, we'll arrange fer a **drop shipment**. We c'n rely on 'ar manufacturer ta **track** id if we need to an' Kevin won't cost us more money!

LET'S LEARN!

VOCABULARY

The following words and expressions were used in the previous dialogues. Let's take a closer look at what they mean.

CD-B: TRACK 14

bill of lading *n.* a document that specifies the terms and special instructions from the shipper to the transportation company.

> **EXAMPLE:** Our client wants the shipment delivered to the back of his building. Make sure to put that on the **bill of lading**.
>
> **TRANSLATION:** Our client wants the shipment delivered to the back of his building. Make sure to note that on the **document which specifies the terms between the transportation company and us**.
>
> **"REAL SPEAK":** 'Ar client wants the shipment delivered ta the back 'ev 'is building. Make sher da put thad on the **bill 'ev lading**.
>
> *Also:* **B/L** *abbrev.*
>
> *Note 1:* **air waybill** *n.* a document that specifies the terms and special instructions from the shipper to the transporter of merchandise sent by air.
>
> *Note 2:* **inland bill of lading** *n.* a document that specifies the terms and special instructions from the shipper to the transporter of merchandise going by truck or train to an exporter's international shipper.
>
> *Note 3:* **ocean bill of lading** *n.* a document that specifies the terms and special instructions from the shipper to the transporter of merchandise going by ship to another country.
>
> **NOW YOU DO IT:** (use "**bill of lading**" in a sentence)

COD *exp.* (an abbreviation for "**C**ollect **O**n **D**elivery") requiring payment by the addressee at the time of delivery.

> **EXAMPLE:** I had the package shipped **COD**, but I didn't have any money when it arrived, so they wouldn't give it to me.
>
> **TRANSLATION:** I had the package shipped **requiring payment by the addressee at the time of delivery**, but I didn't have any money when it arrived, so they wouldn't give it to me.
>
> **"REAL SPEAK":** I had the package shipped **C-O-D**, but I didn' 'ave any money when id arrived, so they wouldn' give it ta me.
>
> *Note:* Many people think *COD* means "cash on delivery."
>
> **NOW YOU DO IT:**
>
> (use "**COD**" in a sentence)

commercial invoice *n.* a document, used for international shipping, which indicates the sender, customer, description of the shipment, where the products were produced, and the replacement cost of each item (not the actual amount the shipper is charging the customer).

> **EXAMPLE:** Always make sure to attach a **commercial invoice** and two copies to the outside of all packages being shipped overseas. It's a customs requirement!
>
> **TRANSLATION:** Always make sure to attach a **document which gives special information about international shipments** and two copies to the outside of all packages being shipped overseas. It's a customs requirement!
>
> **"REAL SPEAK":** Ahweez make sher do attach a **commercial invoice** 'n two copies ta the outside 'ev all packages being shipped overseas. It's a customs requirement!
>
> **NOW YOU DO IT:**
>
> (use "**commercial invoice**" in a sentence)

container *n.* a large shipping receptacle (usually made of steel) designed to be loaded and unloaded from transport vehicles without unpacking.

> **EXAMPLE:** Put the products in a **container** instead of shipping them separately. It'll cost less and be easier to transport!
>
> **TRANSLATION:** Put the products in a **large shipping crate** instead of shipping them separately. It'll cost less and be easier to transport!
>
> **"REAL SPEAK":** Put the prod'cts in a **c'ntainer** instead 'a shipping 'em sep'rit'ly. Id'll cos' less money 'n be easier da transport!
>
> **NOW YOU DO IT:**
>
> (use "**container**" in a sentence)

---

dock *n.* • **1.** (for land transportation) a platform at an industrial location which allows merchandise to be loaded or unloaded to the transportation vehicle • **2.** (for ships) an area at the shore where a ship rests.

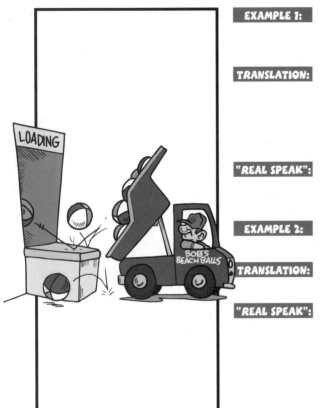

EXAMPLE 1: Kirk's company moved to a new building, but they don't have any **docks**. When they get product shipments, they have to unload the crates and carry them inside!

TRANSLATION: Kirk's company moved to a new building, but they don't have any **platforms which allow goods to be directly loaded or unloaded**. When they get product shipments, they have to unload the crates and carry them inside!

"REAL SPEAK": Kirk's comp'ny moved ta a new building, b't they don't 'ave any **docks**. When they get produc' shipments, they hafta unload the crates 'n carry 'em inside!

EXAMPLE 2: The ship carrying our supplies just arrived. Charles, take the truck to the **dock** and pick it up.

TRANSLATION: The ship carrying our supplies just arrived. Charles, take the truck to the **ship's resting area** and pick it up.

"REAL SPEAK": The ship carrying 'ar supplies just arrived. Charles, take the truck ta the **dock** 'n pick id up.

NOW YOU DO IT:
(use "**dock**" in a sentence)

drop shipment *exp.* a shipment made directly from the manufacturer to the customer.

EXAMPLE: The school wants to use our books for their next semester which starts in just two weeks! To save time, let's arrange for a **drop shipment** from our printer.

TRANSLATION: The school wants to use our books for their next semester which starts in just two weeks! To save time, let's arrange for a **shipment sent directly to the customer** from our printer.

"REAL SPEAK": The school wants ta use 'ar books fer their nex' semester which starts 'n jus' two weeks! Ta save time, let's arrange fer a **drop shipment** fr'm 'ar prin(t)er.

Variation: **drop ship (to)** *v.* to send a shipment directly from the manufacturer to the customer.

NOW YOU DO IT:
(use "**drop shipment**" in a sentence)

FOB *exp.* (an abbreviation for "**F**ree **O**n **B**oard") a shipping term specifying at what point the buyer starts paying for the transportation costs.

EXAMPLE: You don't need to pay the transportation company to pick up the shipment from our warehouse in Los Angeles. The shipping terms are **FOB** Los Angeles.

TRANSLATION: You don't need to pay the transportation company to pick up the shipment from our warehouse in Los Angeles. The shipping terms are **that the buyer will pay for the transportation costs starting in** Los Angeles.

"REAL SPEAK": Ya don't need da pay the transpertation company ta pick up the shipment fr'm 'ar warehouse 'n Los Angeles. The shipping terms 'er **FOB** Los Angeles.

NOW YOU DO IT:

(use "**FOB**" in a sentence)

freight forwarder *n.* a company which prepares shipping and insurance documents, and arranges deliveries of shipments going overseas.

EXAMPLE: The shipment won't be ready for us to send to Tokyo until Saturday. Call the **freight forwarder** and tell them to change the shipping date to Wednesday.

TRANSLATION: The shipment won't be ready for us to send to Tokyo until Saturday. Call the **company which prepares documents and arranges cargo deliveries for domestic manufacturers** and tell them to change the shipping date to Wednesday.

"REAL SPEAK": The shipment won't be ready fer us ta sen' ta Tokyo 'til Saderday. Call the **freight forwerder** 'n tell 'im da change the shipping date ta Wen'sday.

NOW YOU DO IT:

(use "**freight forwarder**" in a sentence)

gross weight *n.* the entire weight of a shipment, including packing and containers.

EXAMPLE: Tell Maureen to include the weight of the packing materials when she calculates the **gross weight**. She forgot last time.

TRANSLATION: Tell Maureen to include the weight of the packing materials when she calculates the **entire weight of the shipment**. She forgot last time.

"REAL SPEAK": Tell Moreen ta include the wade 'a the packing materials when she calculates the **gross weight**. She fergot las' time.

NOW YOU DO IT:

(use "**gross weight**" in a sentence)

lift gate *n.* a piece of machinery attached to the back of a truck that allows merchandise to be lowered to the ground, used when the delivery destination doesn't have an elevated dock.

EXAMPLE: Nathan bought a new truck for the company, but forgot to buy one with a **lift gate**. It will be very hard to unload shipments because we don't have an elevated dock!

TRANSLATION: Nathan bought a new truck for the company, but forgot to buy one with a **piece of machinery attached to the back that allows merchandise to be lowered to the ground**. It will be very hard to unload shipments because we don't have an elevated dock!

"REAL SPEAK": Nathan bod a new truck fer the comp'ny, b't fergot ta buy one with a **lift gate**. Id'll be very hard da unload shipments b'cuz we don'ave 'n elevated dock!

NOW YOU DO IT:
(use "**lift gate**" in a sentence)

pallet *n.* a reusable platform, typically made of wood, on which products are stacked so that they can be moved as a single unit.

EXAMPLE: Stack the boxes on a **pallet**. It will be easier to load the shipment onto the truck as a single unit.

TRANSLATION: Stack the boxes on a **reusable wooden platform**. It will be easier to load the shipment onto the truck as a single unite.

"REAL SPEAK": Stack the boxes on a **pallet**. Id'll be easier da load the shipment onto the truck 'ez a single unit.

Synonym: **skid** *n.*

NOW YOU DO IT:
(use "**pallet**" in a sentence)

shrinkwrap • **1.** *n.* a plastic covering wrapped tighty around two or more items in order to secure them • **2.** *v.* to wrap packages tightly in plastic in order to secure them.

EXAMPLE 1: If you don't have any more **shrinkwrap**, you can strap all the boxes together. That should secure them.

TRANSLATION: If you don't have any more **plastic wrapping**, you can strap all the boxes together. That should secure them.

"REAL SPEAK": If ya don'ave any more **shrinkwrap**, you c'n strap all the boxes tagether. That should secure th'm.

EXAMPLE 2: The shipment was damaged during transport because Bob forgot to **shrinkwrap** the packages!

TRANSLATION: The shipment was damaged during transport because Bob forgot to **wrap** the packages **tightly in plastic**!

"REAL SPEAK": The shipment w'z damage' during transport b'cuz Bob fergot ta **shrinkwrap** the packages!

NOW YOU DO IT:
(use "**shrinkwrap**" in a sentence)

Shipping and International Trade Slang & Jargon

tare weight *n.* the weight of an empty shipping container or packing crate.

EXAMPLE: The customer needs to know the weight of all the products we're shipping. So make sure to subtract the **tare weight** from the weight of the entire shipment.

TRANSLATION: The customer needs to know the weight of all the products we're shipping. So make sure to subtract the **weight of the empty packing crate** from the weight of the entire shipment.

"REAL SPEAK": The custamer needs ta know the wade 'ev all the produc's w'r shipping. So make sher da subtract the **tare weight** fr'm the wade 'a the entire shipment.

NOW YOU DO IT:

(use "**tare weight**" in a sentence)

track (to) *v.* to electronically document a parcel's journey to its destination.

EXAMPLE: The client claims he didn't receive the package. Luckily we **tracked it**, and we know that someone in his office signed for the package yesterday!

TRANSLATION: The client claims he didn't receive the package. Luckily we **electronically documented its journey to its destination**, and we know that someone in his office signed for the package yesterday!

"REAL SPEAK": The client claims 'e didn' receive the package. Luckily we **tracked it**, an' we know th't someone in 'is office signed f'r the package yesterday!

NOW YOU DO IT:

(use "**track**" in a sentence)

LET'S PRACTICE!

A. CREATE YOUR OWN STORY - *(Part 1)*

Follow the instructions below and write down your answer in the space provided. When you have finished answering all the questions, transfer your answers to the story on the next page. Make sure to match the number of your answer with the numbered space in the story. Remember: The funnier your answers, the funnier your story will be!

1. Write down a thing in plural form *(pencils, potatoes, toothbrushes, etc.)*: _____

2. Write down a city *(New York City, Moscow, Tokyo)*: _____

3. Write down a thing in plural form *(pencils, potatoes, toothbrushes, etc.)*: _____

4. Write down an adjective *(big, small, strange, etc.)*: _____

5. Write down a verb ending in "-ing" *(golfing, dancing, running, etc.)*: _____

6. Write down an animal *(dog, octopus, kangaroo)*: _____

7. Write down a place *(restaurant, library, market, etc.)*: _____

8. Write down a mythical place *(Atlantis, the Moon, Oz)*: _____

9. Write down a thing in plural form *(books, worms, peanuts, etc.)*: _____

10. Write down a noun *(pizza, fish, chair, etc.)*: _____

11. Write down an occupation *(accountant, teacher, doctor, etc.)*: _____

12. Write down an adjective starting with the letter "L" *(lazy, lonely, limp, etc.)*: _____

B. CREATE YOUR OWN STORY - *(Part 2)*

Once you've filled in the blanks, read your story aloud. If you've done Part 1 correctly, your story should be hilarious!

SPEAKING

SHIPPING WORLD WEEKLY

THE WEEKLY NEWSPAPER OF THE SHIPPING & INTERNATIONAL TRADE INDUSTRY

"Ask Ed"

by Edward Shippington
Shipping and Trade Expert

Dear Ed...

Last week, I sent out a shipment of [1.] to a client in [2.]. Well, I forgot to **shrinkwrap** the items before I put them on a **pallet**. That's not a big mistake, right?

The client also wanted some [3.], and you know those are so [4.]. I decided to call our **freight forwarder** to make sure I was [5.] them correctly. He reminded me to include the **commercial invoice** and **bill of lading**. But, the guy didn't tell me how to calculate the **tare weight** and **gross weight**. What a [6.]! Anyway, I put the shipment in a **container** and took it to the **dock** in the back of the [7.]. The client wanted the items shipped **FOB** warehouse and **COD**. Not a problem, except that I **tracked** the shipment, and it ended up in [8.] with a group of [9.]!

I should have made a **drop shipment**, so the packages could arrive to the customer faster. After all of that, I got fired from my job. Now I need to find a new [10.]. My question is, do you think I'd make a good [11.]? Sincerely,

[12.] Larry

Shipping and International Trade Slang & Jargon

C. WHAT WOULD YOU DO IF SOMEONE SAID...?

What would you do in response to the words in white italics?
Choose your answer by placing an "X" in the box.

CD-B: TRACK 15

1.	*The destination building doesn't have a dock.*	I would... ☐ a. call a nurse instead ☐ b. use a truck with a lift gate ☐ c. take a vacation
2.	*We don't have any more containers!*	I would... ☐ a. cancel the order ☐ b. hope that more people arrive ☐ c. put the shipment in a crate instead
3.	*I need the gross weight of the shipment.*	I would... ☐ a. give the total weight ☐ b. give the weight of just the products ☐ c. give the weight of just the crate
4.	*You agreed to COD terms, and the shipment just arrived.*	I would... ☐ a. say thank you and take the shipment ☐ b. pay for the shipment ☐ c. refuse the shipment
5.	*The client wants you to track the shipment.*	I would... ☐ a. get in my car and follow it ☐ b. find the shipment electronically ☐ c. go jogging
6.	*Our customer wants us to arrange a drop shipment.*	I would... ☐ a. send the items from the manufacturer ☐ b. send the items from our warehouse ☐ c. send the items from a competitor
7.	*Instead of sending each box separately, shrink-wrap them together.*	I would... ☐ a. make the items smaller ☐ b. wrap the items in pretty paper ☐ c. wrap the items tightly in plastic
8.	*For all shipments going overseas, include a commercial invoice.*	I would... ☐ a. watch commercials on television ☐ b. detail all the products to be sent ☐ c. include payment in the shipment
9.	*Ship these products FOB Tokyo.*	I would... ☐ a. pay for the shipping costs to Tokyo ☐ b. make the customer pay for the shipping ☐ c. fly to Tokyo
10.	*Bring me another pallet! I just used my last one.*	I would... ☐ a. bring a sleeping bag ☐ b. bring a paintbrush and paints ☐ c. bring a wooden platform

Shipping and International Trade Slang & Jargon

D. "ACROSS" WORD PUZZLE

Fill in the crossword puzzle by choosing the correct word from the list below.

CD-B: TRACK 16

CONTAINER	LADING
DOCK	SHRINKWRAP
DROP	TARE
FORWARDER	TRACK

1. Make a [_____] shipment to Denver. It'll be faster.

2. Put the items in a [_____] for shipping.

3. The package never arrived! We need to [_____] it!

4. [_____] weight refers to the weight of an empty crate.

5. Unload the truck at the [_____] behind the building.

6. [_____] the books so we can send them as one unit.

7. The bill of [_____] says we need to deliver the products no later than noon.

8. Ask our freight [_____] to help us ship this crate to Russia.

Shipping and International Trade Slang & Jargon

More Shipping and International Trade Slang & Jargon

If your **freight forwarder** (*company which prepares shipments going overseas*) informs you that a **dock walloper** (*thief*) has just taken the **cargo** (*merchandise*) from your **container** (*shipping receptacle*), you may not know whether or not to be concerned. This type of slang and jargon can even be confusing to most native speakers. But one thing for sure — if you're involved in any type of international trade, understanding the following terms is essential!

Note that in this section, the abbreviation USPS (*United States Postal Service*) will be frequently used.

at sight *exp.* specifying that payment is due when the customer comes to pick up the shipment.

> **EXAMPLE:** I told the buyer that our payment terms are **at sight**, but they didn't bring any money when they came to pick up the shipment!

> **TRANSLATION:** I told the buyer that our payment terms are **payment due upon presentation**, but they didn't bring any money when they came to pick up the shipment!

> **"REAL SPEAK":** I told the buyer th'd 'ar payment terms 'er **at sight**, b't they didn' bring any money when they came da pick up the shipment!

back order (to) *exp.* to order something that will be shipped as soon as it is available.

> **EXAMPLE:** I ordered some more shipping supplies, but they were out of boxes. They should be getting some more next week, so I **back ordered** a few hundred.

> **TRANSLATION:** I ordered some more shipping supplies, but they were out of boxes. They should be getting some more next week, so I **ordered** a few hundred **to be shipped to us as soon as they're available**.

> **"REAL SPEAK":** I ordered s'm more shipping supplies, b't they were oudda boxes. They should be gedding s'm more next week, so I **back ordered** a few hundred.

> *Variation:* **back order (to place/put on)** *exp.* to send merchandise to a customer as soon as it is available.

bonded warehouse *n.* a warehouse authorized by customs for storage of goods where payment of taxes is deferred until the goods are removed.

> **EXAMPLE:** We can't afford to pay the taxes on the shipment, so we'll have to keep it in a **bonded warehouse** until we have enough money.

> **TRANSLATION:** We don't have enough money to pay the duties on the shipment, so we'll have to keep it in a **warehouse authorized by customs for storage of goods where payment of taxes is deferred until the goods are removed** until we have enough money.

> **"REAL SPEAK":** We can' afford da pay the taxes on the shipment, so we'll hafta keep id in a **bonded warehouse** until we have anuf money.

booking *n.* a reservation with a sea freight company for the transportation of cargo.

> **EXAMPLE:** Barbara made a **booking** for the shipment. It needs to be taken to the ship by Thursday.
>
> **TRANSLATION:** Barbara made a **reservation with a sea freight company** for the shipment. It needs to be taken to the ship by Thursday.
>
> **"REAL SPEAK":** Barb'ra made a **booking** fer the shipment. It needs ta be taken ta the ship by Thursday.

bulk rate *n.* a less expensive price for mailing a large number of the same items at the same time.

> **EXAMPLE:** We paid the **bulk rate** on the postcards because we mailed so many and prepared them correctly. We saved a lot of money!
>
> **TRANSLATION:** We paid the **less expensive price** on the postcards because we mailed so many and prepared them correctly. We saved a lot of money!
>
> **"REAL SPEAK":** We paid the **bulk rade** on the postcards b'cuz we mailed so many an' prepared th'm cerrectly. We saved a lodda money!

cargo *n.* merchandise loaded into a large vehicle (such as an airplane, ship, truck, etc.).

> **EXAMPLE:** I've never loaded so much **cargo** before. It must weigh more than the truck!

> **TRANSLATION:** I've never loaded so much **merchandise to be transported** before. It must weigh more than the truck!
>
> **"REAL SPEAK":** I've never loaded so much **cargo** b'fore. It must weigh more th'n the truck!

carrier *n.* an individual or private company that transports shipments to most destinations around the world.

> **EXAMPLE:** Pauline hired a **carrier** to deliver the package because the U.S. Post Office was closed.
>
> **TRANSLATION:** Pauline hired a **private transportation company** to deliver the package because the U.S. Post Office was closed.
>
> **"REAL SPEAK":** Pauline hired a **carrier** ta deliver the package b'cuz the U-S Post Office w'z closed.

Certificate of Origin *n.* a legal document proving the origin of imported goods.

> **EXAMPLE:** Did this shipment come from Chile or Argentina? Check the **Certificate of Origin**.

> **TRANSLATION:** Did this shipment come from Chile or Argentina? Check the **document containing proof of the origin of imported goods**.
>
> **"REAL SPEAK":** Did this shipment come fr'm Chile 'er Argentina? Check the **Certificade 'ev Origin**.
>
> *Note:* A *Certificate of Origin* is used for customs or foreign exchange purposes or both.

Shipping and International Trade Slang & Jargon

certified mail *n.* a service offered by the USPS which provides the sender with a receipt proving that the item arrived at its destination.

> **EXAMPLE:** I always send invoices via **certified mail**. That way I know when my clients received them.

> **TRANSLATION:** I always send invoices via **a service offered by the USPS which provides me with a receipt**. That way I know when my clients received them.

> **"REAL SPEAK":** I ahweez send invoices via **cerdified mail**. That way I know wh'n my clients received th'm.

CIA *abbrev.* (an abbreviation for "**C**ash **I**n **A**dvance") payment terms that specify that full payment must be made before shipment of products.

> **EXAMPLE:** The president wants all payment terms to be **CIA** because one of our clients refused to pay for a shipment last year.

> **TRANSLATION:** The president wants all payment terms to be **full payment made before shipment of products** because one of our clients refused to pay for a shipment last year.

> **"REAL SPEAK":** The president wants all payment terms ta be **CIA** b'cuz one 'ev 'ar clients refused ta pay fer a shipment last year.

consignee *n.* the person to whom merchandise is delivered.

> **EXAMPLE:** We have a shipment of computers to deliver. Jennifer Topaz is the **consignee**. Let's make sure she'll be there to accept the delivery.

> **TRANSLATION:** We have a shipment of computers to deliver. Jennifer Topaz is the **person to whom we are making the delivery**. Let's make sure she'll be there to accept the delivery.

> **"REAL SPEAK":** We 'ave a shipment 'ev c'mpuders ta deliver. Jennifer Topaz 'ez the **consignee**. Let's make sher she'll be there da accept the delivery.

consolidator *n.* an agent who accepts shipments (from different shippers) going to one destination in order to qualify for less expensive rates.

> **EXAMPLE:** Send our shipment to the **consolidator**. It will be much cheaper if it's shipped to England with other packages.

> **TRANSLATION:** Send our shipment to the **agent who accepts shipments going to one destination to qualify for less expensive rates**. It will be much cheaper if it's shipped to England with other packages.

> **"REAL SPEAK":** Send 'ar shipment ta the **c'nsolidader**. Id'll be much cheaper if it's ship' ta England with other packages.

customs *n.* • **1.** the government agency responsible for collecting taxes on imports and exports • **2.** the tax on imports and exports.

> **EXAMPLE 1:** Every shipment must be examined by **customs** to verify its contents.

> **TRANSLATION:** Every shipment must be examined by **the government agency responsible for collecting taxes on imports and exports** to verify its contents.

> **"REAL SPEAK":** Ev'ry shipment mus' be examined by **customs** ta verify its contents.

> **EXAMPLE 2:** The **customs** on imported alcohol is very high, so it's usually cheaper to buy domestic alcohol.

> **TRANSLATION:** The **actual tax** on imported alcohol is very high, so it's usually cheaper to buy domestic alcohol.

> **"REAL SPEAK":** The **customs** on imported alcohol's very high, so it's ujally cheaper da buy damestic alcahol.

DDC n. (an abbreviation for "**D**estination **D**elivery **C**harge") the amount of delivery charges owed by the addressee upon receipt of the shipment.

> **EXAMPLE:** The package is arriving with a **DDC**. Do you have enough money to pay for it?

> **TRANSLATION:** The package is arriving with a **destination delivery charge**. Do you have enough money to pay for it?

> **"REAL SPEAK":** The package's arriving with a **D-D-C**. Do ya have anuf money da pay for it?

dock walloper n. a thief who steals cargo before it has been unloaded from the ship.

> **EXAMPLE:** We lost five shipments last year because of **dock wallopers**. We need better security!

> **TRANSLATION:** We lost five shipments last year because of **thieves who steal cargo**. We need better security!

> **"REAL SPEAK":** We lost five shipments last year b'cuz 'ev **dock wallipers**. We need bedder securidy.

draft n. a written order directing a person (or company) to pay a specified sum of money to a specified person (or company).

> **EXAMPLE:** Nina wrote a bank **draft** to move money to our office in South Africa.

> **TRANSLATION:** Nina wrote an **order directing the** bank **to pay a specified sum of money to a specified person** to move money to our office in South Africa.

> **"REAL SPEAK":** Nina rode a **bank draf'** ta move money ta 'ar office 'n South Africa.

> *Synonym:* **Bill of Exchange** n.

drawee n. a person (or company) who is responsible for paying the sum of money specified on a *draft* (see previous entry).

> **EXAMPLE:** Make sure Brendan is listed as the **drawee** on the *draft*. I'm worried that he won't pay for the shipment.

> **TRANSLATION:** Make sure Brendan is listed as the **individual responsible for the specified amount** on the *draft*. I'm worried that he won't pay for the shipment.

> **"REAL SPEAK":** Make sher Brendan's listed as the **drawee** on the *draft*. I'm worried thad 'e won't pay fer the shipment.

drawer n. the person (or company) who issues a *draft* and receives payment of the specified sum of money from the *drawee*.

> **EXAMPLE:** Mindy is listed as the **drawer** on the *draft*, but she's on vacation. We can't receive the payment until she comes back!

> **TRANSLATION:** Mindy is listed as the **individual that signs a draft and receives payment of the specified amount** on the *draft*, but she's on vacation. We can't receive the payment until she comes back!

> **"REAL SPEAK":** Mindy's listed as the **drawer** on the *draft*, b't she's on vacation. We can't receive the payment 'til she comes back!

duty *n.* a charge collected by a country's government on imported goods entering the country by mail.

> **EXAMPLE:** Don't forget that we have to pay the **duty** in addition to the shipping fees when we send packages out of the country.

> **TRANSLATION:** Don't forget that we have to pay the **charge collected by a country's government on imported goods entering the country by mail** in addition to the shipping fees when we send packages out of the country.

> **"REAL SPEAK":** Don't ferget that we hafta pay the **dudy** in addition ta the shipping fees when we sen' packages outta the country.

duty drawback *n.* a customs law which refunds duties (or taxes) on imported components used to manufacture exports.

> **EXAMPLE:** The shipment of car parts we received qualifies for **duty drawback**, since we'll be exporting the cars after they're built.

> **TRANSLATION:** The shipment of car parts we received qualifies for **refund of duties on imported components used to manufacture exports**, since they'll be exporting the cars after they're built.

> **"REAL SPEAK":** The shipmen' 'ev car parts we received qualifies fer **dudy drawback**, since we'll be expording the cars after they're built.

export • **1.** *n.* a product manufactured domestically and sold to another country • **2.** *v.* to send domestic products or services out of the country for sale in another country.

> **EXAMPLE 1:** We can make a lot of money if we sell these motorcycles as **exports**. There are countries that don't make any of their own.

> **TRANSLATION:** We can make a lot of money if we sell these motorcycles as **products manufactured domestically and sold to another country**. There are countries that don't make any of their own.

> **"REAL SPEAK":** We c'n make a lodda money if we sell these modercycles 'ez **exports**. There 'er countries th't don't make any 'a their own.

> **EXAMPLE 2:** Some of our technology is too secret to **export** to other countries.

> **TRANSLATION:** Some of our technology is too secret to **send** to other countries.

> **"REAL SPEAK":** Some 'ev 'ar technology's too secret ta **export** ta other countries.

Express Mail *n.* a USPS mail class that provides faster delivery service.

> **EXAMPLE:** The package didn't arrive today because Carrie forgot to send it via **Express Mail**.

> **TRANSLATION:** The package didn't arrive today because Carrie forgot to send it via **a USPS mail class that provides faster delivery service**.

> **"REAL SPEAK":** The package didn't arrive today because Carrie forgot to send it via **Express Mail**.

First-Class Mail *n.* a USPS class of mail that receives the fastest non-Express Mail service.

> **EXAMPLE:** Tell Walter to send the letters via **First-Class Mail**. Our clients need to receive them quickly.

> **TRANSLATION:** Tell Walter to send the letters via **a USPS class of mail that receives the fastest non-Express Mail service**. Our clients need to receive them quickly.

"REAL SPEAK": Tell Walter da sen' the ledders via **Firs'-Class Mail**. 'Ar clients need da receive th'm quickly.

flat rack *n.* a platform designed with the flexibility to carry oversized cargo which can be loaded from the sides and top.

EXAMPLE: Load the packages onto **flat racks** for shipping. They are too big to fit into the containers.

TRANSLATION: Load the packages onto **platforms designed with flexibility to carry oversized cargo** for shipping. They are too big to fit into the containers.

"REAL SPEAK": Load the packages onta **flat racks** fer shipping. They'er too big da fid inta the containers.

handling charge *n.* an additional amount of money added to the shipping charges which pays for time and materials used to prepare a shipment.

EXAMPLE: Don't forget to include the **handling charge** on the invoice. It takes a lot of time to package these items.

TRANSLATION: Don't forget to include **an additional amount of money to the shipping charges which pays for time and materials used to prepare the shipment** on the invoice. It takes a lot of time to package these items.

"REAL SPEAK": Don't ferget ta include the **handling charge** on the invoice. It takes a lodda time da package these idems.

import • **1.** *n.* a product manufactured in another country and sold domestically • **2.** *v.* to bring foreign products or services into the country for sale domestically.

EXAMPLE 1: **Imports** generally cost more than domestic products because of the high shipping fees from one country to another.

TRANSLATION: **Products manufactured in another country and sold domestically** generally cost more than domestic products because of the high shipping fees from one country to another.

"REAL SPEAK": **Imports** generally cost more th'n damestic produc's b'cuz 'a the high shipping fees fr'm one country to another.

EXAMPLE 2: America **imports** a lot of cars from Germany and Japan.

TRANSLATION: America **brings into our country** a lot of cars from Germany and Japan.

"REAL SPEAK": America **imports** a lodda cars fr'm Germany 'n Japan.

Insured Mail *n.* a USPS service that reimburses the sender for lost, damaged, or stolen mail.

EXAMPLE: I sent the holiday gifts via **Insured Mail**. Now the USPS will have to pay me if any are lost.

TRANSLATION: I sent the holiday gifts via **a USPS service that provides payment for lost parcels**. Now the USPS will have to pay me if any are lost.

Shipping and International Trade Slang & Jargon

"REAL SPEAK": I sent the holiday gifts via **Insured Mail**. Now the U-S-P-S'll hafta pay me 'ef any 'er lost.

L/C *n.* (an abbreviation for "**L**etter of **C**redit") a bank's letter which guarantees payment to a named payee when terms specified in the letter are met.

EXAMPLE: We need payment guaranteed by **L/C** because it's too difficult to prosecute foreign distributors if they don't pay.

TRANSLATION: We need payment guaranteed by **Letter Credit** because it's too difficult to prosecute foreign distributors if they don't pay.

"REAL SPEAK": We need payment guaranteed by **L-C** b'cuz it's too difficult ta prosecute foreign distribuders if they don't pay.

lead time *n.* the time required to produce something before it can be shipped to its destination.

EXAMPLE 1: I need your company to print twenty thousand annual reports for us. How much **lead time** will you need?

TRANSLATION: I need your company to print twenty thousand annual reports for us. How much **time** will you need **to produce it before it's ready to ship**?

"REAL SPEAK": I need jer comp'ny da print twen'y thousand annual reports fer us. How much **lead time** will ya need?

manifest *n.* a list of all shipments that were made during a specific period of time.

EXAMPLE 1: I can't remember whether or not we sent the shipment to Kenny's Shoes today. Do you have the **manifest** for today?

TRANSLATION: I can't remember whether or not we sent the shipment to Kenny's Shoes today. Do you have the **list of all the shipments we made** for today?

"REAL SPEAK": I can't remember whether 'er not we sent the shipment ta Kenny's Shoes taday. Do ya have the **manifest** fer taday?

money order *n.* a check issued by a bank which guarantees payment to the payee.

EXAMPLE: Tell the customer we don't accept personal checks, only credit cards and **money orders**.

TRANSLATION: Tell the customer we don't accept personal checks, only credit cards and **checks issued by a bank**.

"REAL SPEAK": Tell the cusdamer we don' accept personal checks, only credit cards 'n **money orders**.

net weight *n.* the weight of the contents of a shipment excluding the weight of the container, pallet, skid, crate or other receptacle.

EXAMPLE: I need the **net weight** for the shipment, so let's subtract the weight of the container from the total weight.

TRANSLATION: I need the **weight of the contents only for the shipment**, so let's subtract the weight of the container from the total weight.

"REAL SPEAK": I need the **net weight** fer the shipment, so let's subtract the wade 'a the c'ntainer fr'm the todal weight.

on hand *n.* available, in stock.

EXAMPLE: Our customer just ordered thirty computers. Do we have enough **on hand**?

TRANSLATION: Our customer just ordered thirty computers. Do we have enough **available**?

"REAL SPEAK": 'Ar custamer just ordered thirdy c'mpuders. Do we have anuf **on hand**?

packing list n. a document listing the contents only (without the prices) in a particular shipment.

> **EXAMPLE:** Make sure that the number of items on the **packing list** matches what we actually received.

> **TRANSLATION:** Make sure that the number of items on the **document listing the contents** matches what we actually received.

> **"REAL SPEAK":** Make sher th't the number 'ev idems on the **packing list** matches what we akshelly received.

> *Variation:* **packing slip** n.

POD exp. (an abbreviation for "**P**roof **O**f **D**elivery") the delivery receipt of a shipment indicating the name of the person who signed for a package with the date and time of delivery.

> **EXAMPLE:** We received the **POD** for last week's shipment, so we know it arrived in Toronto safely.

> **TRANSLATION:** We received the **delivery receipt indicating the date and time of delivery** for last week's shipment, so we know it arrived in Toronto safely.

> **"REAL SPEAK":** We r'ceived the **P-O-D** fer las' week's shipment, so we know id arrived 'n Teron(t)o safely.

postmark n. a cancellation mark indicating the date of shipment and the specific postal office that has processed the item.

> **EXAMPLE:** The **postmark** on this package says it was mailed from Los Angeles almost three weeks ago, but it just arrived today!

> **TRANSLATION:** The **cancellation mark** on this package says it was mailed from Los Angeles almost three weeks ago, but it just arrived today!

> **"REAL SPEAK":** The **pos'mark** on this package says it w'z mailed fr'm Los Angeles almos' three weeks ago, b'd it just arrived taday!

pouch n. a cloth bag used by the USPS to transport First-Class Mail, Registered Mail, or Express Mail.

> **EXAMPLE:** That postal worker dropped her **pouch** and all the letters fell out!

> **TRANSLATION:** That postal worker dropped her **cloth bag used to transport mail** and all the letters fell out!

> **"REAL SPEAK":** That posdal worker dropper 'er **pouch** 'n all the ledders fell out!

Priority Mail n. a class of mail used by the USPS which guarantees faster delivery than typical service.

> **EXAMPLE:** Henry didn't send the letter via **Priority Mail**. The client won't receive it for days!

> **TRANSLATION:** Henry didn't send the letter via **a class of mail used by the USPS which guarantees faster delivery than typical service**. The client won't receive it for days!

> **"REAL SPEAK":** Henry didn't send the ledder via **Prioridy Mail**. The client won't receive it fer days!

pro forma invoice n. an invoice indicating the amount the customer will need to pay before the product is shipped.

> **EXAMPLE:** Send Mr. Jenson a **pro forma invoice**. He paid late for the last shipment, so I want our money paid in advance this time.

TRANSLATION: Send Mr. Jenson **an invoice indicating the amount he'll need to pay before we can ship the product**. He paid late for the last shipment, so I want our money paid in advance this time.

"REAL SPEAK": Sen' Mister Jenson a **pro forma invoice**. He paid late fer the las' shipment, so I wan' 'ar money paid 'n advance this time.

purchasing agent n. a person (or company) who purchases merchandise on behalf of an organization.

EXAMPLE: We need to buy more computers but we have to go through our **purchasing agent** to get them, and she's on vacation.

TRANSLATION: We need to buy more computers but we have to go through our **agent, who purchases merchandise on behalf of our organization** to get them, and she's on vacation.

"REAL SPEAK": We need da buy more c'mpuders b't we hafta go through 'ar **purchasing agent** ta get th'm, an' she's on vacation.

purchase order n. a legal document that guarantees payment within a specified period of time for the items listed.

EXAMPLE: We just received a **purchase order** from International Business Systems for fifty office chairs. Let's deliver the chairs tomorrow and give them the invoice at the same time.

TRANSLATION: We just received a **legal document that guarantees payment** from International Business Systems for fifty office chairs. Let's deliver the chairs tomorrow and give them the invoice at the same time.

"REAL SPEAK": We jus' r'ceived a **purchase order** fr'm In(t)ernational Bizness Systems fer fifdy office chairs. Let's deliver the chairs tamorrow 'n give 'em the invoice 'it the same time.

Variation: **P.O.** n.

Note: In place of a *purchase order* (which is a physical piece of paper), often a company will just supply the seller with a purchase order number (*P.O. number*) over the phone.

quotation n. a projected cost for a product or service given to a customer (so that the customer can decided whether or not to make the purchase).

EXAMPLE: We got **quotations** from three different companies for the items we need. Let's hire the least expensive company.

TRANSLATION: We got **projected costs** from three different companies for the items we need. Let's hire the least expensive company.

"REAL SPEAK": We got **quotations** fr'm three diff'rent comp'nies fer the idems we need. Let's hire the least expensive company.

Variation: **[price] quote** n.

registered mail n. a service offered by the USPS where mail is electronically documented (see: *to track*, p. 156) at each point on its route so as to assure safe delivery.

EXAMPLE: I sent the letter via **registered mail** because the last letter I sent never arrived in San Francisco.

TRANSLATION: I sent the letter via **the service offered where mail is electronically documented at each piont on its route** because the last letter I sent never arrived in San Francisco.

"REAL SPEAK": I sent the ledder via **registered mail** b'cuz the las' ledder I sent never arrived 'n San Fr'ncisco.

return receipt n. a card signed by the addressee of an item and mailed back to the sender as proof of delivery.

EXAMPLE: When Vincent sent the letter, he requested a **return receipt**. That way he'll know if the client received it.

TRANSLATION: When Vincent sent the letter, he requested **to have a card signed by the addressee of the item mailed back to him as proof of delivery**. That way he'll know if the client received it.

"REAL SPEAK": When Vincent sent the ledder, he requested a **return receipt**. That way he'll know 'ef the client received it.

SASE *exp.* (an abbreviation for "**S**elf-**A**ddressed **S**tamped **E**nvelope") a pre-stamped envelope addressed back to the sender.

EXAMPLE: Wedding invitations always contain an **SASE**. That way guests can respond with little effort and without having to pay for postage.

TRANSLATION: Wedding invitations always contain an **self-addressed stamped envelope**. That way guests can respond with little effort and without having to pay for postage.

"REAL SPEAK": Wedding invitations ahweez c'ntain 'n **S-A-S-E**. That way guess' c'n respond w'th liddle effert and without havin' da pay fer postage.

"We need it yesterday!" *exp.* "We need it immediately (and yesterday would have been preferable)!"

EXAMPLE: I need to place an order and **we need it yesterday**!

TRANSLATION: I need to place an order and **we need it immediately**!

"REAL SPEAK": I need da place 'n order 'n **we need it yesterday**!

TANYA TRAVELS LIGHT

Business Travel Slang & Jargon

THIS LESSON FEATURES **15** NEW SLANG WORDS & IDIOMS

LET'S WARM UP!

MATCH THE PICTURES

As a fun way to get started, see if you can guess the meaning of the new slang words and expressions on the opposite page by using the pictures below and following the context of the sentences.

Business Travel Slang & Jargon

1. I need a vacation. I think I'll **fly stand-by** to Las Vegas tomorrow.
   - ☐ fly standing up
   - ☐ fly when there is an available seat in the airplane

2. I'm too scared to fly on **puddle jumpers**!
   - ☐ small airplanes
   - ☐ airplanes that skim across water

3. I told Janet I'd meet her at the **gate**, but she's not here.
   - ☐ passageway to the airplane
   - ☐ security checkpoint

4. How can you carry so much luggage? You need to **travel light**!
   - ☐ travel with light luggage
   - ☐ travel with few pieces of luggage

5. I just earned a free ticket through the airline's **frequent flyer plan**!
   - ☐ program for pilots
   - ☐ discount program for people who fly often

6. This flight to New Orleans has **connections** in Atlanta and Miami.
   - ☐ scheduled airplane changes
   - ☐ maintenance stops

7. We can **board** the plane now. We'll be in Hawaii in just a few hours!
   - ☐ enter
   - ☐ exit

8. Is this a **nonstop flight**?
   - ☐ flight without scheduled stops along the way
   - ☐ flight that never ends

9. I just **booked** a hotel room in Cancun.
   - ☐ researched
   - ☐ reserved

10. I had a six-hour **layover** in St. Louis on my way to Seattle.
    - ☐ meeting
    - ☐ stop

11. I want a **window seat**. It's relaxing to watch the clouds.
    - ☐ seat by a window
    - ☐ seat made of glass

12. On most airplanes, there is a strict limit of just one **carry-on**!
    - ☐ piece of luggage you're allowed to take onto the plane
    - ☐ child per family

13. Did you buy a **round-trip ticket** or are you staying in Florida?
    - ☐ ticket around the world
    - ☐ ticket that includes travel back to your point of departure

14. Johnson **has jet lag** because of his long flight from London. Give him some time to sleep before the meeting.
    - ☐ has severe fatigue
    - ☐ has a fear of flying

15. I took a **red-eye** from Salt Lake City, so that I could be at the meeting this morning.
    - ☐ flight for people with red eyes
    - ☐ an overnight flight

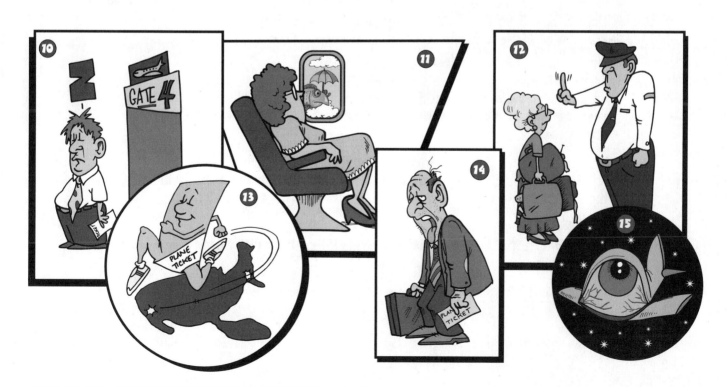

LET'S TALK!

A. DIALOGUE USING SLANG & IDIOMS

The words introduced on the first two pages are used in the dialogue below. See if you can understand the conversation. *Note:* The translation of the words in boldface is on the right-hand page.

CD-B: TRACK 17

Tanya: I need to **book a flight** to Los Angeles right away! I'd like a **round-trip ticket** and a **window seat**. I **travel light**, so I only have one **carry-on**.

Dave: No problem. We have a **red-eye** available, if you don't mind having **jet lag**. Or you can **fly stand-by** on a **puddle jumper**, but you'll have to make two **connections** with a three-hour **layover** in Pittsburgh.

Tanya: Well, I was hoping for a **nonstop flight**, but this will give me more miles for my **frequent flyer plan**. Okay. I'll take it.

Dave: Fine. You can **board** the plane in just a few minutes at **gate** 7A.

B. DIALOGUE TRANSLATED INTO STANDARD ENGLISH

LET'S SEE HOW MUCH YOU REMEMBER!
Just for fun, move around in random order to the words and
expressions in boldface below. See if you can remember their
slang equivalents without looking at the left-hand page!

Tanya: I need to **reserve a flight** to Los Angeles right away. I'd like a **ticket that includes travel back here** and a **seat by a window**. I **travel with only a few pieces of luggage**, so I only have one **small bag to take onto the plane**.

Dave: No problem. We have an **overnight flight** available if you don't mind having **severe fatigue due to air travel**. Or you can **be on a passenger waiting list for an available seat** on a **small airplane**, but you'll have to make two **airplane changes** with a three-hour **stop** in Pittsburgh.

Tanya: Well, I was hoping for a **flight without scheduled stops along the way**, but this will give me more miles for my **special discount program for people who fly often**. Okay. I'll take it.

Dave: Fine. You can **enter** the plane in just a few minutes at **passageway** 7A.

Business Travel Slang & Jargon

C. DIALOGUE USING "REAL SPEAK"

The dialogue below demonstrates how the slang conversation on the opposite page would *really* be spoken by native speakers!

CD-B: TRACK 17

Tanya: I need da **book a flight** ta L.A. ride away! I'd like a **roun'-trip ticked** and a **window seat**. I **travel light**, so I only have one **carry-on**.

Dave: No problem. We have a **red-eye** available, if ya don't mind having **jet lag**. Or ya c'n **fly stan'-by** on a **puddle jumper**, but chu'll hafta make two **connections** with a three-hour **layover** 'n Pittsburgh.

Tanya: Well, I w'z hoping fer a **nonstop flight**, b't this'll give me more miles fer my **frequent flyer plan**. Okay. A'll take it.

Dave: Fine. You c'n **board** the plane 'n just a few minutes 'it **gate** 7A.

LET'S LEARN!

VOCABULARY

The following words and expressions were used in the previous dialogues. Let's take a closer look at what they mean.

CD-B: TRACK 18

board (to) *v.* to enter a ship or airplane.

EXAMPLE: If Donald doesn't **board** the airplane right now, it will leave without him!

TRANSLATION: If Donald doesn't **enter** the airplane right now, it will leave without him!

"REAL SPEAK": If Donald doesn' **board** the airplane right now, id'll leave withoud 'im!

NOW YOU DO IT:
(use "**board**" in a sentence)

book [a hotel, flight, room, etc.] (to) *v.* to reserve.

EXAMPLE: I **booked my flight** to Greece, but I haven't found a hotel with an available room yet! Where will I sleep when I get there?

TRANSLATION: I **reserved my flight** to Greece, but I haven't found a hotel with an available room yet! Where will I sleep when I get there?

"REAL SPEAK": I **booked my flight** ta Greece, b'd I haven' found a hotel with 'n available room yet! Where'll I sleep when I get there?

NOW YOU DO IT:
(use "**book**" in a sentence)

carry-on *n.* a small bag, or piece of luggage, which one is permitted to take onto the plane.

EXAMPLE: Jenna has three **carry-ons**, but the airline will only let her take one on the plane. She always overpacks!

TRANSLATION: Jenna has three **carry-ons**, but the airline will only let her take one on the plane. She always overpacks!

"REAL SPEAK": Jenna has three **carry-ons**, but the airline'll only ledder take one on the plane. She always overpacks!

NOW YOU DO IT:
(use "**carry-on**" in a sentence)

connection *n.* a point during a trip where one must change airplanes.

EXAMPLE: Poor Alice has to make two **connections** on her trip to Boston! The plane has to stop in Denver and Chicago.

TRANSLATION: Poor Alice has to make two **airplane changes** on her trip to Boston! The plane has to stop in Denver and Chicago.

"REAL SPEAK": Poor Alice hasta make two **connections** on 'er trip ta Bost'n! The plane hasta stop in Denver an' Chicago.

NOW YOU DO IT:
(use "**connection**" in a sentence)

fly stand-by (to) *exp.* to be on a passenger waiting list for an available seat.

EXAMPLE: Joseph forgot to make reservations, so now he has to **fly stand-by**. If the flight is full, he won't get a seat!

TRANSLATION: Joseph forgot to make reservations, so now he has to **be on a passenger waiting list for an available seat**. If the flight is full, he won't get a seat!

"REAL SPEAK": Joseph fergot ta make reservations, so now 'e hasta **fly stan'-by**. If the flight's full, 'e won't ged a seat!

NOW YOU DO IT:
(use "**fly stand-by**" in a sentence)

frequent flyer plan *n.* a special program that offers free flights or discounts to people who fly often.

EXAMPLE: Adam has to travel every week for work, so he joined a **frequent flyer plan**. Now he gets free plane tickets for every 10,000 miles he flies.

TRANSLATION: Adam has to travel every week for work, so he joined a **special program that offers free flights to people who fly often**. Now he gets free plane tickets for every 10,000 miles he flies.

"REAL SPEAK": Adam hasta travel ev'ry week fer work, so 'e joined a **frequent flyer plan**. Now 'e gets free plane tickets fer ev'ry ten thousan' miles 'e flies.

NOW YOU DO IT:
(use "**frequent flyer plan**" in a sentence)

gate *n.* the passageway through which passengers enter or exit an airplane.

EXAMPLE: Bob's plane leaves from this **gate**, but I saw him walking in the other direction. He's going to miss his flight!

TRANSLATION: Bob's plane leaves from this **passageway**, but I saw him walking in the other direction. He's going to miss his flight!

"REAL SPEAK": Bob's plane leaves fr'm this **gate**, b'd I saw 'im walking in the other direction. He's gonna miss 'is flight!

Note: The term *gate* can also refer to the area near the passageway where people wait.

NOW YOU DO IT:

(use "**gate**" in a sentence)

jet lag (to have) *exp.* to have severe fatigue due to the time change between one's point of departure and one's destination.

EXAMPLE: Ken couldn't concentrate during the meeting because he **had jet lag** from his long flight from Iceland.

TRANSLATION: Ken couldn't concentrate during the meeting because he **was severely fatigued** from his long flight from Iceland.

"REAL SPEAK": Ken couldn' concentrate during the meeding b'cuz 'e **had jet lag** from 'is long flight fr'm Icel'nd.

NOW YOU DO IT:

(use "**jet lag**" in a sentence)

layover *n.* a stop in one or more cities when traveling by air.

EXAMPLE: Olivia was supposed to be here by now, but her plane had a three-hour **layover** in Pittsburgh.

TRANSLATION: Olivia was supposed to be here by now, but her plane had a three-hour **stop** in Pittsburgh.

"REAL SPEAK": Olivia w'z saposta to be here by now, b'd 'er plane had a three-hour **layover** 'n Pittsburgh.

NOW YOU DO IT:

(use "**layover**" in a sentence)

nonstop flight *n.* a flight made without scheduled stops along the way.

EXAMPLE: Charlie won't fly unless he can reserve a **nonstop flight**. He hates waiting while the plane makes stops in other cities.

TRANSLATION: Charlie won't fly unless he can reserve a **flight without scheduled stops along the way**. He hates waiting while the plane makes stops in other cities.

"REAL SPEAK": Charlie won't fly unless 'e c'n r'serve a **nonstop flight**. He hates waiding while the plane makes stops 'n other cidies.

Synonym: **direct flight** *n.*

NOW YOU DO IT:

(use "**nonstop flight**" in a sentence)

puddle jumper *n.* a small airplane used for short flights.

EXAMPLE: I don't like to fly on **puddle jumpers**! I only feel safe on big airplanes.

TRANSLATION: I don't like to fly on **small airplanes**! I only feel safe on big airplanes.

"REAL SPEAK": I don' like ta fly on **puddle jumpers**! I only feel safe on big airplanes.

NOW YOU DO IT:

(use "**puddle jumper**" in a sentence)

red-eye *n.* an overnight flight whose passengers arrive at their destination with red eyes from staying awake.

EXAMPLE: Harvey fell asleep in the meeting because he took a **red-eye** from Boston to get here on time.

TRANSLATION: Harvey fell asleep in the meeting because he took an **overnight flight** from Boston to get here on time.

"REAL SPEAK": Harvey fell asleep 'n the meeding b'cuz 'e took a **red-eye** da get here on time.

NOW YOU DO IT:

(use "**red-eye**" in a sentence)

round-trip ticket *n.* a ticket that includes travel to one's destination and back again.

EXAMPLE:	Elliot forgot to buy a **round-trip ticket**. Now he's in Chicago and there are no seats available for his return trip home!
TRANSLATION:	Elliot forgot to buy a **ticket that includes travel to one's destination and back again**. Now he's in Chicago and there are no seats available for his return trip home!
"REAL SPEAK":	Elliot fergot ta buy a **roun'-trip ticket**. Now 'e's 'n Chicago 'n there 'er no seats available for 'is r'turn trip home!

NOW YOU DO IT:
(use "**round-trip ticket**" in a sentence)

travel light (to) *exp.* to travel with only one or two pieces of luggage.

EXAMPLE:	I wish my boss would **travel light**, but he always takes at least three pieces of luggage whenever we travel, and he makes me carry them!
TRANSLATION:	I wish my boss would **travel with just one piece of luggage**, but he always takes at least three pieces of luggage whenever we travel, and he makes me carry them!
"REAL SPEAK":	I wish my boss 'ed **travel light**, b'd 'e ahweez takes 'it least three pieces 'ev luggage wh'never we travel, an' 'e makes me carry th'm!

NOW YOU DO IT:
(use "**travel light**" in a sentence)

window seat *n.* a seat on an airplane or train located next to the window.

EXAMPLE:	I wanted the **window seat** but Johnson took it. Now he'll get to enjoy the view instead of me!
TRANSLATION:	I wanted the **seat next to the window** but Johnson took it. Now he'll get to enjoy the view instead of me!
"REAL SPEAK":	I wan'ed the **window seat** b't Johnson took it. Now 'e'll get ta enjoy the view 'nstead 'a me!

NOW YOU DO IT:
(use "**window seat**" in a sentence)

Business Travel Slang & Jargon

LET'S PRACTICE!

A. TRUTH OR LIE

Read the conversation each person is having on the phone, then read their actual thoughts in the bubble. Decide if the person is telling the truth or a lie by checking the appropriate box.

CD-B: TRACK 19

B. FIND THE DEFINITION

Write the definition of the slang word(s) in boldface choosing from the definition list below.

CD-B: TRACK 20

DEFINITIONS

✔ a point during a trip where one must change airplanes

✔ a small airplane

✔ the passageway through which passengers enter or exit the airplane

✔ to travel with just a few pieces of luggage

✔ a special discount program for people who fly often

✔ a stop in one or more cities when traveling by air

✔ to enter a plane, ship, or train

✔ to be on a passenger waiting list for an available seat

✔ to reserve (a seat on an airplane, a hotel, etc.)

✔ a seat on a plane or train that's located by a window

✔ a ticket that includes travel to one's destination and back again

✔ a flight made without scheduled stops along the way

✔ a small piece of luggage one takes onto the plane

✔ to have severe fatigue due to the time change during one's flight

✔ an overnight flight

1. **round-trip ticket** *n.* _____

2. **jet lag (to have)** *exp.* _____

3. **frequent flyer plan** *n.* _____

4. **board (to)** *exp.* _____

5. **gate** *n.* _____

6. **layover** *n.* _____

7. **nonstop flight** *n.* _____

8. **window seat** *v.* _____

9. **book [a hotel, flight, etc.] (to)** *exp.* _____

10. **fly stand-by (to)** *exp.* _____

11. **connection** *n.* _____

12. **puddle jumper** *n.* _____

13. **red-eye** *n.* _____

14. **travel light (to)** *exp.* _____

15. **carry-on** *n.* _____

C. FIND-THE-WORD GRID

Fill in the blanks with the most appropriate word using the list. Next, find and circle the word in the grid below. The answers may be spelled vertically or horizontally.

CD-B: TRACK 21

BOARD	FREQUENT	LAYOVER	PUDDLE	RED-EYE
CARRY-ONS	GATE	LIGHT	STAND-BY	WINDOW

1. If you want to fly to Syracuse, you'll have to take a _____ jumper.

2. I fly twice a month. I need to join a _____ flyer plan!

3. Terry has six pieces of luggage! He should learn how to travel _____ !

4. This flight has a four-hour _____ in Detroit before flying to Springfield.

5. I'm bored. Maybe I can fly _____ and get tickets to Hawaii for the weekend.

6. Did Holly _____ the ship? I wanted to say good-bye before she left!

7. I have three _____ , but the airline only lets you bring two bags on the plane.

8. Under new security rules, only passengers can go to the _____.

9. I'm exhausted! I took a _____ , so I could be here for your speech this morning!

10. I'll get sick if I don't get a _____ seat on the train tomorrow!

FIND-THE-WORD GRID

T	N	F	R	I	A	K	C	E	D	G	R	G	E	W	D	S	T	M	A	T
H	W	A	L	L	E	G	R	L	I	G	H	T	A	B	T	E	D	E	M	A
V	I	D	L	R	S	O	S	L	A	M	U	P	F	I	R	C	S	L	O	R
Y	N	J	T	R	E	I	G	A	L	F	R	E	Q	U	E	N	T	U	V	V
E	D	O	W	C	A	R	R	Y	O	N	S	E	A	O	D	S	A	N	E	E
I	O	U	G	C	U	A	B	O	A	R	D	D	I	R	E	T	N	C	N	T
Q	W	P	A	D	N	S	E	V	R	M	R	M	N	G	Y	O	D	H	G	O
U	C	N	T	I	H	L	E	E	D	P	U	D	D	L	E	W	B	O	S	D
E	U	E	E	N	E	R	H	R	N	E	C	B	O	N	I	A	Y	S	O	E
I	T	D	W	D	D	H	T	M	R	E	E	L	W	S	E	Z	O	I	S	A

THE SLANGMAN FILES

More Business Travel Slang & Jargon

Traveling for business can certainly be frustrating, but not half as much as being unable to understand the everyday jargon that goes along with it. For example, if the flight attendant announces that your **ETA** (*estimated time of arrival*) has been changed due **head winds** (*wind blowing in the opposite direction of the airplane, decreasing its speed*) and an unexpected **layover** (*stop in a city*), you may not know whether or not to celebrate or panic.

The following list is sure to help you understand just about any airport official!

aisle seat *n.* a seat on an airplane or train located next to the aisle.

> **EXAMPLE:** Looking out the window makes Heather feel sick, so she always requests an **aisle seat** when she flies.

> **TRANSLATION:** Looking out the window makes Heather feel sick, so she always requests a **seat located next to the aisle** when she flies.

> **"REAL SPEAK":** Looking out the window makes Heather feel sick, so she ahweez reques'n **aisle seat** when she flies.

bag *n.* a piece of luggage.

> **EXAMPLE:** Thomas lost one of his **bags** at the airport. Now he doesn't have any new shirts to wear during the conference!

> **TRANSLATION:** Thomas lost one of his **pieces of luggage** at the airport. Now he doesn't have any new shirts to wear during the conference!

> **"REAL SPEAK":** Thomas lost one 'ev 'is **bags** 'it the airport. Now 'e doesn'ave any new shirts ta wear during the conf'rence!

baggage claim *n.* the area of the airport where one recovers one's luggage after a flight.

> **EXAMPLE:** The flight arrives at noon, but then Monica needs to wait for her luggage at **baggage claim**. That could take another twenty minutes or more!

> **TRANSLATION:** The flight arrives at noon, but then Monica needs to wait for her luggage at **the area of the airport where one recovers one's luggage after a flight**. That could take another twenty minutes or more!

> **"REAL SPEAK":** The flide arrives 'it noon, b't then Monica needs ta wait fer her luggage 'it **baggage claim**. That could take another twen'y minutes 'er more!

barf bag *n.* a bag used for air sickness, usually found in the back pocket of the seat in front of the passenger.

> **EXAMPLE:** Victor always gets sick when he flies, so he holds the **barf bag** during the flight just in case he needs it.

> **TRANSLATION:** Victor always gets sick when he flies, so he holds the **bag used for air sickness** during the flight just in case he needs it.

> **"REAL SPEAK":** Victer ahweez gets sick when 'e flies, so 'e holds the **barf bag** during the flight just 'n case 'e needs it.

> *Note:* The verb *to barf* is slang for "to vomit."

boarding pass *n.* a ticket issued by the airline that contains one's seat number and is used to gain admittance onto an airplane.

> **EXAMPLE:** The airline employees wouldn't let Lucille onto the plane because she lost her **boarding pass**!

> **TRANSLATION:** The airline employees wouldn't let Lucille onto the plane because she lost her **ticket issued by the airline**!

> **"REAL SPEAK":** The airline employees wouldn' let Lucille onta the plane b'cuz she lost 'er **boarding pass**!

booked solid (to be) *exp.* said of a hotel, passenger ship, airplane, etc. that has no more space available; to be completely full.

> **EXAMPLE:** The hotel Sam wanted to stay at was **booked solid**. He had to find another place to stay during his trip to Kansas City.

> **TRANSLATION:** The hotel Sam wanted to stay at was **completely full**. He had to find another place to stay during his trip to Kansas City.

> **"REAL SPEAK":** The hotel Sam wan'ed da stay at w'z **booked solid**. He had da find another place ta stay during 'is trip ta Kansas Cidy.

bumped off an airplane, train, etc. (to get) *v.* to lose one's seat in an airplane, train, etc.

> **EXAMPLE:** Wendel **got bumped off** the flight. Now he's going to miss our afternoon meeting in Fresno!

> **TRANSLATION:** Wendel **lost his seat on** the flight. Now he's going to miss our afternoon meeting in Fresno!

> **"REAL SPEAK":** Wendel **got bumped off** the flight. Now 'e's gonna miss 'ar afternoon meeding 'n Fresno!

> *Note:* When using **bumped off**, it's important to follow it with an object, such as *the flight* (as seen in the example). If you simply say, *I was bumped off*, this means "I was killed by gangsters" since *to bump someone off* is gangster slang!

> *Variation 1:* **bumped from an airplane, train, etc. (to get)** *exp.*

> *Variation 2:* **bumped (to get)** *adj.*

bumped up (to be) *v.* to get upgraded from one's current airfare class to a higher class for free, usually due to lack of space in the current class.

> **EXAMPLE:** Adam was **bumped up** to first class at no extra cost because there were no seats left in the cheaper section of the plane.

TRANSLATION: Adam was **moved** to first class at no extra cost because there were no seats left in the cheaper section of the plane.

"REAL SPEAK": Adam w'z **bumped up** ta firs' class 'it no extra cost b'cuz there were no seats left 'n the cheaper section 'a the plane.

business class *n.* a section of the airplane containing seats intended for business travelers, with more room per person than the cheaper seats (located in *coach*, p. 185), but with less room than the expensive seats (located in *first class*, p. 187).

EXAMPLE: Devon always pays the extra money to sit in **business class** because he's over six feet tall.

TRANSLATION: Devon always pays the extra money to sit in the **section of the airplane containing seats intended for business travelers** because he's over six feet tall.

"REAL SPEAK": Devon ahweez pays the extra money da sit 'n **bizness class** b'cuz 'e's over six feet tall.

cabin *n.* the passenger section of the inside of an airplane.

EXAMPLE: I hope they turn off the lights in the **cabin**. It will make it easier to sleep during the flight.

TRANSLATION: I hope they turn off the lights in the **passenger section of the airplane**. It will make it easier to sleep during the flight.

"REAL SPEAK": I hope they turn off the lights 'n the **cabin**. Id'll make id easier da sleep during the flight.

check into a hotel (to) *exp.* to register at a hotel upon arrival and receive one's room key.

EXAMPLE: Hilary didn't have time to **check into the hotel** before the conference started, so she had to carry her luggage with her all morning.

TRANSLATION: Hilary didn't have time to **register at the hotel and receive her room key** before the conference started, so she had to carry her luggage with her all morning.

"REAL SPEAK": Hilary didn'ave time da **check inta the hotel** b'fore the conf'rence starded, so she had da carry 'er luggage with 'er all morning.

check one's luggage (to) *exp.* to give one's luggage to an airline employee for transportation to one's destination.

EXAMPLE: Daniel **checked his luggage** as soon as he got to the airport. He didn't want to carry it any longer than necessary.

TRANSLATION: Daniel **gave his luggage to an airline employee for transportation to his destination** as soon as he got to the airport. He didn't want to carry it any longer than necessary.

"REAL SPEAK": Daniel **checked 'is luggage** 'ez soon 'ez 'e got ta the airport. He didn' wanna carry id any longer th'n necessary.

chopper *n.* a helicopter.

EXAMPLE: Ian took the company's **chopper** to get to a meeting on the other side of town.

TRANSLATION: Ian took the company's **helicopter** to get to a meeting on the other side of town.

"REAL SPEAK": Ian took the comp'ny's **chopper** da get to a meeding on the other side 'ev town.

coach *n.* the section of the airplane containing the cheapest seats.

EXAMPLE: The company is so poor that even the president has to sit in **coach** when he flies!

TRANSLATION: The company is so poor that even the president has to sit in **the section of the airplane containing the cheapest seats** when he flies!

"REAL SPEAK": The comp'ny's so poor th'd even the president has ta sid in **coach** when 'e flies!

cockpit *n.* the area of the airplane where the pilot and copilot sit.

> **EXAMPLE:** For security reasons, no one is allowed to visit the **cockpit** during a flight.
>
> **TRANSLATION:** For security reasons, no one is allowed to visit the **area of the airplane where the pilot and copilot sit** during a flight.
>
> **"REAL SPEAK":** Fer securidy reasons, no one's allowed da visit the **cockpit** during a flight.

come in for a landing (to) *exp.* to begin landing an airplane.

> **EXAMPLE:** We started to **come in for a landing** but there was another plane in the way. We had to circle over the airport for an extra thirty minutes!
>
> **TRANSLATION:** We started to **begin landing** but there was another plane in the way. We had to circle over the airport for an extra thirty minutes!
>
> **"REAL SPEAK":** We starded da **come in fer a landing** b't there w'z another plane 'n the way. We had da circle over the airport fer 'n extra thirdy minutes!

commuter *n.* a person who travels regularly for his or her job.

> **EXAMPLE:** I pity **commuters** like Gregory. He has to travel between Los Angeles and San Diego every day!
>
> **TRANSLATION:** I pity **people who travel regularly for their jobs** like Gregory. He has to travel between Los Angeles and San Diego every day!

> **"REAL SPEAK":** I pidy **commuders** like Gregory. He hasta travel b'tween Los Angeles 'n San Diego ev'ry day!

concierge *n.* a hotel employee who assists guests by storing their luggage, taking and delivering messages, making reservations for restaurants, etc.

> **EXAMPLE:** The **concierge** helped Malcolm find a nice restaurant for dinner since he wasn't familiar with Seattle.
>
> **TRANSLATION:** The **hotel employee who assists guests** helped Malcolm find a nice restaurant for dinner since he wasn't familiar with Seattle.
>
> **"REAL SPEAK":** The **concierge** helped Malc'm find a nice rest'rant fer dinner since 'e wasn't familiar with Seattle.

ETA *n.* (an abbreviation for "**E**stimated **T**ime of **A**rrival") the time when an airplane, train, etc. is due to arrive at its destination.

> **EXAMPLE:** My **ETA** is seven o'clock in the morning. You'll have to get up very early if you want to meet me at the airport when I arrive.

> **TRANSLATION:** My **estimated time of arrival** is seven o'clock in the morning. You'll have to get up very early if you want to meet me at the airport when I arrive.

> **"REAL SPEAK":** My **E-T-A** 'ez seven a'clock 'n the morning. You'll hafta ged up very early if ya wanna meet me 'it the airport wh'n I arrive.

ETD *n.* (an abbreviation for "**E**stimated **T**ime of **D**eparture") the time when an airplane, train, etc. is due to depart for its destination.

> **EXAMPLE:** Let's eat lunch. There are two hours before my **ETD**, and I'm really hungry!

> **TRANSLATION:** Let's eat lunch. There are two hours before my **estimated time of departure**, and I'm really hungry!

> **"REAL SPEAK":** Let's eat lunch. There 'er two hours b'fore my **E-T-D**, an' I'm really hungry!

exit row *n.* the row of airplane seats located next to an exit door.

> **EXAMPLE:** You're not allowed to sit in the **exit row** unless you're physically capable of opening the exit door if there's an emergency.

> **TRANSLATION:** You're not allowed to sit in the **row of seats located next to an exit door** unless you're physically capable of opening the exit door if there's an emergency.

> **"REAL SPEAK":** Y'r nod allowed da sid in the **exit row** unless y'r physic'lly capable 'ev opening the exit door 'ef there's 'n amergency.

first class *n.* the section of the airplane containing the most expensive seats that offer passengers more room, better food, and more personal attention.

> **EXAMPLE:** Whenever Tabitha flies, she always sits in **first class** because she's rich.

> **TRANSLATION:** Whenever Tabitha flies, she always sits in **the section of the airplane containing the most expensive seats** because she's rich.

> **"REAL SPEAK":** Wh'never Tabitha flies, she ahweez sits 'n **firs' class** b'cuz she's rich.

flight attendant *n.* an airline employee who assists passengers during the flight.

> **EXAMPLE:** I could never be a **flight attendant**. They have to be friendly and helpful regardless of how rude the plane's passengers are!

> **TRANSLATION:** I could never be an **airline employee who assists passengers during the flight**. They have to be friendly and helpful regardless of how rude the plane's passengers are!

> **"REAL SPEAK":** I could never be a **flide attendant**. They hafta be frien'ly 'n helpful regardless 'ev how rude the plane's passengers are!

fogged in (to be) *exp.* said of a condition where an airplane is unable to depart due to low visibility from excessive fog.

> **EXAMPLE:** We'll have to postpone the meeting until Helen returns. Her plane is **fogged in** at the airport in Denver.
>
> **TRANSLATION:** We'll have to postpone the meeting until Helen returns. Her plane is **unable to depart due to low visibility from excessive fog** at the airport in Denver.
>
> **"REAL SPEAK":** We'll hafta postpone the meeding 'til Helen r'turns. Her plane's **fogged in** 'it the airport 'n Denver.

get in (to) *v.* to arrive.

> **EXAMPLE:** The boss's plane **gets in** around noon, but you should be at the airport early! She gets very angry if she has to wait for her ride home.
>
> **TRANSLATION:** The boss's plane **arrives** around noon, but you should be at the airport early! She gets very angry if she has to wait for her ride home.
>
> **"REAL SPEAK":** The boss's plane **gets in** aroun' noon, b't chu should be 'it the airpord early! She gets very angry if she hasta wait fer her ride home.

head wind *n.* a wind blowing in the opposite direction of the airplane or ship, causing a decrease in its speed.

> **EXAMPLE:** Carl's flight was supposed to arrive an hour ago, but a **head wind** slowed down the plane. Let's eat dinner without him.
>
> **TRANSLATION:** Carl's flight was supposed to arrive an hour ago, but a **wind blowing in the opposite direction of the airplane** slowed down the plane. Let's eat dinner without him.
>
> **"REAL SPEAK":** Carl's flight w'z sapposta arrive 'n hour ago, b'd a **head wind** slowed down the plane. Let's eat dinner without 'im.

hijack (to) *v.* to take control of a vehicle by force, usually to reach an alternate destination.

> **EXAMPLE:** Joel made a joke about **hijacking** the plane, and the security guards arrested him!
>
> **TRANSLATION:** Joel made a joke about **taking control of the plane by force**, and the security guards arrested him!
>
> **"REAL SPEAK":** Joel made a joke about **hijacking** the plane, an' the securidy guards arrested 'im!

in-flight movie or meal *n.* a movie or meal that is offered to passengers during a flight.

> **EXAMPLE:** Earl didn't have time to eat lunch before his flight. Luckily the airline served an **in-flight meal**.

> **TRANSLATION:** Earl didn't have time to eat lunch before his flight. Luckily the airline served a **meal during the flight**.
>
> **"REAL SPEAK":** Earl didn'ave time da eat lunch b'fore 'is flight. Luckily the airline served 'n **in-flight meal**.

jet setter *n.* a person who travels frequently, often to exotic or fashionable locations.

> **EXAMPLE:** Robert has traveled all over the world and has seen so many fascinating places. I want to be a **jet setter** like him!

TRANSLATION: Robert has traveled all over the world and has seen so many fascinating places. I want to be a **person who travels frequently** like him!

"REAL SPEAK": Robert's traveled all over the world an'ez seen so many fascinading places. I wanna be a **jet sedder** like him!

jumbo jet *n.* a large airplane intended for long flights.

EXAMPLE: I love to watch the **jumbo jets** at the airport. I'm always amazed that such huge structures can fly.

TRANSLATION: I love to watch the **large airplanes** at the airport. I'm always amazed that such huge structures can fly.

"REAL SPEAK": I love da watch the **jumbo jets** 'it the airport. I'm ahweez amazed th't such huge structures c'n fly.

leg of the flight *exp.* a part of a journey.

EXAMPLE: They served us lunch during the first **leg of the flight** from New York City to Chicago, but we only got a snack when we flew from Chicago to Seattle.

TRANSLATION: They served us lunch during the first **part of the journey** from New York City to Chicago, but we only got a snack when we flew from Chicago to Seattle.

"REAL SPEAK": They served us lunch during the first **leg 'ev the flight** fr'm New York City ta Chicago, b't we only god a snack when we flew fr'm Chicago ta Seaddle.

moving sidewalk *n.* a type of flat escalator that moves people forward.

EXAMPLE: I'm so glad this airport has **moving sidewalks**! I broke my leg last week and it's hard to walk long distances.

TRANSLATION: I'm so glad this airport has **flat escalators**! I broke my leg last week and it's hard to walk long distances.

"REAL SPEAK": I'm so glad this airport has **moving sidewalks**! I broke my leg las' week 'n it's hard da walk long distences.

Synonym: **people-mover** *n.*

nose-dive *n.* a sudden, swift drop made by an airplane.

EXAMPLE: Flying is very safe. We don't need to worry...unless the plane starts a **nose-dive**!

TRANSLATION: Flying is very safe. We don't need to worry...unless the plane starts a **sudden, swift drop**!

"REAL SPEAK": Flying's very safe. We don't need da worry...unless the plane starts a **nose-dive**!

Also: **nose-dive (to)** *v.*

on board (to be) *n.* to be inside an airplane, train, ship, etc.

EXAMPLE: Is Katherine **on board** the airplane already? I didn't get to say good-bye!

TRANSLATION: Is Katherine **inside** the airplane already? I didn't get to say good-bye!

"REAL SPEAK": Is Kath'rine **on board** the airplane ahready? I didn' get ta say guh-bye!

overbook (to) *v.* said of an airline (hotel, train, etc.) that makes more reservations than they can accommodate.

EXAMPLE: They **overbooked** the flight to Dallas. Some passengers will have to wait three hours for the next flight.

TRANSLATION: They **made more reservations for** the flight to Dallas **than the airplane can accommodate**. Some passengers will have to wait three hours for the next flight.

"REAL SPEAK": They **overbooked** the flight ta Dallas. Some passengers'll hafta wait three hours fer the nex' flight.

overhead compartment n. the storage locker above one's seat on an airplane, train, etc.

EXAMPLE: Before the flight begins, you must place your luggage under a seat or in the **overhead compartment**.

TRANSLATION: Before the flight begins, you must place your luggage under a seat or in the **storage locker above your seat**.

"REAL SPEAK": B'fore the flight begins, you mus' place yer luggage under a seed 'er in the **overhead compartment**.

skycap n. an airport employee who helps travelers with their luggage at an airport.

EXAMPLE: Larry brought so much luggage that he had to ask a **skycap** for help.

TRANSLATION: Larry brought so much luggage that he had to ask an **airport employee who helps travelers with their luggage** for help.

"REAL SPEAK": Larry brought so much luggage thad 'e had da ask a **skycap** fer help.

Synonym: **porter** n.

tail wind n. a wind blowing in the same direction as the airplane or ship, causing an increase in its speed.

EXAMPLE: Because of the strong **tail wind**, we're going to arrive in St. Louis twenty minutes early!

TRANSLATION: Because of the strong **wind blowing in the same direction as our airplane**, we're going to arrive in St. Louis twenty minutes early!

"REAL SPEAK": B'cuz 'a the strong **tail wind**, w'r gonna arrive 'n Saint. Louis twen'y minutes early!

take off (to) v. to depart into the air.

EXAMPLE: I love to sit in the airport and watch the planes **take off**.

TRANSLATION: I love to sit in the airport and watch the planes **depart into the air**.

"REAL SPEAK": I love ta sit 'n the airport 'n watch the planes **take off**.

take one's seat (to) *exp.* to sit in one's assigned seat.

> **EXAMPLE:** Please **take your seat**. We need to see how many seats are still available.

> **TRANSLATION:** Please **sit in your assigned seat**. We need to see how many seats are still available.

> **"REAL SPEAK":** Please **take yer seat**. We need ta see how many seats 'er still available.

taxi (to) *v.* said of an airpane which travels slowly on the ground before takeoff or after landing.

> **EXAMPLE:** We landed at ten o'clock exactly, but the plane **taxied** for fifteen minutes before we could exit.

> **TRANSLATION:** We landed at ten o'clock exactly, but the plane **traveled slowly on the ground** for fifteen minutes before we could exit.

> **"REAL SPEAK":** We landed 'it ten a'clock exactly, b't the plane **taxied** fer fifteen minutes b'fore we could exit.

terminal *n.* a station where passengers begin or end their journey.

> **EXAMPLE:** After the plane landed, William got lost in the **terminal** trying to find his rental car agency.

> **TRANSLATION:** After the plane landed, William got lost in the **station** trying to find his rental car agency.

> **"REAL SPEAK":** After the plane landed, William got lost 'n the **terminal** trying da find 'is ren'al car agency.

turbulence *n.* the unstable flow of air around an airplane which causes it to shake.

> **EXAMPLE:** The pilot made us buckle our seatbelts because of the **turbulence**.

> **TRANSLATION:** The pilot made us buckle our seatbelts because of the **unstable flow of air around the airplane which caused it to shake**.

> **"REAL SPEAK":** The pilot made us buckle 'ar seatbelts b'cuz 'a the **turbulence**.

wake-up call *n.* a phone call made at a specified time in order to wake someone.

> **EXAMPLE:** I forgot my alarm clock, so I'll need a **wake-up call** if I want to be at my morning meeting on time!

> **TRANSLATION:** I forgot my alarm clock, so I'll need a **phone call to wake me** if I want to be at my morning meeting on time!

> **"REAL SPEAK":** I fergot my alarm clock, so a'll need a **wake-up call** 'ef I wanna be 'it my morning meeding on time!

ROGER GETS THE INSIDE TRACK!

Sports Terms Used in Business

THIS LESSON FEATURES **15** NEW SLANG WORDS & IDIOMS

LET'S WARM UP!

MATCH THE PICTURES

As a fun way to get started, see if you can guess the meaning of the new slang words and expressions on the opposite page by using the pictures below and following the context of the sentences.

1. You already finished the report? You're **home free** at next week's meeting!
   - ❑ going to win a free house
   - ❑ assured of success

2. Have you heard about the new **game plan**? We're going to make a lot of money next year!
   - ❑ strategy
   - ❑ football slogan

3. I forgot to finish the report last night! I should have **kept my eye on the ball**.
   - ❑ stayed focused
   - ❑ watched basketball on T.V.

4. I used to **bat a thousand** but I've made a lot of mistakes recently.
   - ❑ make a $1,000 a week
   - ❑ be very successful

5. Since Jane left, we've all been **jockeying for position**. I want her old job!
   - ❑ maneuvering ourselves to get an advantage
   - ❑ gambling

6. Valerie missed her meeting with the president. She really **dropped the ball**!
   - ❑ failed to complete her responsibilities
   - ❑ deserves a promotion

7. Dan made the first sale this month. He loves to be **first out of the gate**.
   - ❑ the first person to eat
   - ❑ the first person to start something

8. Joe thought he was getting a raise, but he got fired! He was **way off-base**!
   - ❑ totally wrong
   - ❑ at another building

9. Stewart **calls the shots** since he got promoted.
   - ❑ bought a gun
   - ❑ makes the decisions

10. I want to be a **team player**, but I prefer doing things my way!
    - ❑ person who works well with others
    - ❑ a baseball player

11. Kathy **jumped the gun** and announced her promotion too early!
    - ❑ acted violently
    - ❑ acted prematurely

12. We're **down to the wire** on the project. We have to finish today!
    - ❑ close to the point where the project is due
    - ❑ out of supplies

13. Ned told me to **shape up or ship out**. I need to try harder!
    - ❑ lose weight or take a trip
    - ❑ improve my performance or leave

14. Ed's been selling cars for 30 years. Now he has **the inside track**.
    - ❑ the advantage
    - ❑ the best office

15. Paul **fumbled**! He calculated all of the numbers wrong, and the boss is really angry!
    - ❑ tripped and fell
    - ❑ made a mistake

Sports Terms Used in Business

LET'S TALK!

A. DIALOGUE USING SLANG & IDIOMS

The words introduced on the first two pages are used in the dialogue below. See if you can understand the conversation. *Note:* The translation of the words in boldface is on the right-hand page.

CD-B: TRACK 22

Linda: Did you hear about Roger? He normally **bats a thousand**, but when his project came **down to the wire**, he really **dropped the ball**. I don't **call the shots**, but in my opinion Roger will have to **shape up or ship out**. Management won't tolerate a **fumble** like that.

Tom: You're **way off-base**. Other people are already **jockeying for position**, but I think they're **jumping the gun**. Roger is a **team player**, and if he is **first out of the gate** with a better **game plan**, then he still has **the inside track** for a promotion.

Linda: Maybe you're right. If Roger **keeps his eye on the ball**, he'll be **home free**!

Sports Terms Used in Business

B. DIALOGUE TRANSLATED INTO STANDARD ENGLISH

LET'S SEE HOW MUCH YOU REMEMBER!
Just for fun, move around in random order to the words and
expressions in boldface below. See if you can remember their
slang equivalents without looking at the left-hand page!

Linda: Did you hear about Roger? He normally **is extremely successful**, but when his
project came **very close to the moment when it was due**, he really **failed
to accomplish his responsibilities**. I don't **make the rules**, but in my
opinion Roger will have to **improve his performance or leave the
company**. Management won't tolerate a **mistake** like that.

Tom: You're **totally wrong**. Other people are already **maneuvering themselves
in order to gain an advantage**, but I think they're **acting prematurely**.
Roger is a **person who works well with others**, and if he is **the first
person** with a better **strategy**, then he still has **the advantage** for a promotion.

Linda: Maybe you're right. If Roger **stays focused**, he'll be **assured of attaining his
goals**!

C. DIALOGUE USING "REAL SPEAK"

The dialogue below demonstrates how the slang conversation on the opposite page would *really* be spoken by native speakers!

CD-B: TRACK 22

Linda: Didja hear about Roger? He normally **bats a thouz'nd**, b't when 'is project came **down da the wire**, he really **dropped the ball**. I don't **call the shots**, b'd 'n my opinion Roger'll hafta **shape up 'er ship out**. Management won't tolerade a **fumble** like that.

Tom: Y'r **way off-base**. Other people 'er already **jockeying fer position**, b'd I think they're **jumping the gun**. Roger's a **team player**, an' if 'e's **first oudda the gate** with a bedder **game plan**, then 'e still has **the inside track** fer a pr'motion.

Linda: Maybe y'r right. If Roger **keeps his eye on the ball**, he'll be **home free**!

LET'S LEARN!

VOCABULARY

The following words and expressions were used in the previous dialogues. Let's take a closer look at what they mean.

CD-B: TRACK 23

bat a thousand (to) *exp.* to be extremely successful.

> **EXAMPLE:** Sheila is **batting a thousand** at her new job. She sold more cars than anyone else!
>
> **TRANSLATION:** Sheila is **extremely successful** at her new job. She sold more cars than anyone else!
>
> **"REAL SPEAK":** Sheila's **badding a thouz'nd** ad 'er new job. She sold more cars th'n anyone else!
>
> *Origin:* In baseball, one thousand is a perfect batting percentage, an ideal that is impossible to achieve.
>
> **NOW YOU DO IT:**
> (use "**bat a thousand**" in a sentence)

Sports Terms Used in Business

call the shots (to) *exp.* to be in charge; to make the decisions.

EXAMPLE:	Don't tell me what to do. Mr. Livingston **calls the shots** here, not you!
TRANSLATION:	Don't tell me what to do. Mr. Livingston **is in charge** here, not you!
"REAL SPEAK":	Don't tell me what ta do. Mr. Livingston **calls the shots** here, not you!
Origin:	From pool, where a player announces the target pocket for each shot.
Synonym:	**run the show (to)** *exp.*

NOW YOU DO IT:

(use "**call the shots**" in a sentence)

down to the wire (to be) *exp.* to be very close to the moment when a task is due.

EXAMPLE:	We're **down to the wire**. Everyone has to work late tonight.
TRANSLATION:	We're **very close to the moment when our task is due**. Everyone has to work late tonight.
"REAL SPEAK":	W'r **down da the wire**. Ev'ryone hasta work late t'night.
Origin:	In horse racing, the wire is at the finish line.

NOW YOU DO IT:

(use "**down to the wire**" in a sentence)

drop the ball (to) *exp.* to fail to complete one's responsibilities.

EXAMPLE:	Samantha was supposed to schedule the meeting, but she **dropped the ball** and forgot to do it.
TRANSLATION:	Samantha was supposed to schedule the meeting, but she **failed to complete her responsibilities** and forgot to do it.
"REAL SPEAK":	Samantha w'z suppozed ta schedule the meeding, but she **dropped the ball** an' fergot ta do it.
Origin:	If a player drops the ball during a game, the game must stop until the ball is once again put into play.

NOW YOU DO IT:

(use "**drop the ball**" in a sentence)

Sports Terms Used in Business

first out of the gate (to be) *exp.* to be the first person to begin something.

EXAMPLE: The boss asked for new money-making ideas, and Gary was the **first out of the gate**. He made five suggestions right away.

TRANSLATION: The boss asked for new money-making ideas, and Gary was the **first person to begin**. He made five suggestions right away.

"REAL SPEAK": Th' boss asked fer new money-making ideas, an' Gary w'z the **first oudda the gate**. He made five suggestions ride away.

Origin: In horse racing, this refers to a horse which leaves the starting gate first after the starting signal.

NOW YOU DO IT:

(use "**first out of the gate**" in a sentence)

fumble (to) *v.* to make a mistake.

EXAMPLE: This project is extremely important to the company. We can't afford to **fumble**.

TRANSLATION: This project is extremely important to the company. We can't afford to **make a mistake**.

"REAL SPEAK": This projec's extremely important ta the comp'ny. We can' afford da **fumble**.

Origin: In football, when a player drops the ball during the action, it's called a *fumble*.

NOW YOU DO IT:

(use "**fumble**" in a sentence)

game plan *n.* strategy.

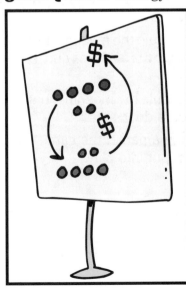

EXAMPLE: We need a good **game plan** if we're going to attract new clients this month.

TRANSLATION: We need a good **strategy** if we're going to attract new clients this month.

"REAL SPEAK": We need a good **game plan** if w'r gonna attract new clients this month.

Origin: In football, this refers to the strategy devised by the coach which dictates the actions for the game.

NOW YOU DO IT:

(use "**game plan**" in a sentence)

Sports Terms Used in Business

home free (to be) *exp.* to be assured of attaining one's goal.

EXAMPLE: Carol worked very hard on this project, so I think we're **home free**.

TRANSLATION: Carol worked very hard on this project, so I think we're **assured of attaining our goals**.

"REAL SPEAK": Car'l worked very hard on this proj'ct, so I think w'r **home free**.

Origin: In baseball, said of a player who is certain to reach home base and score a point.

NOW YOU DO IT:

(use "**home free**" in a sentence)

inside track (to have the) *exp.* to have the advantage.

EXAMPLE: Mathew **has the inside track** for getting a promotion because he's good friends with the president.

TRANSLATION: Mathew **has the advantage** for getting a promotion because he's good friends with the president.

"REAL SPEAK": Mathew **has the inside track** fer gedding a pr'motion b'cuz 'e's good frenz w'th the president.

Origin: In track and field, the runner on the inside track has an advantage over the others because he or she has the shortest distance to run.

NOW YOU DO IT:

(use "**have the inside track**" in a sentence)

jockey for position (to) *exp.* to maneuver oneself in order to gain an advantage.

EXAMPLE: Todd and Ian are always **jockeying for position**. They should concentrate more on doing their jobs than on getting promoted!

TRANSLATION: Todd and Ian are always **maneuvering themselves in order to gain an advantage**. They should concentrate more on doing their jobs than on getting promoted!

"REAL SPEAK": Todd 'n Ian 'er ahweez **jockeying fer position**. They should concentrate more on doing their jobs th'n on gedding pr'moded!

Origin: In horse racing, jockeys maneuver their horses in an attempt to gain a better position in the race.

NOW YOU DO IT:

(use "**jockey for position**" in a sentence)

Sports Terms Used in Business

jump the gun (to) *exp.* to act prematurely.

EXAMPLE: Michael started celebrating before he got the promotion. He shouldn't have **jumped the gun**!

TRANSLATION: Michael started celebrating before he got the promotion. He shouldn't have **acted prematurely**!

"REAL SPEAK": Michael starded celebrating b'fore 'e got the pr'motion. He shouldn'ev **jumped the gun**!

Origin: In track and field, said of a runner who starts running before the traditional starting gun is fired.

NOW YOU DO IT:

(use "**jump the gun**" in a sentence)

keep one's eye on the ball (to) *exp.* to stay focused on the task one is performing.

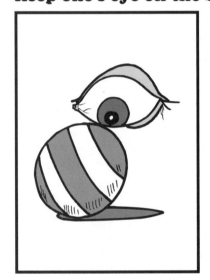

EXAMPLE: Sharon has a lot of projects to complete, so she needs to **keep her eye on the ball**.

TRANSLATION: Sharon has a lot of projects to complete, so she needs to **stay focused on the task she is performing**.

"REAL SPEAK": Sharon has a lodda projects ta complete, so she needs ta **keep 'er eye on the ball**.

Origin: In baseball, a batter who watches the ball closely has the best chance of hitting it.

NOW YOU DO IT:

(use "**keep your eye on the ball**" in a sentence)

off-base (to be [way]) *exp.* to be totally wrong.

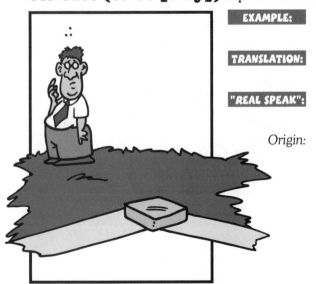

EXAMPLE: Frank said we'd be profitable in two months, but he was **way off-base**! It will take us two years to make a profit.

TRANSLATION: Frank said we'd be profitable in two months, but he was **totally wrong**! It will take us two years to make a profit.

"REAL SPEAK": Frank said we'd be profidable 'n two munts, b'd 'e w'z **way off-base**! Id'll take us two years ta make a profit.

Origin: In baseball, a player who is not touching a base (*off-base*) is vulnerable to being tagged out.

NOW YOU DO IT.

(use "**off base**" in a sentence)

shape up or ship out (to) *exp.* to improve one's performance or leave the company.

> **EXAMPLE:** Brad slept through another meeting. The boss told him to **shape up or ship out**.
>
> **TRANSLATION:** Brad slept through another meeting. The boss told him to **improve his performance or leave the company**.
>
> **"REAL SPEAK":** Brad slept through another meeding. The boss told 'im da **shape up 'er ship out**.
>
> **NOW YOU DO IT:**
> (use "**shape up or ship out**" in a sentence)

team player *n.* a person who works well with others.

> **EXAMPLE:** William is a **team player**. He enjoys working with other people, and everyone thinks he's a great person.
>
> **TRANSLATION:** William is a **person who works well with others**. He enjoys working with other people, and everyone thinks he's a great person.
>
> **"REAL SPEAK":** William's a **team player**. He enjoys working w'th other people, 'n ev'ryone thinks 'e's a great person.
>
> *Origin:* In general sports, *team players* value the team's success more than their own success.
>
> *Note:* In the business world, groups of employees are often referred to as *teams*. The use of this word is supposed to instill a feeling of cooperation and loyalty among the members of the *team*.
>
> **NOW YOU DO IT:**
> (use "**team player**" in a sentence)

Sports Terms Used in Business

LET'S PRACTICE!

A. CORRECT OR INCORRECT?

Decide if the words in boldface have been used correctly or incorrectly by checking the appropriate box.

CD-B: TRACK 24

1. I always **jockey for position** when I exercise.
   ❑ CORRECT   ❑ INCORRECT

2. Maureen **fumbled** when she made an insulting remark in front of his wife!
   ❑ CORRECT   ❑ INCORRECT

3. I always have **the inside track** because I like to drive very fast.
   ❑ CORRECT   ❑ INCORRECT

4. I like to **call the shots** because I'm allergic to alcohol.
   ❑ CORRECT   ❑ INCORRECT

5. Evan **jumped the gun** and bought a new house before his raise was approved!
   ❑ CORRECT   ❑ INCORRECT

6. I'm a **team player** which is why I'm always assigned to projects by myself.
   ❑ CORRECT   ❑ INCORRECT

7. If you have a lot of tasks, just **keep your eye on the ball** until they're all finished.
   ❑ CORRECT   ❑ INCORRECT

8. I've made so many mistakes this year that I'm **batting a thousand**!
   ❑ CORRECT   ❑ INCORRECT

9. Take this package **down to the wire** and mail it.
   ❑ CORRECT   ❑ INCORRECT

10. I'm **home free** on this project because I already finished most of the work.
    ❑ CORRECT   ❑ INCORRECT

11. What's your **game plan** for getting a promotion?
    ❑ CORRECT   ❑ INCORRECT

12. My brother wants to join the Navy. I told him to **shape up or ship out**.
    ❑ CORRECT   ❑ INCORRECT

13. If Brandon **drops the ball** again, I'll get promoted instead of him!
    ❑ CORRECT   ❑ INCORRECT

14. I'm usually the **first out of the gate** because I'm always late.
    ❑ CORRECT   ❑ INCORRECT

15. Trisha wants a promotion. Now she's going **off base** to buy a present for the boss.
    ❑ CORRECT   ❑ INCORRECT

Sports Terms Used in Business

B. BLANK-BLANK

Fill in the blank in Column A with the correct word or phrase from Column B. Each answer can only be used once.

COLUMN A	COLUMN B
1. Ted was supposed to write the report, but he went home instead. He really _____!	**shape up or ship out**
2. The boss isn't sure who to hire for the project, so Jason and David are both _____.	**down to the wire**
3. I love working with Sally because she's a _____ _____. We always complete our work on time.	**team player**
4. Brendan was late for work again, so I told him he'd better _____!	**batting a thousand**
5. We need to be _____ with new products for the computer market.	**jumped the gun**
6. I don't want to _____. It's too stressful to make all the decisions.	**inside track**
7. We have to work all night because we're _____ on this project!	**fumbled**
8. I have a good _____ for making more money. I'm going to advertise in all the local newspapers.	**dropped the ball**
9. I only have another five minutes of work left to do on my report. I'm _____!	**jockeying for position**
10. I'm friends with the boss' wife, so I have the _____ for getting a bonus at Christmas.	**call the shots**
11. Daryl wants to buy more computers, but I think he's _____. We should fix the ones we have first.	**home free**
12. Hannah _____ last week when she skipped an important meeting to have lunch with her mother.	**game plan**
13. Patrick sold another six cars today. He's been _____ lately!	**way off base**
14. Rick _____ and hired Kelly before the boss gave her approval.	**first out of the gate**

Sports Terms Used in Business

C. TRUE OR FALSE

Decide whether or not the definition of the words in boldface
is true or false by checking an "X" in the correct box.

CD-B: TRACK 26

1. **fumble (to)** *v.* to drop papers or supplies on the floor, usually after tripping.
   ❏ TRUE ❏ FALSE

2. **team player** *n.* a person who works well with others.
   ❏ TRUE ❏ FALSE

3. **off base (to be [way])** *exp.* to get lost while trying to follow directions.
   ❏ TRUE ❏ FALSE

4. **jump the gun (to)** *exp.* to act prematurely.
   ❏ TRUE ❏ FALSE

5. **home free (to be)** *exp.* to be assured of success.
   ❏ TRUE ❏ FALSE

6. **inside track (to have the)** *exp.* to own the best car, suit, or office.
   ❏ TRUE ❏ FALSE

7. **bat a thousand (to)** *exp.* to be extremely successful.
   ❏ TRUE ❏ FALSE

8. **game plan** *n.* rules for playing games such as chess and checkers.
   ❏ TRUE ❏ FALSE

9. **call the shots (to)** *exp.* to make the decisions.
   ❏ TRUE ❏ FALSE

10. **keep one's eye on the ball (to)** *exp.* to stay focused.
    ❏ TRUE ❏ FALSE

11. **drop the ball (to)** *exp.* to fail to complete one's responsibilities.
    ❏ TRUE ❏ FALSE

12. **jockey for position (to)** *exp.* to wear bright silk clothes in order to get promoted.
    ❏ TRUE ❏ FALSE

13. **down to the wire (to be)** *exp.* to be close to the time when a task is due.
    ❏ TRUE ❏ FALSE

14. **first out of the gate (to be)** *exp.* to be the first person to exit an airplane.
    ❏ TRUE ❏ FALSE

15. **shape up or ship out (to)** *exp.* to improve one's performance or leave the company.
    ❏ TRUE ❏ FALSE

Sports Terms Used in Business

More Sports Terms Used in Business

Since sports are such an important part of American culture, it's not surprising that sports terms and expressions have become part of our everyday speech. Without knowledge of this jargon, you're clearly at a disadvantage in any business negotiation. Now the **ball's in your court** (*it's up to you*) — if you **dive right in** (*begin immediately*) and study the following list, you'll surely **clear a big hurdle** (*overcome a big obstacle*) and **hit a home run** (*become extremely successful*) in your next meeting or negotiation!

ball in one's court (to have the) *exp.* to be responsible for taking the next action.

> **EXAMPLE:** I told our potential client how much it would cost him to hire us for the project. Now **the ball's in his court**.

> **TRANSLATION:** I told our potential client how much it would cost him to hire us for the project. Now **he's responsible for taking the next action**.

> **"REAL SPEAK":** I told 'ar patential client how much it would cost 'im da hire us fer the project. Now **the ball's 'n his court**.

> *Origin:* In tennis, players take their turn when the ball is in their court (on their side of the net).

ballpark figure *exp.* an estimate.

> **EXAMPLE:** I don't have the actual numbers, but I can give you a **ballpark figure**.

> **TRANSLATION:** I don't have the actual numbers, but I can give you an **estimate**.

> **"REAL SPEAK":** I don'ave the actual numbers, b'd I c'n give you a **ballpark figure**.

blow the whistle on someone (to) *exp.* to inform on someone.

> **EXAMPLE:** Karen saw John stealing office supplies, so she **blew the whistle** on him and got him fired.

> **TRANSLATION:** Karen saw John stealing office supplies, so she **informed on him** and got him fired.

> **"REAL SPEAK":** Karen saw John stealing office supplies, so she **blew the whistle** on 'im 'n god 'im fired.

> *Origin:* In many sports, the referee blows a whistle to indicate an illegal play.

> *Also:* **whistle-blower** *n.* an informant (*see p. 66*).

bounce something off someone (to) *exp.* to test someone's reaction to an idea.

> **EXAMPLE:** I need to find a solution to my problem. Can I **bounce some ideas off you**?

TRANSLATION: I need to find a solution to my problem. Can I **test your reaction to some ideas**?

"REAL SPEAK": I need da find a solution ta my problem. C'n I **bounce s'm ideas off ya**?

Origin: When a ball is thrown at a wall it bounces back, just like an idea that is presented to another person bounces back with that person's opinion.

clear a hurdle (to) *exp.* to overcome an obstacle.

EXAMPLE: Rachel hates talking in public. She really **cleared a hurdle** when she gave that speech yesterday.

TRANSLATION: Rachel hates talking in public. She really **overcame an obstacle** when she gave that speech yesterday.

"REAL SPEAK": Rachel hates talking 'n public. She really **cleared a hurdle** when she gave that speech yesterday.

Origin: In track and field, a runner who jumps over a hurdle without knocking it over is said to clear the hurdle.

come in a close second (to) *exp.* to be the second choice for something by a very small margin.

EXAMPLE: We chose Adam's company to be our supplier, but Martha's company **came in a close second**.

TRANSLATION: We chose Adam's company to be our supplier, but Martha's company **was the second choice by a very small margin**.

"REAL SPEAK": We chose Adam's comp'ny da be 'ar supplier, b't Martha's comp'ny **came in a close second**.

Origin: In track and field, a competitor who fails to win the race by a small margin comes in a close second.

come out of left field (to) *exp.* to be completely unexpected.

EXAMPLE: Hilary's promotion **came out of left field**. She just started working here two weeks ago!

TRANSLATION: Hilary's promotion **was completely unexpected**. She just started working here two weeks ago!

"REAL SPEAK": Hilary's pr'motion **came oudda lef' field**. She jus' starded working here two weeks ago!

dive [right] in (to) *exp.* to begin a task immediately.

EXAMPLE: We don't have time to train you. You'll have to **dive right in**.

TRANSLATION: We don't have time to train you. You'll have to **begin the task immediately**.

"REAL SPEAK": We don'ave time da train you. You'll hafta **dive ride in**.

Origin: In swimming, to dive into the water without hesitation.

even keel (to be on an) *exp.* to be steady and well-balanced.

> **EXAMPLE:** Last week, Debbie and Bill were fighting, but this week they're **on an even keel**.
>
> **TRANSLATION:** Last week, Debbie and Bill were fighting, but this week they're **steady and well-balanced**.
>
> **"REAL SPEAK":** Las' week, Debbie 'n Bill were fiding, b't this week they're **on 'n even keel**.
>
> *Origin:* In sailing, the keel is the bottom part of the boat which runs from the front to the back, whose function is to balance the boat.

field [a call] (to) *exp.* to answer a telephone call intended for someone else.

> **EXAMPLE:** Georgia had to **field a call** while her boss was at a doctor's appointment.

> **TRANSLATION:** Georgia had to **answer a telephone call** while her boss was at a doctor's appointment.
>
> **"REAL SPEAK":** Georgia had da **field a call** while 'er boss w'z ad a docter's appointment.
>
> *Origin:* In baseball, to catch a ball hit after being into the outfield and throw it back to the appropriate person.

free rein (to have) *exp.* to be allowed to do anything you want without having to get permission.

> **EXAMPLE:** In my new job, I **have free rein** to hire any assistant I want.

> **TRANSLATION:** In my new job, I **am allowed** to hire any assistant I want **without having to get permission**.
>
> **"REAL SPEAK":** In my new job, I **have free rein** da hire any assistant I want.
>
> *Origin:* In horse racing, when a horse's reins are pulled back, the horse slows down. But when the reins are completely loose, the horse is free to move as quickly as it can.

get one's feet wet (to) *exp.* to begin slowly.

> **EXAMPLE:** Donna wants to work at our London office, but I think she should **get her feet wet** in Baltimore first.
>
> **TRANSLATION:** Donna wants to work at our London office, but I think she should **begin slowly** in Baltimore first.
>
> **"REAL SPEAK":** Donna wants ta work 'id 'ar London office, b'd I think she should **ged 'er feet wet** 'n Baltimore first.
>
> *Origin:* In swimming, it's common to test the water first before jumping in.

get the ball rolling (to) *exp.* to begin.

> **EXAMPLE:** We don't have much time, so let's **get the ball rolling** as soon as possible.
>
> **TRANSLATION:** We don't have much time, so let's **begin** as soon as possible.
>
> **"REAL SPEAK":** We don'ave much time, so let's **get the ball rolling** 'ez soon 'ez possible.

go a few rounds with someone (to) *exp.* to argue for a while with someone.

> **EXAMPLE:** Carol and Bill couldn't agree on the project strategy, but after **going a few rounds**, they finally decided what to do.
>
> **TRANSLATION:** Carol and Bill couldn't agree on the project strategy, but after **arguing for a while**, they finally decided what to do.

Sports Terms Used in Business

"REAL SPEAK": Carol 'n Bill couldn' agree on the project stradegy, b'd after **going a few rounds**, they fin'lly decided what ta do.

Origin: In boxing, the match is divided into rounds.

go down with the ship (to) *exp.* to stay with a project or company until it collapses.

EXAMPLE: The company isn't doing well. I think it's time to look for a new job or **go down with the ship**.

TRANSLATION: The company isn't doing well. I think it's time to look for a new job or **stay with the company until it collapses**.

"REAL SPEAK": The comp'ny isn' doing well. I think it's time da look fer a new job 'er **go down w'th the ship**.

Origin: In the Maritime tradition, a captain stayed on his ship even when it was sinking.

good track record (to have a) *exp.* to have a personal history of being successful and experienced.

EXAMPLE: I think we should hire Shelley for the job. She has a **good track record** in this type of work.

TRANSLATION: I think we should hire Shelley for the job. She has a **personal history of being successful and experienced** in this type of work.

"REAL SPEAK": I think we should hire Shelley fer the job. She 'as a **good track record** 'n this type 'a work.

hard to call (to be) *exp.* to be difficult to determine.

EXAMPLE: It's **hard to call** whether Tony or Laurie would make a better boss. They both have a lot of great qualities.

TRANSLATION: It's **difficult to determine** whether Tony or Laurie would make a better boss. They both have a lot of great qualities.

"REAL SPEAK": It's **hard da call** whether Tony 'er Laurie 'ed make a bedder boss. They both have a lodda great qualidies.

Origin: In many sports, a play which has no obvious ruling is considered *hard to call* by the referee.

Also: **make the call (to)** *exp.* to make a difficult decision.

heavyweight *n.* an important and powerful person.

EXAMPLE: Marcus controls our whole department and the president listens to everything he says. He's a real **heavyweight**.

TRANSLATION: Marcus controls our whole department and the president listens to everything he says. He's a real **important and powerful person**.

Sports Terms Used in Business

"REAL SPEAK": Marcus controls 'ar whole department an' the president listens ta ev'rything 'e says. He's a real **heavyweight**.

Origin: In boxing, a boxer whose weight puts him in the largest category, heavyweights.

Antonym: **lightweight** *n.*

hit a home run (to) *exp.* to achieve a great success.

EXAMPLE: The client loved Peter's work and wants him to do their next project, too. He really **hit a home run**.

TRANSLATION: The client loved Peter's work and wants him to do their next project, too. He really **achieved a great success**.

"REAL SPEAK": The client loved Peder's work 'n wants 'im da do their nex' project, too. He really **hid a home run**.

Origin: In baseball, a home run is a type of hit that allows the batter to score a point (call a *run* in baseball jargon).

huddle (to) *v.* to have a private meeting.

EXAMPLE: Let's **huddle** before the big meeting. We need to plan our strategy.

TRANSLATION: Let's **have a private meeting** before the big meeting. We need to plan our strategy.

"REAL SPEAK": Let's **huddle** b'fore the big meeding. We need da plan 'ar stradegy.

Origin: In football, the players form a tight circle (known as a huddle) to discuss strategy for the upcoming play.

in deep water (to be) *exp.* to be in big trouble.

EXAMPLE: Daniel is **in deep water** because he couldn't answer any of the boss' questions in the meeting this morning.

TRANSLATION: Daniel is **in big trouble** because he couldn't answer any of the boss' questions in the meeting this morning.

"REAL SPEAK": Daniel's **'n deep wadder** b'cuz 'e couldn' answer any 'a the boss' questions 'n the meeding th's morning.

Origin: In swimming, a swimmer in deep water risks exhaustion and drowning because there is no place to rest.

in the ballpark (to be) *exp.* to be within acceptable limits.

EXAMPLE: The sale price isn't as low as we wanted, but it's **in the ballpark**.

TRANSLATION: The sale price isn't as low as we wanted, but it's **within acceptable limits**.

"REAL SPEAK": The sale price isn'ez low 'ez we wan'ed, b'd it's **'n the ballpark**.

Origin: In baseball, a ball that is hit, but doesn't leave the stadium, is said to be *in the ballpark*.

in the homestretch (to be) *exp.* to be close to completion.

EXAMPLE: We're **in the homestretch**! Just one more night of working late and we'll be finished.

TRANSLATION: We're **close to completion**! Just one more night of working late and we'll be finished.

Sports Terms Used in Business

"REAL SPEAK": W'r **'n the homestretch**! Jus' one more night 'ev working late 'n we'll be finished.

Origin: In horse racing, the *homestretch* is the final distance the horses must cross to reach the finish line.

in the same league as someone or something (to be) *exp.* to be at the same level as someone (in skill, beauty, rank, etc.).

EXAMPLE: I'm not **in the same league as Phil**. He's got a lot of experience and I'm new to this type of work.

TRANSLATION: I'm not **at the same level as Phil**. He's got a lot of experience and I'm new to this type of work.

"REAL SPEAK": I'm nod **in the same league 'ez Phil**. He's god a lod 'ev experience 'n I'm new da this type 'a work.

Origin: In many sports, there is a hierarchy of levels, or leagues. A team only plays other teams in its own league.

jump off the deep end (to) *exp.* to go crazy.

EXAMPLE: After working in a stressful job for ten years, Al **jumped off the deep end**.

TRANSLATION: After working in a stressful job for ten years, Al **went crazy**.

"REAL SPEAK": After working in a stressful job fer ten years, Al **jumped off the deep end**.

Origin: In swimming, when a swimmer jumps into the deep end of the pool, he or she has no way of knowing how deep it is and, consequently, the full extent of the risk.

Synonym: **go off the deep end (to)** *exp.*

left at the gate (to be) *exp.* to be surpassed by a large margin.

EXAMPLE: Mark was **left at the gate** when Sally sold five cars before he sold even one.

TRANSLATION: Mark was **surpassed by a large margin** when Sally sold five cars before he sold even one.

"REAL SPEAK": Mark w'z **left 'it the gate** wh'n Sally sold five cars b'fore 'e sold even one.

Origin: In horse racing, any horse that doesn't leave the starting gate with the others has been left at the gate.

Synonym: **left in the dust (to be)** *exp.*

make a splash (to) *exp.* to become very successful (and get a lot of attention).

EXAMPLE: I hear Sally **made a splash** in the marketing department with her great new ideas.

TRANSLATION: I hear Sally **became very successful** in the marketing department with her great new ideas.

"REAL SPEAK": I hear Sally **made a splash** 'n the markeding department with 'er great new ideas.

Origin: In swimming, someone who jumps into the water and makes a big splash gains attention.

neck and neck (to be) *exp.* to be even in a contest.

EXAMPLE: Samuel and Ramone are **neck and neck**. It's hard to say which one of them will be promoted first.

TRANSLATION: Samuel and Ramone are **even in the contest**. It's hard to say which one of them will be promoted first.

"REAL SPEAK": Samuel 'n Ramone 'er **neck 'n neck**. It's hard da say which one 'ev 'em'll be pr'moded first.

Origin: In horse racing, two horses that are running at the same speed are said to be neck and neck.

pace oneself (to) *exp.* to adjust one's speed in order to have enough energy to accomplish the entire task.

EXAMPLE: Vince has been working late every day for the last month. He should **pace himself**. There's still a lot to do!

TRANSLATION: Vince has been working late every day for the last month. He should **adjust his speed in order to have enough energy to accomplish the entire task**. There's still a lot to do!

"REAL SPEAK": Vince's been working lade ev'ry day fer the last month. He should **pace 'imself**. There's still a lot ta do!

Origin: In track and field, runners must run fast enough to win but slow enough not to exhaust themselves. This is called *pacing*.

pinch hit (to) *exp.* to take someone's place.

EXAMPLE: Jane is sick. Ryan will have to **pinch hit** for her in today's meeting.

TRANSLATION: Jane is sick. Ryan will have to **take her place** for her in today's meeting.

"REAL SPEAK": Jane's sick. Ryan'll hafta **pinch hit** fer her in taday's meeding.

Origin: In baseball, a player who replaces a less capable player at bat during a critical point of the game.

play by the rules (to) *exp.* to conduct oneself without breaking the rules, either legally or ethically.

EXAMPLE: James will lie in order to get a promotion, but I like to **play by the rules**.

TRANSLATION: James will lie in order to get a promotion, but I like to **conduct myself without breaking the rules**.

"REAL SPEAK": James'll lie 'n order da ged a pr'motion, b'd I like ta **play by the rules**.

Origin: Every sport has rules under which the team members must play, or they risk being disqualified.

Synonym: **play fair (to)** *exp.*

referee (to) *v.* to mediate between two or more people.

EXAMPLE: Dennis and Liz need to work together without fighting. I won't always be here to **referee** them.

TRANSLATION: Dennis and Liz need to work together without fighting. I won't always be here to **mediate between** them.

"REAL SPEAK": Dennis 'n Liz need da work tagether w'thout fiding. I won' ahweez be here da **referee** th'm.

right off the bat *exp.* instantly.

EXAMPLE: I didn't like Neal **right off the bat**. He started telling me what to do on his first day!

TRANSLATION: I didn't like Neal **instantly**. He started telling me what to do on his first day!

"REAL SPEAK": I didn' like Neal **ride off the bat**. He starded telling me what ta do on 'is firs' day!

Origin: In baseball, when the ball comes in direct contact with the bat, it is sent forward in an instant.

right out of the chute (to be) *exp.* to be inexperienced.

EXAMPLE: Don't ask Rebecca for the answer. She's **right out of the chute** and doesn't know anything yet.

TRANSLATION: Don't ask Rebecca for the answer. She's **inexperienced** and doesn't know anything yet.

"REAL SPEAK": Don' ask Rebecca fer the answer. She's **ride oudda the chute** 'n doesn' know anything yet.

Origin: In horse racing, a horse that speeds out of the starting gate is said to be *right out of the chute.*

roll with the punches (to) *exp.* to accept something unpleasant without fighting back.

EXAMPLE: I know the boss is always mean to you, but just try to **roll with the punches**. He's retiring in just one more week.

TRANSLATION: I know the boss is always mean to you, but just try to **accept it without fighting back**. He's retiring in just one more week.

"REAL SPEAK": I know the boss 'ez ahweez mean da you, b't jus' try da **roll w'th the punches**. He's retiring 'n jus' one more week.

Origin: In boxing, if a boxer *rolls with the punches* (literally, "to allow one's body to move in the direction of the punches without resisting"), he is less likely to get hurt.

rough seas ahead (to have) *exp.* to have many difficulties and challenges in the near future.

EXAMPLE: Our company has **rough seas ahead**. If we don't make enough money this year, we'll have to close.

TRANSLATION: Our company has **many difficulties and challenges in the near future**. If we don't make enough money this year, we'll have to close.

"REAL SPEAK": 'Ar comp'ny has **rough seas ahead**. If we don't make anuf money this year, we'll hafta close.

run interference for someone (to) *exp.* to block a potential problem from going to someone else.

EXAMPLE: I'm going to **run interference for Monica** because the boss is angry at her. If I talk to him first, maybe he'll relax.

TRANSLATION: I'm going to **block a potential problem from going to Monica** because the boss is angry at her. If I talk to him first, maybe he'll relax.

"REAL SPEAK": I'm gonna **run innerference fer Monica** b'cuz the boss 'ez angry ad 'er. If I talk to 'im first, maybe he'll relax.

Origin: In football, players who run interference stop their teammates from being tackled by the opposing team.

run with the ball (to) *exp.* to assume responsibility with great enthusiasm.

EXAMPLE: The boss gave me a new assignment and I'm going to **run with the ball**.

TRANSLATION: The boss gave me a new assignment and I'm going to **assume responsibility with great enthusiasm**.

"REAL SPEAK": The boss gay me a new assignment an' I'm gonna **run w'th the ball**.

Sports Terms Used in Business

saved by the bell (to be) *exp.* to get out of a bad situation due to luck.

> **EXAMPLE:** The boss was just about to yell at me when he got called into a meeting. I was **saved by the bell**!

> **TRANSLATION:** The boss was just about to yell at me when he got called into a meeting. I was **saved from a bad situation due to luck**!

> **"REAL SPEAK":** The boss w'z just about ta yell 'it me when 'e got called into a meeding. I w'z **saved by the bell**!

> *Origin:* In boxing, the moment the bell rings, the boxers must stop fighting. For the losing boxer, he is often saved from getting more injuries.

score (to) *exp.* to make a favorable impression; to succeed.

> **EXAMPLE:** Heather **scored** with the boss by completing her project two weeks early.

> **TRANSLATION:** Heather **made a favorable impression** with the boss by completing her project two weeks early.

> **"REAL SPEAK":** Heather **scored** w'th the boss by compleding 'er project two weeks early.

> *Also:* **score big [time] (to)** *exp.*

> *Also:* **score points (to)** *exp.*

sink or swim (to) *exp.* to fail or succeed.

> **EXAMPLE:** You'll either **sink or swim** at this company. If you sell enough computers, you'll make a lot of money. If you don't sell enough, you'll get fired.

> **TRANSLATION:** You'll either **fail or succeed** at this company. If you sell enough computers, you'll make a lot of money. If you don't sell enough, you'll get fired.

> **"REAL SPEAK":** You'll either **sink 'er swim** 'it this comp'ny. If ya sell anuf compuders, you'll make a lodda money. If ya don't sell anuf, you'll get fired.

> *Origin:* In swimming, if one doesn't try to swim, one sinks and drowns.

skating on thin ice (to be) *exp.* to be in a risky situation.

> **EXAMPLE:** I'm **skating on thin ice**. If I'm late to work one more time, I'll be fired!

> **TRANSLATION:** I'm **in a risky situation**. If I'm late to work one more time, I'll be fired!

> **"REAL SPEAK":** I'm **skading on thin ice**. If I'm late ta work one more time, a'll be fired!

> *Origin:* In skating, a skater must always be careful not to skate on thin ice or he/she risks falling through it.

smooth sailing (to be) *exp.* to be easy.

> **EXAMPLE:** The most difficult part of this project is over. It will be **smooth sailing** from now on.

> **TRANSLATION:** The most difficult part of this project is over. It will be **easy** from now on.

> **"REAL SPEAK":** The mos' difficult pard 'ev this project 'ez over. Id'll be **smooth sailing** fr'm now on.

strike out (to) *exp.* to fail.

> **EXAMPLE:** Every time Edward asks the boss for a raise, he **strikes out**.

> **TRANSLATION:** Every time Edward asks the boss for a raise, he **fails**.

> **"REAL SPEAK":** Ev'ry time Edward asks the boss fer a raise, he **strikes out**.

> *Origin:* In baseball, this refers to a player who misses the ball three times and earns an *out* for his team.

> *Also:* **"Three strikes and you're out!"** *exp.* "If you make three mistakes, you don't get any more chances!"

Origin: In football, when a player gets the ball, he must run as fast as possible.

tackle a problem (to) *exp.* to try aggressively to solve a problem.

> **EXAMPLE:** We need to **tackle this problem**. It's costing us money every day!
>
> **TRANSLATION:** We need to **try aggressively to solve this problem**. It's costing us money every day!
>
> **"REAL SPEAK":** We need da **tackle this problem**. It's costing us money ev'ry day!

> *Origin:* In football, a player who tackles a member of the opposing team removes that person (who could be a problem) from the action.

take a time out (to) *exp.* to stop the proceedings momentarily.

> **EXAMPLE:** Brad needs to research some numbers. Let's **take a time out** and meet again when he's ready.
>
> **TRANSLATION:** Brad needs to research some numbers. Let's **stop the proceedings momentarily** and meet again when he's ready.
>
> **"REAL SPEAK":** Brad needs da research s'm numbers. Let's **take a time out** 'n meed again when 'e's ready.
>
> *Origin:* In many sports, calling a time out stops the game for a short time so that the team may rest or discuss strategy.

> *Note:* Parents commonly give their misbehaving children a *time out*, which is a period of time when the children are made to be still and quiet in an effort to get them to calm down.

take the wind out of one's sails (to) *exp.* to cause someone to lose his or her enthusiasm.

> **EXAMPLE:** Lorraine was almost finished with the project when the boss added six more tasks. That really **took the wind out of her sails**.
>
> **TRANSLATION:** Lorraine was almost finished with the project when the boss added six more tasks. That really **caused her to lose her enthusiasm**.
>
> **"REAL SPEAK":** Lorraine w'z almos' finished w'th the project when the boss added six more tasks. That really **took the wind oud 'ev 'er sails**.
>
> *Origin:* In sailing, a sailboat loses speed when it has no wind to propel it.

test the water (to) *exp.* to examine something more closely before proceeding.

> **EXAMPLE:** We need to **test the water** on this new product before we start selling it.
>
> **TRANSLATION:** We need to **examine** this new product more closely before we start selling it.
>
> **"REAL SPEAK":** We need da **test the wadder** on this new product b'fore we start selling it.
>
> *Origin:* In swimming, people often test the temperature of the water before they dive in.

throw someone a curve (to) *exp.* (short for "to throw someone a curve ball") to surprise someone, usually in a negative way.

> **EXAMPLE:** The boss really **threw me a curve** when he asked about my family. We've only talked about the company before!
>
> **TRANSLATION:** The boss really **surprised me** when he asked about my family. We've only talked about the company before!

"REAL SPEAK": The boss really **threw me a curve** when 'e ast' about my fam'ly. We've only talked about the comp'ny b'fore!

Origin: In baseball, when the pitcher throws a ball that curves unexpectedly, it makes the ball harder to hit.

throw in the towel (to) *exp.* to quit.

EXAMPLE: I can't keep working so many hours. I'm going to **throw in the towel** if this doesn't stop.

TRANSLATION: I can't keep working so many hours. I'm going to **quit** if this doesn't stop.

"REAL SPEAK": I can't keep working so many hours. I'm gonna **throw 'n the towel** 'ef this doesn' stop.

Origin: In boxing, the manager of the losing boxer throws a towel into the ring to signify defeat and stop the fight.

touch base with someone (to) *exp.* to make contact with someone.

EXAMPLE: I need to **touch base with Gary** before we go to lunch. I need to ask him a few questions about the meeting this morning.

TRANSLATION: I need to **contact Gary** in order to exchange information before we go to lunch. I need to ask him a few questions about the meeting this morning.

"REAL SPEAK": I need da **touch base w'th Gary** b'fore we go da lunch. I need da ask 'im a few questions about the meeding th's morning.

Origin: In baseball, the runner must make contact with each base in order to score a point.

ANSWERS TO LESSONS 1-10

LESSON 1 - KYLE'S MAKING BIG BUCKS

LET'S WARM UP!

1. work routine
2. working day and night
3. boss
4. a lot of money
5. trying to earn the favor of
6. trespassed into shelley's area of authority
7. a bar with after-work specials
8. getting promoted
9. a small amount of money
10. work very hard

LET'S PRACTICE!

A. CHOOSE THE RIGHT WORD

1. bucks
2. nosed
3. chicken
4. climb
5. daily
6. happy
7. down
8. toes
9. dog
10. clock

B. CONTEXT EXERCISE

1. doesn't make sense
2. makes sense
3. doesn't make sense
4. doesn't make sense
5. makes sense
6. makes sense
7. doesn't make sense
8. doesn't make sense
9. makes sense

C. CREATE YOUR OWN SENTENCE (SUGGESTIONS FOR ANSWERS)

1. Let's go to happy hour and have a drink!
2. I make chicken feed.
3. Because she brown nosed the boss.
4. He's really climbing the corporate ladder!
5. Yes! I want to make big bucks!
6. Then you'd better knuckle down!
7. Because she's top dog.
8. He's been working around the clock on a project.
9. She's been stepping on my toes a lot lately.
10. Yes! I'm very tired of the daily grind.

D. COMPLETE THE PHRASE

1. grind
2. top
3. feed
4. knuckle
5. toes
6. brown
7. ladder
8. hour
9. clock

LESSON TWO - DEBBIE TALKS SHOP

LET'S WARM UP!

1. talking about work
2. hasty decision
3. general guideline
4. improvising
5. became proficient at
6. gave me some advice
7. in summary
8. thinking about the problem carefully
9. made himself appear more competent than Paul
10. time allotted for eating lunch

LET'S PRACTICE!

A. FIND THE MISSING WORDS

Ken: Do you have time to talk **shop**? I've been going over the information in my **head**, but I just can't get the **hang** of this new procedure. Do you have time to give me **pointers**?

Shelley: Sure, no problem. Okay. As a **rule** of thumb, you should always think before you speak, don't make any **snap** judgments when talking to clients, don't **show up** the other employees by making them look foolish in front of the client, and don't take your lunch **break** when you're scheduled to have a meeting. That's the new procedure in a **nutshell**.

Ken: Guess I can't just fly by the **seat** of my pants anymore. Thanks!

B. CREATE YOUR OWN NEWSPAPER COLUMN

Remember, be as creative as your own imagination!

C. MATCH THE SENTENCES

1. E	5. J	9. C	
2. F	6. H	10. I	
3. G	7. D		
4. A	8. B		

LESSON THREE – LISA GETS A FAIR SHAKE

LET'S WARM UP!

1. E	5. A	9. D	
2. C	6. J	10. I	
3. F	7. H		
4. G	8. B		

LET'S PRACTICE!

A. WHAT DOES IT MEAN?

1. someone or something outdated

2. to become violently angry

3. a new employee

4. to do most of the work

5. to give someone an opportunity to succeed

6. a group of traditionally-minded executives

7. a company's mood

8. a day when employees are allowed to wear casual clothes

9. to update one's résumé

10. an Internet company

B. COMPLETE THE FAIRY TALE

Once upon a time, there was a young girl named Cinderella who moved to the big city. Unfortunately, she had no idea how expensive rent and cost of living were and needed to find a good-paying job right away, so she quickly _____polished_____ her résumé.

The next morning, Cinderella got her first job interview with a dot **com**. Just as she was ready to leave, she stopped suddenly, looked down at her clothes, and began to cry. "I can't go to a job interview dressed in these old clothes," she thought. "And I can't afford to buy new ones!"

Oh, she was so sad! But suddenly a voice from behind her said, "I'll help you dress for your interview. What's a Fairy Godmother for?" Cinderella could hardly believe her eyes! "Now. Let's get you dressed. What's the corporate _____culture_____ of the office?" asked the Fairy Godmother. Cinderella had no idea. "Well, since today is Friday, it's probably a **dress-down** day, so let's put you into a silk top and slacks." With that, the Fairy Godmother waved her magic wand and Cinderella was instantly dressed in beautiful gown! But the Fairy Godmother added, "Just remember to come back before sunset or your clothes will suddenly disappear." "I'll remember," said Cinderella.

When she arrived at her interview, she knew right away that it was an _____old boy's_____ club and that she may not be given a fair _____shake_____ at the interview. They told her that she would have to do the _____lion's_____ share of the work using an old _____dinosaur_____ of a computer. In fact, it made the last marketing manager go _____postal_____ and quit! But that didn't scare Cinderella. After a long interview, the executives still weren't convinced that she would be the right person for the job.

Tired and losing hope, Cinderella forgot about the time and the sun was starting to set. In an instant, her clothes disappeared! The executives were clearly stunned. Then, after a moment, they all said at the same time, "You're hired! It'll be good to get some new _____blood_____ in here!" And with her new salary, Cinderella could finally afford to live on the upper east side in a charming converted brownstone.

C. CONTEXT EXERCISE

1. C
2. H
3. E
4. B

5. J
6. I
7. F
8. A

9. D
10. G

D. COMPLETE THE PHRASEE

Cheryl: I love my new job! We have a dress-**down** day every Friday, free lunch once a week, and most important, there's no favoritism. Everyone gets a **fair** shake. That's why the company has such a great corporate **culture**.

Laura: You're really lucky! My company is very different. It's an old boys' **club** where there's absolutely no respect for women. The women do the lion's **share** of the work and don't make much money. Sometimes I feel if I don't get out of there, I'm going to go **postal**!

Cheryl: Your executives sound like **dinosaurs**! You should **polish** your résumé and come to work for my dot **com**. We always need **new** blood.

LESSON FOUR – BILL REINVENTS THE WHEEL

LET'S WARM UP!

1. everything
2. the latest date by which it must be completed
3. hierarchy of company executives
4. executives

5. very big problem
6. informant
7. person with the least power
8. solving a problem that has already been solved

9. overall strategy
10. created a large new problem
11. talk
12. official forms and procedures

LET'S PRACTICE!

A. CHOOSE THE RIGHT WORD

1. totem
2. red
3. blower
4. big
5. worms
6. chain

7. interface
8. wax
9. wheel
10. situation
11. ups
12. drop

C. CROSSWORD PUZZLE

B. MATCH THE COLUMN

1. F
2. N
3. P
4. I
5. C
6. K

7. L
8. A
9. H
10. J
11. D
12. E

LESSON FIVE – TRACEY DEFENDS THE THIRD WORLD

LET'S WARM UP!

1. False
2. True
3. False

4. True
5. True
6. False

7. False
8. True
9. False

10. False
11. False
12. False

LET'S PRACTICE!

A. I KNOW THE ANSWER, BUT WHAT'S THE QUESTION?

1. Does your company operate in America and Mexico?
2. Why is it so important to you to make a lot of money?
3. Is England a wealthy country?
4. Do you work for the World Trade Organization?
5. Why does it cost so much to ship items to India?
6. Is it difficult to travel from America to Canada?

B. FIND YOUR PERFECT MATCH

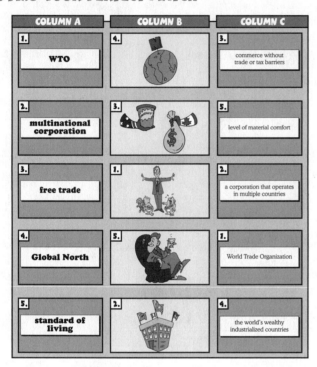

COLUMN A	COLUMN B	COLUMN C
1. WTO	4.	3. commerce without trade or tax barriers
2. multinational corporation	3.	5. level of material comfort
3. free trade	1.	2. a corporation that operates in multiple countries
4. Global North	5.	1. World Trade Organization
5. standard of living	2.	4. the world's wealthy industrialized countries

C. IMAGINE THAT...

In this section, you could have many possible answers. Remember, respond to each situation by making a complete sentence using one of the groups of words in the word list AND using each group only once. Be as creative as you'd like!

D. YOU'RE THE AUTHOR

Chandler: If we remove all the trade **barriers** to international trade, then the rich countries of the Global **North** are just going to get richer.

Rachel: Yes, but the **deregulation** of trade will also help the poor countries of the **Third** World, at least that's what the **WTO** has been saying.

Chandler: I think **free** trade is definitely a good thing. As boundary **erosion** increases, the world is becoming more of a global **village**. We should encourage this **globalization** as much as possible.

Rachel: Yes, but poverty should be a **transcultural** concern. I want everyone to have a better **standard** of living, not just the rich multinational **corporations**.

LESSON SIX – CAROLYN IS A LAME DUCK!

LET'S WARM UP!

1. politically neutral
2. politician currently in office
3. congress
4. vague and misleading
5. conservative
6. principles
7. voting locations
8. won
9. criticizing his opponent
10. won by an overwhelming number of votes
11. defended his beliefs
12. political partner
13. politician who has no reason to work hard
14. election

LET'S PRACTICE!

A. THE UNFINISHED CONVERSATION (SUGGESTIONS FOR ANSWERS)

1. I'd rather just waffle on the issue.
2. Yes. My opponent is terrible, so I have the election wrapped up.
3. You're just mudslinging because you want her opponent to win.
4. Cordelia got more votes, so she won the race.
5. I'm going to Capitol Hill to watch a session of congress.

B. CHOOSE THE RIGHT WORD

1. running
2. platform
3. waffles
4. Hill
5. landslide
6. duck
7. polls
8. wing
9. mudslinging
10. incumbent
11. stand
12. road

C. COMPLETE THE STORY

Hello! I'm a candidate for president, and I hope you'll vote for me! I spent ten years on __Capitol Hill__ where I __took a stand__ on many important issues. My __running mate__ is a __right wing__ politician with a strong __platform__. My opponent is the __incumbent__. I don't like to __mudsling__, but you should know that he __waffles__ on most issues and usually takes a __middle-of-the-road__ approach. When he loses the election, I'm sure he'll be a __lame duck__ until I start. I have this election __wrapped up__, but please go to the __polls__ on election day and vote for me in this presidential __race__. We'll definitely __win by a landslide__!

D. CREATE YOUR OWN SENTENCE (SUGGESTIONS FOR ANSWERS)

1. He has a middle-of-the-road approach.
2. She's a lame duck! I wish the new Mayor could start right now.
3. Yes, she's always been right wing.
4. He picked Marty as his running mate.
5. I agree. He has the election wrapped up.
6. Yes, you need to take a stand on the issue.
7. He's the incumbent, so I think he has the advantage.
8. It should be an exciting race!
9. You can vote at the polls.
10. Yes, she won by a landslide!

LESSON SEVEN – KELLY MADE A KILLING

LET'S WARM UP!

1. J
2. E
3. C
4. A
5. L

6. N
7. H
8. M
9. G
10. K

11. I
12. F
13. B
14. C

LET'S PRACTICE!

A. CREATE YOUR OWN SENTENCE (SUGGESTIONS FOR ANSWERS)

1. Yes! I made a killing by day trading with tech stocks.
2. I think you should buy a mutual fund or some blue-chip stocks. They're relatively safe investments.
3. You should buy and hold your stocks. Maybe you'll have a stock split in a few months and make some money!
4. Don't spend your entire nest egg on high-risk stocks or you could definitely take a beating!
5. I love to play the market so I have a lot of different stocks, bonds, and other investments in my portfolio.
6. Sure, but I think you should go long and diversify. Don't put all your money in one place.

B. TRUE OR FALSE

1. False
2. True
3. False
4. False
5. True
6. False
7. False
8. False
9. True
10. False

C. YOU'RE THE AUTHOR

Clarisse: I just took a **beating** in the stock market! I lost all of my nest **egg** on a **high**-risk **tech** stock! I was going to buy and **hold** but I decided to **day** trade instead. What a mistake!

Franklin: Do you have any **blue**-chip stocks or mutual **funds** in your **portfolio**? If you're going to **play** the market, you need to **diversify** more. You can make a **killing** with a stock **split**, but that only happens when you go **long**.

Clarisse: Thanks for the advice!

D. CROSSWORD PUZZLE

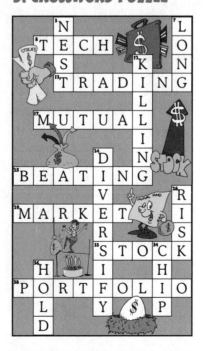

LESSON EIGHT – FRANK TRACKS THE PALLET
LET'S WARM UP!

1. False
2. True
3. False
4. False
5. False

6. True
7. True
8. False
9. True
10. False

11. False
12. True
13. False
14. False

LET'S PRACTICE!
A. & B. CREATE YOUR OWN STORY

In this section, you could have many possible answers. Remember, the more creative you are, the funnier your story will be!

C. WHAT WOULD YOU DO IF SOMEONE SAID...?

1. b
2. c
3. a
4. b
5. b

6. a
7. c
8. b
9. a
10. c

D. "ACROSS" WORD PUZZLE

1. drop
2. container
3. track
4. tare

5. dock
6. shrinkwrap
7. lading
8. forwarder

LESSON NINE – TANYA TRAVELS LIGHT
LET'S WARM UP

1. fly when there is an available seat in the airplane
2. small airplanes
3. passageway to the airplane
4. travel with few pieces of luggage
5. discount program for people who fly often
6. scheduled airplane changes
7. enter
8. flight without scheduled stops along the way

9. reserved
10. stop
11. seat by a window
12. pieces of luggage you're allowed to take onto
13. ticket that includes travel back to your point of departure
14. has severe fatigue
15. an overnight flight

LET'S PRACTICE!
A. TRUTH OR LIE

1. Lie
2. Truth
3. Lie

4. Truth
5. Lie
6. Truth

B. FIND THE DEFINITION

1. a ticket that includes travel to one's destination and back again
2. to have severe fatigue due to the time change during one's flight
3. a special discount program for people who fly often
4. to enter a plane, ship, or train
5. the passageway through which passengers enter or exit the airplane
6. a stop in one or more cities when traveling by air
7. a flight made without scheduled stops along the way
8. a seat on a plane or train that's located by a window
9. to reserve (a seat on an airplane, a hotel, etc.)
10. to be on a passenger waiting list for an available seat
11. a point during the trip where one must change airplanes
12. a small airplane
13. an overnight flight
14. to travel with just a few pieces of luggage
15. a small piece of luggage one takes onto the plane

C. FIND-THE-WORD GRID

1. PUDDLE
2. FREQUENT
3. LIGHT
4. LAYOVER
5. STAND-BY
6. BOARD
7. CARRY-ONS
8. GATE
9. RED-EYE
10. WINDOW

FIND-THE-WORD GRID

```
T N F R I A K C E D G R G E W D S T M A T
H W A L L E G R L I G H T A B T E D E M A
V I D L R S O S L A M U P F I R C S L O R
Y N J T R E I G A L F R E Q U E N T U V V
E D O W C A R R Y O N S E A O D S A N E E
I O U G C U A B O A R D D I R E T N C N T
Q W P A D N S E V R M R M N G Y O D H G O
U C N T I H L E E D P U D D L E W B O S D
E U E N E R H R N E C B O N I A Y S O E
I T D W D D H T M R E E L W S E Z O I S A
```

LESSON TEN – ROGER GETS THE INSIDE TRACK

LET'S WARM UP!

1. assured of success
2. strategy
3. stayed focused
4. be very successful
5. maneuvering ourselves to get an advantage
6. failed to complete her responsiblities
7. the first person to start something
8. totally wrong
9. makes the decisions
10. person who works well with others
11. acted prematurely
12. close to the point where the project is due
13. improve my performance or leave
14. the advantage
15. made a mistake

LET'S PRACTICE!

A. CORRECT OR INCORRECT?

1. INCORRECT
2. CORRECT
3. INCORRECT
4. INCORRECT
5. CORRECT
6. INCORRECT
7. CORRECT
8. INCORRECT
9. INCORRECT
10. CORRECT
11. CORRECT
12. INCORRECT
13. CORRECT
14. INCORRECT
15. INCORRECT

B. BLANK-BLANK

1. dropped the ball
2. jockey for position
3. team player
4. shape up or ship out
5. first out of the gate
6. call the shots
7. down to the wire
8. game plan
9. home free
10. inside track
11. way off base
12. fumbled
13. batting a thousand
14. jumped the gun

C. TRUE OR FALSE

1. False
2. True
3. False
4. True
5. True
6. False
7. True
8. False
9. True
10. True
11. True
12. False
13. True
14. False
15. True

THE SLANGMAN GUIDE TO

STREET SPEAK 1
THE COMPLETE COURSE IN AMERICAN SLANG & IDIOMS

This book presents dozens of the most popular slang and idioms used in the U.S. as well as in many common situations such as: at a party, at the market, at the movies, on vacation, at the airport, at a restaurant, on the road, at school, on a date, and more! In addition, learn common contractions and reductions used by every native-born American!

Book: 160 pages ISBN: 1-891-888-080 • US $18.95

This 2-Audio CD set, ideal for ear-training, contains the dialogues used in the book, all the exercises, plus each vocabulary section, all spoken in "real speak!"
2-Audio CD set ISBN: 1-891-888-293 • US $35.00

This 2-Audio Cassette set contains the dialogues in the book & a selection of exercises spoken in "real speak!"
2-Audio Cassette set ISBN: 1-891-888-307 • US $25.00

Book and 2-CD set
ISBN: 1-891-888-250 • US $50.00

Book and 2-CD set
ISBN: 1-891-888-277 • US $40.00

STREET SPEAK 3
THE COMPLETE COURSE IN AMERICAN SLANG & IDIOMS

This book examines even more everyday slang & idioms essential for nonnative speakers! Categories include: dating, love, breaking up, hobbies, popular words & expressions taken from sports, popular teen & college slang, popular American television shows, alliterations, proverbs, being politically correct, and more!

Book: 240 pages ISBN: 1-891-888-226 • US $21.95

This 2-Audio CD set, ideal for ear-training, contains the dialogues used in the book, all the exercises, plus each vocabulary section, all spoken in "real speak!"
2-Audio CD set ISBN: 1-891-888-331 • US $35.00

This 2-Audio Cassette set contains the dialogues in the book & a selection of exercises spoken in "real speak!"
2-Audio Cassette set ISBN: 1-891-888-34X • US $25.00

Book and 2-CD set
ISBN: 1-891-888-560 • US $50.00

Book and 2-CD set
ISBN: 1-891-888-569 • US $40.00

STREET SPEAK 2
THE COMPLETE COURSE IN AMERICAN SLANG & IDIOMS

This book explores more popular slang & idioms, with an extra bonus – our new special section called "From The Slangman Files." This fun segment is a handy resource presenting popular slang & idioms which have been grouped in categories such as: fruits & vegetables, colors, initials, body parts, people's first names, food, clothing, numbers, and animals!

Book: 240 pages ISBN: 1-891-888-064 • US $21.95

This 2-Audio CD set, ideal for ear-training, contains the dialogues used in the book, all the exercises, plus each vocabulary section, all spoken in "real speak!"
2-Audio CD set ISBN: 1-891-888-315 • US $35.00

This 2-Audio Cassette set contains the dialogues in the book & a selection of exercises spoken in "real speak!"
2-Audio Cassette set ISBN: 1-891-888-323 • US $25.00

Book and 2-CD set
ISBN: 1-891-888-269 • US$50.00

Book and 2-CD set
ISBN: 1-891-888-285 • US $40.00

DIRTY ENGLISH
A GUIDE TO POPULAR OBSCENITIES IN ENGLISH

This book is a humorous, yet academic, "course" on the most commonly used obscenities, insults, curses, and gestures used in the English language. This book is so complete, we challenge you to find a dirty word or expression that's not in it!

Book: 240 pages ISBN: 1-891-888-234 • US $21.95

This 2-Audio CD set, ideal for ear-training, contains the dialogues used in the book, all the exercises, plus each vocabulary section, all spoken in "real speak!"
2-Audio CD set ISBN: 1-891-888-412 • US $35.00

This 2-Audio Cassette set contains the dialogues in the book & a selection of exercises spoken in "real speak!"
2-Audio Cassette set ISBN: 1-891-888-420 • US $25.00

Book and 2-CD set
ISBN: 1-891-888-48X • US $50.00

Book and 2-CD set
ISBN: 1-891-888-498 • US $40.00

PRICES/AVAILABILITY SUBJECT TO CHANGE

THE SLANGMAN GUIDE TO

BIZ SPEAK 1
SLANG, IDIOMS & JARGON USED IN BUSINESS ENGLISH

Learn dozens of popular slang words and idioms used in virtually every American company. Chapters include: common abbreviations and shortcuts used in business, popular slang and idioms in the workplace, plus slang and jargon used in computer technology, Internet (World Wide Web), marketing, advertising, meetings, negotiations, and more!

Book: 160 pages | **ISBN: 1-891-888-145 • US $21.95**

This 2-Audio CD set, ideal for ear-training, contains the dialogues used in the book, all the exercises, plus each vocabulary section all spoken in "real speak!"

2-Audio CD set | **ISBN: 1-891-888-350 • US $35.00**

This 2-Audio Cassette set contains the dialogues in the book & a selection of exercises spoken in "real speak!"

2-Audio Cassette set | **ISBN: 1-891-888-366 • US $25.00**

BUY THE SET AND SAVE!

Book and 2-CD set
ISBN: 1-891-888-595 • US $50.00

BUY THE SET AND SAVE!

Book and 2-CD set
ISBN: 1-891-888-609 • US $40.00

BIZ SPEAK 2
SLANG, IDIOMS & JARGON USED IN BUSINESS ENGLISH

Learn more popular slang words and idioms used in virtually every American company. Chapters include: more everyday workplace slang & idioms, plus slang & idioms used in international trade, sports terms used in business, business travel, shipping, globalization, "bureaucratese," and more!

Book: 240 pages | **ISBN: 1-891-888-153 • US $21.95**

This 2-Audio CD set, ideal for ear-training, contains the dialogues used in the book, all the exercises, plus each vocabulary section all spoken in "real speak!"

2-Audio CD set | **ISBN: 1-891-888-374 • US $35.00**

This 2-Audio Cassette set contains the dialogues in the book & a selection of exercises spoken in "real speak!"

2-Audio Cassette set | **ISBN: 1-891-888-382 • US $25.00**

BUY THE SET AND SAVE!

Book and 2-CD set
ISBN: 1-891-888-615 • US $50.00

BUY THE SET AND SAVE!

Book and 2-CD set
ISBN: 1-891-888-625 • US $40.00

BIZ SPEAK 3
SLANG, IDIOMS & JARGON USED IN BUSINESS ENGLISH

This final volume includes: more everyday workplace slang & idioms, plus slang & idioms jargon used in finance and banking, human resources, business management, information technology, plus foreign words used in business, terms for being politically correct, and an important and hilarious section on common gestures to avoid at all costs in business!

Book: 240 pages | **ISBN: 1-891-888-161 • US $21.95**

This 2-Audio CD set, ideal for ear-training, contains the dialogues used in the book, all the exercises, plus each vocabulary section all spoken in "real speak!"

2-Audio CD set | **ISBN: 1-891-888-390 • US $35.00**

This 2-Audio Cassette set contains the dialogues in the book & a selection of exercises spoken in "real speak!"

2-Audio Cassette set | **ISBN: 1-891-888-404 • US $25.00**

BUY THE SET AND SAVE!

Book and 2-CD set
ISBN: 1-891-888-633 • US $50.00

BUY THE SET AND SAVE!

Book and 2-CD set
ISBN: 1-891-888-641 • US $40.00

UNDERSTANDING AMERICAN-ENGLISH THROUGH AMERICAN CULTURE
HOW AMERICANS WALK, TALK, ACT, AND THINK!

It's simple. The only way to truly speak American-English like a native is to *think* like an American... to **feel** like an American! Hollywood native, Slangman David Burke, will give you the inside information you're unlikely to find in any other video. Included in the price of the video is:

■ A full, downloadable transcript which can be found on our website, www.slangman.com

■ Activities for the classroom & self-study are also available on our website such as: pair work, group activities, plus exercises for reading, writing, listening, & speaking!

20 minutes | **ISBN: 1-891-888-587 • US $50.00**

SLANGMAN POSTER

The Slangman poster is perfect for the classroom! This big, colorful, 24"x36" poster demonstrates the top ten slang terms and expressions used by teens, in dating, in school, and on television. In addition, students will have hours of fun learning the updated version of *Cinderella*, complete with the most popular slang terms now being used! **ONLY US $5!**

PRICES/AVAILABILITY SUBJECT TO CHANGE

THE SLANGMAN GUIDE  TO

STREET SPANISH 1
THE BEST OF SPANISH SLANG

Become an insider by learning some of the most popular slang used throughout the many Spanish-speaking countries. Entertaining dialogues, word games and drills, crossword puzzles, and word searches will have you understanding the everyday language used on the street, in homes, offices, stores, and among family and friends in no time!

Book: 233 pages   ISBN: 0-471-179-701 • US $15.95

This Audio Cassette contains all the dialogues in the book & a selection of exercises from every lesson.
Audio Cassette   ISBN: 1-891-888-188 • US $12.50

STREET SPANISH 2
THE BEST OF SPANISH SLANG

This entertaining guide will lead you through an exciting domain of imaginative and popular Spanish idioms using dialogues, vocabulary lessons, entertaining word drills and games including crossword puzzles, fill-ins, find-a-word charts, and dictations.

Book: 234 pages   ISBN: 0-471-179-71X • US $15.95

This Audio Cassette contains all the dialogues in the book & a selection of exercises from every lesson.
Audio Cassette   ISBN: 1-891-888-196 • US $12.50

STREET SPANISH 3
THE BEST OF NAUGHTY SPANISH

The third piece to understanding everyday Spanish is to learn popular expletives and obscenities – those back-alley words and phrases constantly used in movies, books, and conversations between native speakers. This is the first step-by-step guide of its kind to explore the most common curses, vulgarities, and obscenities used in many Spanish-speaking countries.

Book: 238 pages   ISBN: 0-471-179-728 • US $15.95

This Audio Cassette contains all the dialogues in the book & a selection of exercises from every lesson.
Audio Cassette   ISBN: 1-891-888-307 • US $12.50

STREET SPANISH
SLANG DICTIONARY & THESAURUS

This unique slang dictionary and thesaurus offers Spanish equivalents and usage tips for over one thousand Spanish terms, including slang, idioms, colloquialisms, and obscenities. It also offers a fun thesaurus featuring Spanish expressions and obscenities, all destined to make you feel like an insider in no time.

Book: 267 pages   ISBN: 0-471-168-343 • US $16.95

STREET FRENCH 1
THE BEST OF FRENCH SLANG

Sacré bleu! This fun guide is the first in a series of books that teach how to speak and understand the real language used daily on the street, in homes, offices, stores, and among family and friends. Entertaining dialogues, word games and drills, crossword puzzles, and word searches will have you sounding like a native in a flash.

Book: 252 pages   ISBN: 0-471-138-983 • US $15.95

This Audio Cassette contains all the dialogues in the book & a selection of exercises from every lesson.
Audio Cassette   ISBN: 1-891-888-005 • US $12.50

STREET FRENCH 2
THE BEST OF FRENCH IDIOMS

This fully-illustrated guide explores some of the most popular idioms used in France! This book is packed with word games, dialogues using idioms, crossword puzzles, find-a-word grids, and special tips guaranteed to make you *au jus* ("up-to-date" or, literally, "juiced up") before you know it!

Book: 268 pages   ISBN: 0-471-138-991 • US $15.95

This Audio Cassette contains all the dialogues in the book & a selection of exercises from every lesson.
Audio Cassette   ISBN: 1-891-888-013 • US $12.50

STREET FRENCH 3
THE BEST OF NAUGHTY FRENCH

This is the first step-by-step guide of its kind to explore the most common curses, crude terms, and obscenities used in France. Chapters include: dating slang, non-vulgar / vulgar insults & put-downs, name-calling, body parts in slang, sexual slang, bodily functions, sounds & smells, plus the many uses of *Merde, & Foutre.*

Book: 239 pages   ISBN: 0-471-138-009 • US $15.95

This Audio Cassette contains all the dialogues in the book & a selection of exercises from every lesson.
Audio Cassette   ISBN: 1-891-888-021 • US $12.50

STREET FRENCH
SLANG DICTIONARY & THESAURUS

This unique slang dictionary and thesaurus offers English equivalents and usage tips for over one thousand French terms, including slang, idioms, colloquialisms, and obscenities. It also offers a fun thesaurus featuring French expressions, obscenities, & slang synonyms for English words and phrases, all destined to make you feel like an insider in no time.

Book: 323 pages   ISBN: 0-471-168-068 • US $16.95

PRICES/AVAILABILITY SUBJECT TO CHANGE

WWW.SLANGMAN.COM

ORDER FORM

SLANGMAN PUBLISHING

12206 Hillslope Street
Studio City, CA 91604 • USA

INTERNATIONAL:
1-818-769-1914

TOLL FREE (US/Canada):
1-877-SLANGMAN
(1-877-752-6462)

Worldwide FAX:
1-413-647-1589

Get the latest news, preview chapters, and shop online at:

WWW.SLANGMAN.COM

QUANTITY	ISBN	TITLE	PRICE	TOTAL
		THE SLANGMAN GUIDE TO		
		THE SLANGMAN GUIDE TO		
		THE SLANGMAN GUIDE TO		
		THE SLANGMAN GUIDE TO		
		THE SLANGMAN GUIDE TO		
		THE SLANGMAN GUIDE TO		
		THE SLANGMAN GUIDE TO		
		THE SLANGMAN GUIDE TO		
		THE SLANGMAN GUIDE TO		
		THE SLANGMAN GUIDE TO		
		THE SLANGMAN GUIDE TO		
		THE SLANGMAN GUIDE TO		
		THE SLANGMAN GUIDE TO		
		THE SLANGMAN GUIDE TO		
		THE SLANGMAN GUIDE TO		
		THE SLANGMAN GUIDE TO		
		THE SLANGMAN GUIDE TO		
		THE SLANGMAN GUIDE TO		
		THE SLANGMAN GUIDE TO		
		THE SLANGMAN GUIDE TO		

Total for Merchandise	
Sales Tax *(California Residents Only add applicable sales tax)*	
Shipping *(See Left)*	
ORDER TOTAL	

prices/availability subject to change

SHIPPING

—Domestic Orders—

SURFACE MAIL
(delivery time 5-7 days).
Add $4 shipping/handling for the first item, $1 for each additional item.

RUSH SERVICE
available at extra charge. Please telephone us for details.

—International Orders—

OVERSEAS SURFACE (delivery time 6-8 weeks).
Add $5 shipping/handling for the first item, $2 for each additional item.

OVERSEAS AIRMAIL available at extra charge. Please phone for details.

Name _____

(School/Company) _____

Street Address _____

City _____ State/Province _____ Postal Code _____

Country _____ Phone _____ Email _____

METHOD OF PAYMENT (CHECK ONE)

☐ Personal Check or Money Order *(Must be in U.S. funds and drawn on a U.S. bank.)*
☐ VISA   ☐ Master Card   ☐ Discover

Credit Card Number

Expiration Date

⬆ **Signature** *(important!)*